*Mondrian in Action*

# Mondrian in Action

OPEN SOURCE BUSINESS ANALYTICS

WILLIAM D. BACK
NICHOLAS GOODMAN
JULIAN HYDE

MANNING
Shelter Island

Manning Publications Co.
20 Baldwin Road
Shelter Island, NY 11964

Development editor:  Susanna Kline
Copyeditor:  Andy Carroll
Proofreader:  Janet Vail
Typesetter:  Gordan Salinovic
Cover designer:  Marija Tudor

ISBN 9781617290985
Printed in the United States of America
1 2 3 4 5 6 7 8 9 10 – MAL – 18 17 16 15 14 13

# brief contents

# contents

# *preface*

I joined Pentaho in 2011 with only a vague notion of business analytics or Mondrian and was told by my boss at the time that I should focus on becoming the Mondrian "expert" on the team. As I do when learning any new technology, my first action was to create a personal project to implement. In addition to my personal efforts, I was also assigned to support several clients dealing with Mondrian-related challenges.

As I started looking at the documentation and learning Mondrian, I quickly discovered that useful information was in multiple places, including the Mondrian site, forums, product websites, best practices, and even just in the heads of people who had been working with Mondrian for a while. To help myself, I began gathering notes together in one location and got the idea that a book on Mondrian would be very helpful.

After some encouragement from various friends and coworkers, I contacted Julian Hyde, who also recommended Nick Goodman for the project. Together we agreed that it was a good idea, so we started checking around for reputable publishers. Since I already had a shelf, both physical and virtual, full of Manning books, it wasn't really a difficult choice.

This book is the work of the authors over the course of more than a year, but contains information created by multiple developers and communities over a decade. If you're already using Mondrian, I hope you'll find this a useful reference and learn a thing or two, particularly about the upcoming Mondrian 4.0. If you're new to Mondrian, then I hope you'll find this a useful learning tool that covers both the basics and advanced topics. No matter where you fall on the Mondrian knowledge scale, I hope you'll find this book and the tools contained in it a useful aid in helping businesses make better decisions.

WILLIAM BACK

# about this book

This book is about Mondrian 4.0 and related technologies. It's organized into chapters based on functionality. Chapters are designed to be standalone in most cases, but it's easier, especially for beginners, to start at the beginning and work through the chapters of interest in order. Depending on your role in the organization, different chapters will be more relevant than others.

### Intended audience

This book is targeted at four general types of users:

The *business analyst* is the person who will use Mondrian to perform analysis. This reader mainly wants to use Mondrian and the related tools, not necessarily understand all of the inner workings, such as configuration and database format.

The *data warehouse architect* is the person who's responsible for setting up the data for Mondrian for business analysts to use. This person makes it possible for analysis to be fast and easy.

The *business intelligence enterprise architect* is responsible for making Mondrian work within the enterprise. This includes installation, configuration, scaling, and security.

Finally, *application developers* will want to learn how to integrate Mondrian in their own applications. Integration approaches include embedding the Mondrian engine into your application as well as using Mondrian's web services to get data.

### Roadmap

Here's what you'll learn in each chapter:

- Chapter 1 introduces you to business analytics and why you'd want to use a tool like Mondrian. After reading this chapter you should have an understanding of the problem that Mondrian is trying to solve. You'll also understand how Mondrian fits into the larger business analytics architecture.

- Chapter 2 gives you a high-level overview of Mondrian and how it works to support the enterprise. This chapter provides general context for most of the rest of the book. By reading this chapter you should understand what Mondrian can do for your organization.

- Chapter 3 introduces the concept of star schemas and data marts. This chapter explains why and how to organize the data for maximum effectiveness with Mondrian. After finishing this chapter you'll understand why certain data organization is better than others and how to create data marts for your solution.

- Chapter 4 presents the fundamentals of the Mondrian schema. This schema logically describes the data in the database. You'll be able to create your own schemas for analysis after reading this chapter.

- Chapter 5 expands on chapter 4 and looks at advanced schema features. It includes features such as parent-child hierarchies and hanger dimensions that allow you to model more complex data. After reading this chapter and chapter 4 you'll know the vast majority of all Mondrian schema features.

- Chapter 6 introduces the concept of roles and security. You'll learn how to restrict access to data for users based on their role—for example, limiting cost information to cost accountants and financial managers.

- Chapter 7 talks about how to maximize Mondrian performance. In particular you'll learn how to create and configure aggregate tables and use advanced in-memory caching features to make analysis with Mondrian even faster.

- Chapter 8 revisits the question of security to include dynamically setting access to data as well as support for multi-tenancy. This chapter is of particular interest to anyone managing a large-scale Mondrian installation with many users, including external clients.

- Chapter 9 talks about how Mondrian is used within Pentaho, the leading open source business analytics framework. You will learn how to use Mondrian as a source for analytics, reporting, and dashboards. This chapter also describes using Mondrian with the Community Dashboard Framework, a popular open source plug-in for Pentaho.

- Chapter 10 is for the developers who want to either embed Mondrian into their application or use it as a source of analytics data. Detailed examples are provided to help you create your own solutions.

- Chapter 11 wraps up the book with an overview of some advanced analytics topics. It shows how to perform advanced analytics within Mondrian and use popular data mining tools. We also place Mondrian in the Big Data landscape.

## Recommended reading

Table 1 shows the chapter likely to be of most interest to each type of reader. That's not to say that the other chapters won't also be of interest, but that these are most relevant.

Table 1   Relevant chapters by reader

| Chapter | Business Analyst | Data Architect | Enterprise Architect | Application Developer |
|---|:---:|:---:|:---:|:---:|
| Chapter 1, "Beyond reporting: business analytics" | ✓ | ✓ | ✓ | ✓ |
| Chapter 2, "Mondrian: a first look" | ✓ | ✓ | ✓ | ✓ |
| Chapter 3, "Creating the data mart" | | ✓ | | |
| Chapter 4, "Multidimensional modeling: making analytics data accessible" | | ✓ | ✓ | |
| Chapter 5, "How schemas grow" | | ✓ | ✓ | |
| Chapter 6, "Securing data" | | ✓ | ✓ | |
| Chapter 7, "Maximizing Mondrian performance" | | ✓ | ✓ | |
| Chapter 8, "Dynamic security" | | | ✓ | ✓ |
| Chapter 9, "Working with Mondrian and Pentaho" | ✓ | ✓ | ✓ | ✓ |
| Chapter 10, "Developing with Mondrian" | | ✓ | | ✓ |
| Chapter 11, "Advanced analytics" | ✓ | | ✓ | |

## Code conventions and downloads

The code in this book is generally in individual listings. When code is inline it'll be specified by code markings to make it easily identifiable. Code is set in a fixed-width font like this.

Note that the listings only show what's necessary to explain something. You should download the software to get the full examples. See appendix A for more information on how to download the software; go to the publisher's website at www.manning.com/ MondrianinAction to download the examples.

## Software requirements

The code in this book, when specific to Mondrian, is for Mondrian 4.0. Most will work with Mondrian 3.5 or later. Mondrian 4.0 will be released as part of Pentaho 5.1 in early 2014. You can currently use Mondrian 4.0 with Saiku, which was used to validate the examples in this book. If you encounter problems with the code examples in this book, please let the authors know in the Manning Author Online forum.

In addition to the software described in appendix A, you'll need a system capable of running Java and a web browser. The code has been tested with Java 1.6, but should also run on Java 1.7 or later. You'll also need a database that's supported by Mondrian, such as MySQL or PostgreSQL.

An IDE that supports HTML, Javascript, XML, and Java, such as IntelliJ Idea or Eclipse, is ideal but not required. You can enter all of the examples in a text editor and compile from the command line. But an IDE will make it a lot easier.

## Author Online

The purchase of *Mondrian in Action* includes free access to a private web forum run by Manning Publications, where you can make comments about the book, ask technical questions, and receive help from the authors and from other users. To access the forum and subscribe to it, point your web browser at www.manning.com/Mondrian-inAction. This page provides information on how to get on the forum once you are registered, what kind of help is available, and the rules of conduct on the forum.

Manning's commitment to our readers is to provide a venue where a meaningful dialogue between individual readers and between readers and the authors can take place. It's not a commitment to any specific amount of participation on the part of the authors, whose contribution to the forum remains voluntary (and unpaid). We suggest you try asking the authors some challenging questions, lest their interest stray!

The Author Online forum and archives of previous discussions will be accessible from the publisher's website as long as the book is in print.

## About the cover illustration

The figure on the cover of *Mondrian in Action* is captioned a "Man from Konavle." The illustration is taken from the reproduction published in 2006 of a 19th-century collection of costumes and ethnographic descriptions entitled *Dalmatia* by Professor Frane Carrara (1812 – 1854), an archaeologist and historian, and the first director of the Museum of Antiquity in Split, Croatia. The illustrations were obtained from a helpful librarian at the Ethnographic Museum (formerly the Museum of Antiquity), itself situated in the Roman core of the medieval center of Split: the ruins of Emperor Diocletian's retirement palace from around AD 304. The book includes finely colored illustrations of figures from different regions of Croatia, accompanied by descriptions of the costumes and of everyday life.

Konavle is a small town located southeast of Dubrovnik, Croatia. The man on the cover is wearing dark blue woolen trousers and an embroidered red vest over a white linen shirt. Over his shoulders is draped a brown woolen shawl, and a gold sash and red leggings complete his outfit. In his hand he holds a long pipe, and pistols and a musket are visible, stuck in his sash and hanging over his shoulder.

At a time when it is hard to tell one computer book from another, Manning celebrates the inventiveness and initiative of the computer business with book covers based on the rich diversity of regional life of two centuries ago, brought back to life by illustrations from collections such as this one.

# *acknowledgments*

We'd like to thank the staff at Manning who helped make this book a reality. First, Bert Bates patiently taught us the fundamentals of telling a story, rather than simply writing dry, technical prose. Nick Chase helped with the technical aspects, fixing errors and answering basic questions that helped move the project along. Immense thanks to Susanna Kline, who not only made the book of much higher quality and guided us through the process, but also kept us going when we didn't want to. Without Susanna's assistance, we'd still be back somewhere in chapter 3, talking about how we should be writing more. A good editor makes a finished product possible. Finally, thanks to the marketing and production teams at Manning for their support, guidance, and encouragement throughout the publication process.

Though it's impossible to list everyone who provided input, we'd specifically like to thank Anthony DeShazor, Will Gorman, and Luc Boudreau for support and guidance as well as technical and operational insights. The Saiku team, and their lead Paul Stoellberger, were very helpful in testing Mondrian 4.0 and ensuring accurate content for this book. Thank you to Kevin Hanrahan who, although new to Mondrian, worked through examples and provided feedback on errors and omissions. We'd also like to thank the management of Pentaho for being supportive of this effort and allowing us to reuse some internal Pentaho content. Thank you also to our colleagues and friends at Pentaho and in the Pentaho and Mondrian community for creating such a great set of technology and tools.

We'd like to thank the reviewers who took time to read the drafts of our manuscript and provide feedback so that we could make the book easier to read and understand.

Many a poorly written section or so-so graphic was improved by input from our reviewers: Aiden Humphreys, Alexander Helf, Barry Polley, Dan McCreary, Filip Rembiałkowski, Garry Turkington, Greg Soulsby, Lorenzo De Leon, Marc-Steffen Kaesz, Mark Newman, Marko Viitanen, Matt Taylor, Nadia Noori, Najib Coutya, Owen Kaser, Ron Steiger, Saeed Alhajyousef, Salvatore Piccione, and Simon (Zihong) Wang. Thanks also to David Fombella Pombal and Gavin Whyte for their careful technical review of the final chapters shortly before they went into production.

### WILLIAM BACK

You always read about how much work writing a book is and how it takes a team. The reality of that fact didn't hit me until I attempted to write a book of my own. My first clue that I was taking on a large project should've been when former authors told me what a great idea it was, but declined to participate. It's a lot of work, and it does take a lot of help.

I have to first thank my wife, Tara, and my children, Lauren and Nathan. They've been very patient in allowing me to spend hours and weekends locked away in my office or talking with my coauthors. Family support is a must because of the time it takes to write a book.

I also want to thank my coauthors, Julian Hyde and Nick Goodman. They had much more experience and background with past versions of Mondrian and provided a lot of insight into how Mondrian can and should be used. The Mondrian 4.0 features in this book would've been impossible to include without Julian's knowledge of the latest version.

### NICHOLAS GOODMAN

It's easy to wonder why anyone would write a book at all; it's immensely time-consuming, requires more effort than anyone thinks or knows, and can be downright frustrating. This book, however, is something I'm proud to have been a part of, and it certainly would not have happened by me alone.

Julian Hyde is a long-time colleague and friend, and I'm grateful we were able to work on this project together. His efforts shepherding Mondrian over the course of a decade are commendable, and his talents numerous. I'm honored that he and Bill asked me to play a small part as coauthor on this much-overdue project.

Bill Back is the heart and soul of this book! His desire to learn, explore, perfect, communicate, and teach are all present, and in no uncertain terms this book wouldn't have made it past a proposal had it not been for his desire to do this project well. If there were a way to make Bill's name 10x the size of mine on the cover, he'd deserve all that extra credit and more!

To my wife, Kathleen, who listened to me complain and wondered why I ever took on this project, but still encouraged me to just "go work on the book for a couple hours" here and there—you are the only reason the team at Manning received any content from me. To my daughter, Emmeline, who was born during the final days of this book—you'll be glad to know that daddy was doing something productive during those middle-of-the-night sessions!

## JULIAN HYDE

I once said I'd never bet my job on a technology about which no one had seen fit to write a book. Thankfully the Mondrian community isn't as conservative as me! Over the past decade, many people have used Mondrian successfully based on information gleaned from forums, the developer mailing list, and the less-than-perfect online documentation. You've helped each other out, and inspired the developers to make Mondrian faster and better. This book is the culmination of a long journey, and is my way of saying thank you for your patience and support.

Mondrian is an open source project, but its chief inspiration was a commercial product: Microsoft Analysis Services. Its architects—Amir and Ariel Netz and Mosha Pasumansky—radically simplified OLAP. Their product had a query language, MDX, and standard interfaces OLE DB for OLAP and XML/A, where all previous products had required building queries using a proprietary API. Their hybrid architecture combined the convenience of ROLAP with the performance and expressive power of MOLAP. Mondrian wouldn't have been possible without their work creating standard languages, APIs, and architectures.

Every open source project is part of a wider movement. Thank you to all open source software developers out there. We use your software every day for development, debugging, builds, and testing, and you probably don't even know it.

Mondrian has a number of crucial "sister projects"; we literally grew up together. The first, JPivot, started when Andreas Voss flew from Germany to meet me in San Francisco. His company wanted to develop a web-based pivot table; they would build it on top of my fledgling Mondrian project and release it open source if I made sure that Mondrian had the features they needed. We shook hands, and that was that. Other projects followed: LucidDB (John Sichi, Rushan Chen, Zelaine Fong); LucidEra Clearview, which became Pentaho Analyzer (Benny Chow); olap4j (Luc Boudreau and Barry Klawans); OpenI (Sandeep Giri); Saiku (Paul Stoellberger and Tom Barber); and CTools (Pedro Alves).

Many people have contributed code to Mondrian, and I'm grateful to them all. We grow best and fastest when developers and architects bring challenging problems, and work with us to solve them. So, thanks to Joe Barnett, Marc Berkowitz, Roland Bouman, Matt Campbell, Matt Casters, Gang Chen, Dan Dosch, Daniel Einspanjer, Richard Emberson, Sarah Gerweck, Will Gorman, Brandon Jackson, Sean McCullough, Eric McDermid, Gretchen Moran, Thomas Morgner, Henry Olson, Kurt Walker, and Sherman Wood.

Open source BI wasn't always with us. Mark Madsen, Seth Grimes, Nicholas Goodman, James Dixon, and Jos van Dongen explained to the world how open source BI, and in particular Mondrian, could change business. And I'd like to thank Richard

Daley and the whole Pentaho team for their faith and investment in Mondrian and open source BI technology.

Writing a book is hard work. Thank you to my coauthors, Bill and Nick, and to our editor Susanna Kline, for their insight, stamina, and patience. And thank you to my brother Justin and my friend Gordon Cameron, who were always happy to discuss dimensional modeling over a beer or two at Barclay's pub. You helped keep me sane.

Building a piece of technology, and now writing a book, requires commitment and sacrifice, not just from the author, but from his family, who are rarely asked or thanked. My son, now 4, has learned the pattern from his mother: yesterday he said, "Are you going to work at your computer again tonight, Daddy?" Thank you to my wife, Pamela, for everything; and to my sons, Sebastian and Theodore, who will love reading their names in print.

# Beyond reporting: business analytics

**This chapter covers**

- The complexity of database-based reports
- Advantages of OLAP reporting tools
- Reasons for using Mondrian

Business analytics is a process for gaining insight into business performance based on the analysis of historical data. Traditionally the tools used for business analytics have been expensive and difficult to maintain. Mondrian, in contrast, is an open source business analytics tool that enables organizations of any size to give business users access to the data for interactive analysis and to create analysis reports without the help of IT or database administrators. Once the data has been set up, users can interact with it directly. This book will present you with the concepts and technical know-how to use Mondrian, including how to organize the data for easy access, how to securely make your data available, and how to integrate this data into other applications.

This first chapter will introduce you to some of the common problems encountered with a report-based approach to analysis. We'll show you the complexity involved in creating database reports and why they're not a good fit for analysis. Then we'll demonstrate how Mondrian can be used to overcome those challenges and explain some of the features that make Mondrian an ideal choice. Finally, we'll provide an overview of the remainder of the book, where we'll expand on all of the aspects of Mondrian and teach you how to use Mondrian effectively for analysis.

## 1.1 *The need for business analytics*

In his book *Moneyball*, Michael Lewis tells the story of how the Oakland A's managed to put together a highly talented and competitive team on one of the lowest budgets in professional baseball. Prior to this time, scouting was done by scouts watching players and going on gut feel as to who would develop into a professional. As the cost of recruiting players skyrocketed, so did the cost of making an error in signing the wrong guy.

Billy Beane, Oakland's general manager, decided that they needed a more analytical approach. He brought in analysts who would study the statistics of college players and identify players who were good candidates, but who had been overlooked by scouts for a variety of reasons. Statistics such as on-base percentage and number of walks per bat became important considerations that weren't considered important before. This gave Oakland an edge in drafting players that other teams didn't recognize as valuable and signing them for less.

Like the Oakland A's, today's businesses need to be able to optimize their spending to maximize return on investment. Controlling aspects of the business such as inventory costs, waste, excess machinery or labor, and returns is no longer optional, but mandatory to survive in the hyper-competitive, intelligence-driven marketplace. And businesses need good tools and processes to make this happen. The A's wrote much of their own software, but that approach is typically very expensive, slow, and risky. With Mondrian, any organization can have access to world-class analytics tools that they can get up and running quickly with a minimum of cost and risk.

Historically, analysis and management of business has been done using spreadsheets, operational databases, and reports. While these approaches are good for viewing predefined data formats, they're not as good for exploring and discovering new information because reports are often difficult and time consuming to create and manipulate. Online analytical processing (OLAP) is a technology that makes business data available with enough structure for business users to easily explore data and discover important data relationships without having to understand database query languages or the organization of a company's operational databases.

The following are some of the types of discoveries companies can make with OLAP tools and how these discoveries help their businesses:

- Discovering that a particular product is in high demand in summer months, but low demand outside of those months. The company can now adjust inventory seasonally to avoid excessive storage costs.
- Finding out that there's a change in demand for services after running ads in various publications. The company can now coordinate advertising and staffing

to be able to meet demand without overstaffing when launching a new advertising campaign.

- Uncovering the fact that the gender and age of visitors to a website differ according to the day and time. This information allows the site to tailor content based on the day and time to reflect different demographics.
- Figuring out when website demand peaks and by how much. The company can now make informed decisions about how to scale without adding too much static capacity, while being able to meet typical demand.

Making sense of the company's data requires tools that allow users to organize and explore the data and discover interesting facts. Mondrian is the engine for such a set of tools.

Mondrian is an open source OLAP engine that provides access to data in a way that's intuitive to users. As an engine, Mondrian can be run in a web container, such as Tomcat or JBoss, or be embedded as part of an application. Mondrian only requires an optional configuration, a schema defining the logical structure of the data, and a database populated with data. Mondrian works with most databases that support Java database connections.

Figure 1.1 shows how Mondrian aids in analysis in a typical deployment. Mondrian sits between the data and uses logical descriptions of the data to provide data for analysis tools and dashboards. The user explores the data graphically based on data properties, rather than through complex queries. Mondrian dynamically translates to the underlying database query format to provide data in a logical, accurate manner.

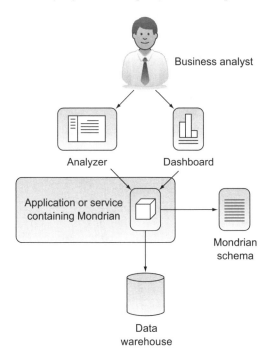

**Figure 1.1  Mondrian is the analytics engine for the business application.**

## 1.2    *Replacing static reports with online analytical processing (OLAP)*

Businesses run on data, and that data is often presented to users in the form of reports. Traditional reports were static and often long, with the important data embedded in a large amount of not-so-important data. Users were also often unable to understand the details behind the data that they did see. They also couldn't drill deeper into the underlying details or into related data.

With modern online reporting, many of these challenges have been overcome, allowing users to reduce data through filters and create links to other reports. But these reports still lack the flexibility to do real analysis, as evidenced by the large number of users who export reports to Excel for further manipulation. This section will present an example of a company struggling under the weight of reports and encountering problems that commonly occur with such systems. In the next section, we'll look at how modern analytics can be applied to overcome these problems and give the power to the users who need the information to make decisions.

Adventure Works is a company that sells bicycling parts and equipment. Their analyst's job is to provide business reports that help the business users manage the business and maximize profits. He spends much of his time exploring data collected from the various business transactions.

> **MAYBE YOU'VE SEEN ADVENTURE WORKS ELSEWHERE?**  If you've worked with other analytics systems, particularly Microsoft Analysis Services (MSAS), you've likely encountered the Adventure Works database before. MSAS has been a leader in business analytics, and Microsoft has led the way with technologies and standards, particularly Multidimensional Expressions (MDX). Mondrian strives to be compliant with these standards as well, so we felt it made sense to use the same data example that Microsoft provides. Note that we've built on the original Adventure Works database, so the data warehouse may be somewhat different than Microsoft's.

The analyst works closely with the database managers to understand the structure of the databases, so he can collect data for reports. When a new report is requested, he'll either create the database query if it's easy, or work with a more experienced database expert. He'll then construct a report based on the data. If the business user likes the report, it's put into production, but more often than not, the user wants small changes, and the analyst has to rework the report. It can take days to get a report correct, and then the user typically wants a different report.

The analyst's users have also been requesting a variety of reports that let them see data at multiple levels and compare different types of data to one another. This means the analyst has to make multiple copies of reports that contain essentially the same data presented at different levels of detail. The users also want to be able to restrict the data and have the ability to click and see greater detail in the data.

Figure 1.2 shows part of the report used by senior management to see the total orders for each city. This lets the managers understand which countries and cities have the largest orders. Listing 1.1 shows the database query that was created to generate the

| State or Province | City | Quantity Ordered | Total Price |
|---|---|---|---|
| England | Warrington | 1 | $ 699.10 |
| England | Watford | 1 | $ 3,578.27 |
| England | West Sussex | 1 | $ 2,181.56 |
| England | Wokingham | 1 | $ 3,578.27 |
| England | Woolston | 1 | $ 3,578.27 |
| England | York | 1 | $ 3,578.27 |
| **Total:** | | | |

**Country: US**

| State or Province | City | Quantity Ordered | Total Price |
|---|---|---|---|
| Alabama | Huntsville | 2 | $ 183.94 |
| Arizona | Chandler | 1 | $ 469.79 |
| Arizona | Gilbert | 1 | $ 602.35 |
| Arizona | Mesa | 3 | $ 1,242.85 |
| Arizona | Phoenix | 1 | $ 28.84 |
| Arizona | Scottsdale | 1 | $ 419.46 |

**Figure 1.2  Orders by city**

report. Note that it requires understanding of the source tables that have the data, how to join the six tables, and SQL syntax.

**Listing 1.1   Query for orders by city**

```
SELECT
     `salesorderdetail`.`OrderQty`,
     `salesorderdetail`.`UnitPrice`,
     `stateprovince`.`Name`,
     `stateprovince`.`CountryRegionCode`,
     `address`.`City`
FROM
     `salesorderheader`
     INNER JOIN `salesorderdetail`
       ON `salesorderheader`.`SalesOrderID` =
         `salesorderdetail`.`SalesOrderID`
     INNER JOIN `customer`
       ON `salesorderheader`.`CustomerID` =
         `customer`.`CustomerID`
     INNER JOIN `customeraddress`
       ON `customer`.`CustomerID` =
         `customeraddress`.`CustomerID`
     INNER JOIN `address`
       ON `customeraddress`.`AddressID` =
         `address`.`AddressID`
     INNER JOIN `stateprovince`
       ON `address`.`StateProvinceID` =
         `stateprovince`.`StateProvinceID`
GROUP BY
     `address`.`City`
ORDER BY
```

```
`stateprovince`.`CountryRegionCode` ASC,
`stateprovince`.`Name` ASC,
`address`.`City` ASC
```

Figure 1.3 displays part of the more detailed report for country- and state-level management, showing who the big customers are for each state or province. Listing 1.2 shows the revised database query for this report. Again, the analyst has to understand the detailed structure of the database to get the data. To make any change to a report, a new query and a new report must be created.

## Customer Sales by City

**Country: US**

State or Province: Idaho

City: Idaho Falls

| LastName | FirstName | OrderQty | UnitPrice |
|----------|-----------|----------|-----------|
| Thompson | Kendra | 1 | $ 72.88 |

City: Lewiston

| LastName | FirstName | OrderQty | UnitPrice |
|----------|-----------|----------|-----------|
| Smith | Margaret | 1 | $ 1,242.85 |

City: Sandpoint

| LastName | FirstName | OrderQty | UnitPrice |
|----------|-----------|----------|-----------|
| Bruner | Shirley | 1 | $ 780.82 |

State or Province: Montana

City: Billings

| LastName | FirstName | OrderQty | UnitPrice |
|----------|-----------|----------|-----------|
| Haines | Betty | 3 | $ 334.06 |
| Smith | Monica | 1 | $ 32.60 |

**Figure 1.3   Orders by customer**

**Listing 1.2   Query for orders by customer**

```
SELECT
      `address`.`City`,
      `contact`.`FirstName`,
      `contact`.`LastName`,
      `salesorderdetail`.`OrderQty`,
      `salesorderdetail`.`UnitPrice`,
      `customeraddress`.`CustomerID`,
      `customer`.`TerritoryID`,
      `stateprovince`.`Name`,
      `stateprovince`.`CountryRegionCode`
FROM
      `address`
      INNER JOIN `customeraddress`
        ON `address`.`AddressID` =
           `customeraddress`.`AddressID`
      INNER JOIN `customer`
        ON `customeraddress`.`CustomerID` =
           `customer`.`CustomerID`
      INNER JOIN `salesorderheader`
```

```
        ON `customer`.`CustomerID` =
          `salesorderheader`.`CustomerID`
    INNER JOIN `salesorderdetail`
        ON `salesorderheader`.`SalesOrderID` =
          `salesorderdetail`.`SalesOrderID`
    INNER JOIN `contact`
        ON `salesorderheader`.`ContactID` =
          `contact`.`ContactID`
    INNER JOIN `stateprovince`
        ON `address`.`StateProvinceID` =
          `stateprovince`.`StateProvinceID`
GROUP BY
    `customeraddress`.`CustomerID`
ORDER BY
    `customer`.`TerritoryID` ASC,
    `address`.`StateProvinceID` ASC,
    `address`.`City` ASC,
    `contact`.`LastName` ASC,
    `stateprovince`.`Name` ASC
```

Lately the requests for new reports and changes have begun to become overwhelming. The Adventure Works analyst is unable to keep up with the requests and is working long hours. Frustrated business users have begun getting their data as a dump from IT and doing analysis in Excel, but the data isn't always up to date, and it's difficult to view from multiple perspectives. In addition to requests for reports, the analyst is now also getting calls to help the users manipulate their data in Excel.

After finishing one particularly complex report with a multitable join query that runs overnight, the analyst comes in to work to find an angry database administrator waiting for him. Apparently the report slowed down the operational database and caused delays in shipments to customers.

Senior managers, happy with their reports, want to share them with regional and store managers, but they only want to let those managers see the data that applies to them. They ask for customized reports for each of the managers. Figure 1.4 shows the report for the USA regional manager. It looks like there are quite a few long days ahead to create all of these reports.

## Sales by City

| State or Province | City | Quantity Ordered | Total Price |
|---|---|---|---|
| **Country: US** | | | |
| Alabama | Birmingham | 1 | $ 209.26 |
| Alabama | Huntsville | 2 | $ 183.94 |
| Arizona | Chandler | 1 | $ 469.79 |
| Arizona | Gilbert | 1 | $ 602.35 |
| Arizona | Mesa | 3 | $ 1,242.85 |
| Arizona | Phoenix | 1 | $ 28.84 |
| Arizona | Scottsdale | 1 | $ 419.46 |
| Arizona | Surprise | 3 | $ 53.99 |

**Figure 1.4   Orders by city for USA**

With the large number of reports and growing number of users, the system is starting to get sluggish and reports are taking a long time to render. This is frustrating to the business users, as they spend more time waiting for reports than analyzing the data.

If the analyst is to stay sane and his business users are to remain happy, there needs to be a better way to do analysis. Fortunately, he stays current in analysis techniques and realizes that an open source OLAP tool, Mondrian, can help him out of this crisis. It will let business users do their own analysis quickly and securely, which should help the bottom line as well as his career.

## 1.3    OLAP to the rescue

Adventure Works wants a solution that allows users to perform their own analysis without waiting for a report to be created or requiring users to consult with a database administrator. They also need a low-cost solution that has minimal upfront risk. Finally, whatever they choose has to be fast so that users can do analysis in minutes rather than days.

There are a number of OLAP tools available, but they decide on Mondrian for the following reasons:

- Mondrian supports user-driven analysis. Users are able to do their own analysis without a lot of help from administrators or report writers.
- Mondrian is a low-cost, low-risk choice. Mondrian is open source and can be downloaded for free. Mondrian also comes bundled with a number of analysis tools and suites that make it easy to install and start using.
- Mondrian is fast. It has a variety of optimization techniques that allow users to perform analysis at the *speed of thought* using interactive tools.
- Mondrian has built-in security capabilities, making it ideal for organizations with sensitive data.
- Mondrian is based on open standards. It runs on a large variety of application servers and works with most major databases. This means Mondrian won't lock you into a proprietary solution.

The rest of this section will elaborate on some of the benefits of Mondrian and how it can solve problems for organizations like Adventure Works.

### 1.3.1    Mondrian lets users drive analysis

Mondrian solves many of the problems related to report-based analysis by removing the need to have database administrators and query writers involved in extracting data. In later chapters, we'll show you how to organize the data and make it easily available to analysts. Once you've done that, users can use graphical tools to access the data. They no longer need to understand the complexity of the data and can spend their time focusing on the analysis and making discoveries that can improve the business.

In Mondrian, data is organized by attributes, such as location and time, so that you can ask questions such as, "What was the increase in sales across all product lines in

North America during 2011?" These data attributes are called *dimensions* in OLAP terminology. Multiple user interfaces provide drag-and-drop abilities for looking at data by these dimensions. You aren't required to know any query languages.

> **WHY PENTAHO** This book relies heavily on examples using Pentaho. This is because Pentaho is the leading supporter of Mondrian and has it embedded in their business analytics server. Although Mondrian is used by a variety of other systems, Pentaho is the most common.

Figure 1.5 shows the Pentaho Analyzer view that allows business intelligence (BI) users to drag objects to the canvas. There's no need to understand the structure of the database or use a query language to do analysis.

Within the dimensions, data can be viewed by *level*, such as sales for a city, country, or region. This allows you to look at data at the level you're interested in, so a national manager can view data at the national level and a regional manager can view data at the regional level.

Figure 1.6 shows orders at the state level created by dragging the Country, State, Quantity Ordered, Price Each, Total, and Year fields to the canvas. As each field is placed on the canvas, the data is updated automatically.

Figure 1.7 shows the same analysis, but at a finer level of detail. In this case, the user dragged the additional fields of City and Customer to the report. This version gives you more detailed information in a matter of seconds or minutes without creating a different query or physical report.

You can easily limit the data using *filters* that only show data based on some rule, such as value, string text, and so on. Mondrian supports filters on all dimensions and

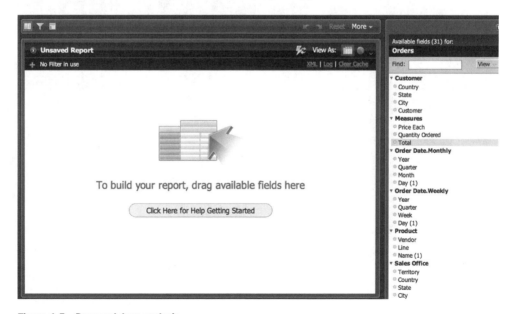

**Figure 1.5 Drag-and-drop analysis**

| Country | State | Year | | | | |
|---|---|---|---|---|---|---|
| | | 2003 | | | 2004 | |
| | | Quantity Ordered | Price Each | Total | Quantity Ordered | Price Each |
| Australia | NSW | 1,140 | $91.99 | $104,872.18 | 803 | $ |
| | Queensland | 336 | $101.20 | $34,003.95 | - | |
| | Victoria | 1,038 | $86.21 | $89,484.72 | 1,429 | $ |
| Austria | Not Available | 20,577 | $90.46 | $1,861,394.73 | 26,627 | $ |
| Belgium | Not Available | 20,577 | $90.46 | $1,861,394.73 | 26,627 | $ |
| Canada | BC | 355 | $96.87 | $34,388.20 | 1,221 | $ |
| | Québec | 145 | $115.80 | $16,790.28 | 287 | $ |
| Denmark | Not Available | 20,577 | $90.46 | $1,861,394.73 | 26,627 | $ |
| Finland | Not Available | 20,577 | $90.46 | $1,861,394.73 | 26,627 | $ |
| France | Not Available | 20,577 | $90.46 | $1,861,394.73 | 26,627 | $ |
| Germany | Not Available | 20,577 | $90.46 | $1,861,394.73 | 26,627 | $ |
| Hong Kong | Not Available | 20,577 | $90.46 | $1,861,394.73 | 26,627 | $ |
| Ireland | Not Available | 20,577 | $90.46 | $1,861,394.73 | 26,627 | $ |
| Italy | Not Available | 20,577 | $90.46 | $1,861,394.73 | 26,627 | $ |
| Japan | Osaka | - | - | - | 692 | $ |
| | Tokyo | - | - | - | 814 | $ |
| New Zealand | Not Available | 20,577 | $90.46 | $1,861,394.73 | 26,627 | $ |
| Norway | Not Available | 20,577 | $90.46 | $1,861,394.73 | 26,627 | $ |

Figure 1.6   State-level orders

| Country | State | City | Customer | Year | |
|---|---|---|---|---|---|
| | | | | 2003 | |
| | | | | Quantity Ordered | Price Each |
| Australia | NSW | Chatswood | Souveniers And Things Co. | 266 | $89.27 |
| | | North Sydney | Anna's Decorations, Ltd | 874 | $92.80 |
| | Queensland | South Brisbane | Australian Gift Network, Co | 336 | $101.20 |
| | Victoria | Glen Waverly | Australian Collectables, Ltd | 447 | $80.90 |
| | | Melbourne | Australian Collectors, Co. | 591 | $91.20 |
| Austria | Not Available | Graz | Mini Auto Werke | 430 | $97.42 |
| | | Salzburg | Salzburg Collectables | 442 | $77.25 |
| Belgium | Not Available | Bruxelles | Petit Auto | - | - |
| | | Charleroi | Royale Belge | 47 | $58.35 |
| Canada | BC | Tsawassen | Royal Canadian Collectables, Ltd. | - | - |
| | | Vancouver | Canadian Gift Exchange Network | 355 | $96.87 |
| | Québec | Montréal | Québec Home Shopping Network | 145 | $115.80 |
| Denmark | Not Available | Kobenhavn | Danish Wholesale Imports | 545 | $98.65 |
| | | Århus | Heintze Collectables | 358 | $96.88 |
| Finland | Not Available | Espoo | Suominen Souveniers | 290 | $95.28 |
| | | Helsinki | Toys of Finland, Co. | 454 | $83.45 |
| | | Oulu | Oulu Toy Supplies, Inc. | 342 | $97.61 |

Figure 1.7   Customer-level orders

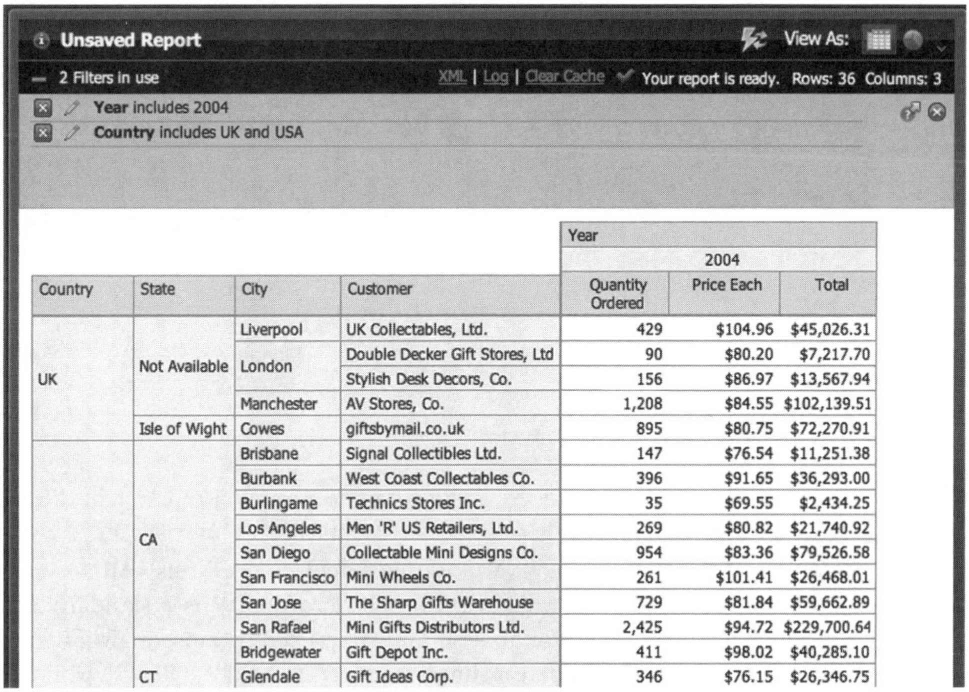


| Country | State | City | Customer | Year 2004 Quantity Ordered | Year 2004 Price Each | Year 2004 Total |
|---|---|---|---|---|---|---|
| UK | Not Available | Liverpool | UK Collectables, Ltd. | 429 | $104.96 | $45,026.31 |
| | | London | Double Decker Gift Stores, Ltd | 90 | $80.20 | $7,217.70 |
| | | | Stylish Desk Decors, Co. | 156 | $86.97 | $13,567.94 |
| | | Manchester | AV Stores, Co. | 1,208 | $84.55 | $102,139.51 |
| | Isle of Wight | Cowes | giftsbymail.co.uk | 895 | $80.75 | $72,270.91 |
| | CA | Brisbane | Signal Collectibles Ltd. | 147 | $76.54 | $11,251.38 |
| | | Burbank | West Coast Collectables Co. | 396 | $91.65 | $36,293.00 |
| | | Burlingame | Technics Stores Inc. | 35 | $69.55 | $2,434.25 |
| | | Los Angeles | Men 'R' US Retailers, Ltd. | 269 | $80.82 | $21,740.92 |
| | | San Diego | Collectable Mini Designs Co. | 954 | $83.36 | $79,526.58 |
| | | San Francisco | Mini Wheels Co. | 261 | $101.41 | $26,468.01 |
| | | San Jose | The Sharp Gifts Warehouse | 729 | $81.84 | $59,662.89 |
| | | San Rafael | Mini Gifts Distributors Ltd. | 2,425 | $94.72 | $229,700.64 |
| | CT | Bridgewater | Gift Depot Inc. | 411 | $98.02 | $40,285.10 |
| | | Glendale | Gift Ideas Corp. | 346 | $76.15 | $26,346.75 |

**Figure 1.8 Filtered data**

values, as well as special filters, such as Top 10 and string-pattern matching. This enables you to tailor the analysis to your needs rather than requiring you to look through a long report that contains a lot of extra data.

Figure 1.8 shows a user filtering a report to just contain the UK and US and the year 2004. The analyst is able to focus on just the relevant information without a query writer needing to create individual reports for each user.

### 1.3.2 *Mondrian is a low-cost, low-risk solution*

Mondrian is an open source project that anyone can download and build. There are no licensing fees or other costs related to using the tool, which makes Mondrian a low-risk option for analytics. Because Mondrian is an engine, you'll also need a server to host it. Fortunately Mondrian runs in a variety of servers, including standalone modes and popular business analytics servers. The most popular of these servers is Pentaho, an open source business analytics suite that has a community edition you can use for free. Mondrian is embedded in the server and acts as the engine for drag-and-drop tools that allow users to easily do analysis.

Figure 1.1 showed how Mondrian acts as the engine for analysis. Figure 1.9 shows how an analytical request from a business user is handled by Mondrian.

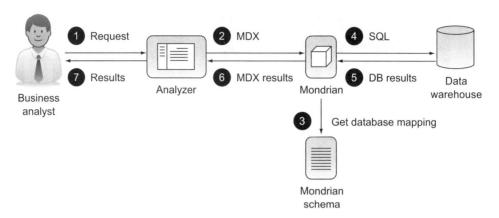

**Figure 1.9   Execution of an analytics query**

1   A business user decides to query some data using a number of different front
    ends, typically a thin-client interface, such as Pentaho Analyzer.

2   The interface creates a Multidimensional Expressions (MDX) query using
    either a web service call or a direct API call. MDX is a standardized general
    query language used for analysis and supported by most analytics engines. The
    advantage of MDX is that it simplifies the calls to the database while also being
    extremely powerful. It's also a common dialect that can be used no matter what
    database the data is stored in. Some user interfaces will allow users to directly
    enter or modify queries in MDX, allowing users who are comfortable with MDX
    syntax to perform more complex queries and use the many functions available
    in MDX.

3   Mondrian uses a logical schema, organized into cubes of dimensions (attributes
    about the data, such as date and location) and measures (the actual data facts,
    such as cost, inventory level, and the like). The schema also provides features
    for performance optimization and security. Mondrian uses this schema to
    retrieve the data either from an in-memory cache or by generating optimized
    database calls. Mondrian automatically creates correct SQL for a wide number
    of databases.

4   Mondrian generates SQL queries based on the metadata description and makes
    a database request.

5   The database returns a result set of data to Mondrian.

6   Mondrian returns the data to the user interface, using a standard API that is
    understood by the visualization tool.

7   Finally, the data is formatted graphically for the user in a tabular format that's
    easy to understand and manipulate.

The entire sequence typically only takes a few seconds, so business users are able to
explore a variety of different alternatives in a single analysis session. Additionally, if

you're using Mondrian as part of the Pentaho BI suite, you can use Mondrian as a source of data for Pentaho reports, enterprise dashboards, and, through direct manipulation in Analyzer, a thin-client front end. This makes Mondrian a very flexible engine for a variety of user-friendly interfaces, while still providing a standard data interface for developers.

> **MONDRIAN MDX** Although Mondrian strives to be compliant with Microsoft's version of MDX, there are a few minor differences. See the Mondrian site for an up-to-date list of differences: http://mondrian.pentaho.com/documentation/mdx.php.

### 1.3.3 *Mondrian is fast*

Mondrian is designed to run quickly. The structure of the OLAP database is designed for performance when doing calculations on large sets of data, with changes in analyses being shown in seconds. Additionally, Mondrian makes use of several optimization techniques, such as in-memory storage of calculations, to further increase speed. And because Mondrian can be embedded in a web application, it can easily be scaled for use by hundreds or thousands of users.

Although the performance gains vary significantly based on the structure of the data warehouse, the use of aggregate tables and in-memory caching can significantly increase performance. For example, one user had a fact table with several hundred million rows and eight dimension tables with up to 25 million rows. Running reports directly using SQL took about 10 minutes each. The addition of Mondrian with aggregations dropped the time to just over 8 seconds. With the addition of caching, these queries dropped to 2.4 seconds on average. Figure 1.10 illustrates the significant gains that can be made by using Mondrian (using Mondrian is more than 100 times faster, in this example).

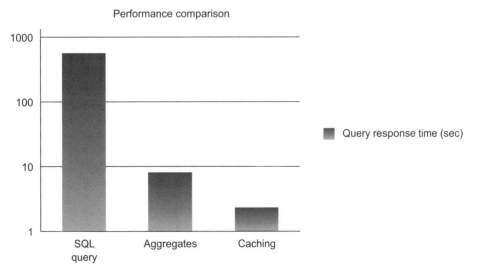

**Figure 1.10   Increased performance with Mondrian**

Because Mondrian is fast, it allows analysts to perform advanced analytics that would be very difficult or slow using SQL. For example, Mondrian has functions that let analysts do linear regression or compare period-over-period performance. It automatically does the calculations at the level desired, without the need to write a different query or program. This makes Mondrian an ideal solution for advanced analytics.

Fast results are essential for interactive analysis. Speed allows analysts to explore the data in a wide variety of ways and to discover things about the business, such as high-selling product lines, inventory problems at warehouses, and what web marketing strategies are effective. In later chapters, we'll show you how to organize the data for maximum performance. We'll also show you how to configure Mondrian to use aggregate tables and caching to further increase performance.

### 1.3.4  *Mondrian is secure*

In addition to performance, enterprises have other considerations when dealing with corporate data, such as restricting access to specific users and supporting tenanted environments with multiple clients. Mondrian uses a role-based approach to restrict data access.

Role-based security means that data is restricted based on a role associated with a user. For example, HR managers may have access to sensitive information about employees that shouldn't be shared with other employees. Financial managers will need to know costs, but inventory managers will only need to know inventory levels. By assigning unique roles to each of these different types of users, Mondrian can have a single analytics database but only show the data needed by each user. Analysis and reporting tools will only get the data appropriate for the particular user, so you don't need separate reports for different roles simply to limit data.

In the chapters on security, we'll show you how to apply roles to restrict access to sensitive data. We'll also show you some advanced approaches that you can use to make roles dynamic and to separate data for multiple clients, securing the data for each in a multi-tenanted environment. This latter feature is useful for organizations that don't just want to use analysis internally, but want to expose the analysis to external clients as well.

### 1.3.5  *Mondrian is based on open standards*

Since Mondrian is built on open technology standards, such as Java and web services, it can run on a wide variety of platforms and be included in both desktop clients and thin clients. This makes it easy to distribute the benefits of Mondrian and OLAP to users around the world. It also means that Mondrian users aren't tied into any particular hardware, operating system, or proprietary software.

Mondrian uses a variety of open, freely available standards. In particular, Mondrian supports the following standards:

- olap4j—An open standard for OLAP via Java
- XMLA—A standard for system-to-system interaction based on SOAP
- XML—A standard markup language that lets you create Mondrian schemas with a simple text editor

Because it supports olap4j and XMLA, it's easy to embed Mondrian and use it to provide a number of solution alternatives, such as interactive analyses, reports, and dashboards.

Mondrian works with most databases, including traditional relational databases such as Microsoft SQL Server, Oracle, PostgreSQL, and MySQL, as well as newer columnar databases, such as Greenplum, Netezza, and LucidDB. This means that although a business will often want to organize the data in ways that get the biggest benefit from Mondrian, they usually won't need a new database solution to do so. Database administrators can also continue to use the systems and tools that they know.

Finally, Mondrian is open source software. You can go online and download not only the binaries, but the source code as well, letting you tailor and extend Mondrian for your needs. Being open source has allowed a community of users and developers to help one another out and contribute ideas back into the project. The community participates in local user groups, online forums, and conferences.

For enterprises that want professional support and additional enterprise functionality, Mondrian is also shipped as part of the Pentaho Enterprise Edition, a complete business analytics platform that includes data warehousing, reporting, and data-mining tools.

Throughout the book, we'll show you how to configure and use a number of tools for Mondrian. We'll also show you how to use Mondrian as a source of analytics information for reports and dashboards. Finally, we'll show you how you can integrate Mondrian into your own applications either directly or using web services.

## 1.4    Summary

This chapter introduced you to business analytics with Mondrian. It covered the problems with report-based analysis and showed how Mondrian can address those problems and how Mondrian fits into the analytics architecture as the engine for analytics. Specifically you saw how Mondrian provides the following:

- User-driven analysis, where the user is free to explore the data
- Increased performance through the structure of the data warehouse, aggregates, and caching
- Enterprise features, such as role-based data access to restrict data to various users and groups

You should now have a good idea of what Mondrian can do and the types of problems it can help solve. You should also understand where Mondrian fits into the overall architecture of a BI solution. Finally, based on your role, you'll know what portions of the rest of the book are most relevant to your needs.

The next chapter will give you a brief tour of Mondrian, showing you how Mondrian provides data to users and how the data is structured and modeled to support analysis. You'll get a chance to run the system and perform analysis using Pentaho and Saiku.

# Mondrian: a first look

2

In the previous chapter, you saw how our fictional Adventure Works company could benefit by moving from a SQL-based reporting solution to one based on OLAP and Mondrian. Adventure Works has now implemented Mondrian inside of Pentaho, an open source business analytics suite. In this chapter, we'll take a look at how they implemented Mondrian and how they can use it for analysis. We'll start with a brief overview of the architecture, and then we'll see some types of things you can do with Mondrian. Finally, we'll talk about how the data gets from your operational systems into Mondrian for analysis.

In addition to learning how Adventure Works is using Mondrian for analysis, you'll be introduced to some user-interface tools that make analysis with Mondrian as simple as dragging and dropping. After reading this chapter, you'll understand the parts that make up a typical Mondrian deployment and how data is organized and described.

## 2.1  *Mondrian's role in analytics*

As we stated in chapter 1, Mondrian is an engine for analytics. It accepts analytical queries and converts them into relational queries, returning the data in a form that supports analytics. But for Mondrian to be useful to business users, it needs some sort of interface and application to run it.

There are a number of common ways that Mondrian can be deployed. It can be set up in an application server to run on its own and provide services. This approach tends not to be very user friendly because it doesn't have a nice graphical user interface. Mondrian can also be embedded in a standalone application. This approach is good for custom applications with a specific purpose but isn't as useful for supporting a wide variety of uses of Mondrian unless you have multiple applications. Finally, Mondrian can be deployed as part of a larger web application that provides tools for users to work with. This approach is the most flexible, but it also requires the most organization and configuration. Fortunately there are solutions that are easily configured and deployed.

Several products use Mondrian as their analytics engine for reporting and analysis, as shown in table 2.1. One such product is Pentaho, a popular open source business analytics server that includes Mondrian and has a variety of plugins to let users directly use Mondrian's capabilities. Pentaho is the largest open source distributor of Mondrian in the world, and it's used by thousands of organizations. Pentaho is also one of the main supporters and contributors to Mondrian, meaning Mondrian will continue to work with Pentaho in the foreseeable future, and new features in Mondrian will be quickly integrated into Pentaho.

**Table 2.1  Some products that use Mondrian**

| Name | Description |
|------|-------------|
| Pentaho Analyzer | Pentaho's enterprise analysis UI that provides interactive analysis with tables and graphs. |
| Pentaho Reporting | A reporting tool that creates pixel-perfect reports using Mondrian data. |
| Community Dashboard Framework | A popular open source dashboard framework for creating interactive dashboards. |
| Saiku | A free open source analytics tool that provides interactive analysis with tables and graphs. Saiku is available as a Pentaho plugin or a standalone product. |

Figure 2.1 shows how Mondrian fits into the architecture of Pentaho. This view is very simplified, but it contains the major parts of a system that uses Mondrian.

- Users interact using web-based tools.
- Mondrian accepts queries from these tools and then uses logical schema matches to generate SQL queries.
- Mondrian then returns the results to the clients for formatting and to display to users.

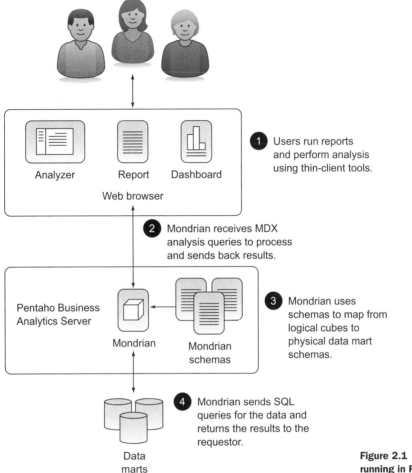

Figure 2.1 **Mondrian running in Pentaho**

Mondrian has been architected to be simple to integrate, yet flexible for a variety of users and interfaces to use.

Now that you know how Mondrian fits into a complete architecture, let's dive in and start to use it.

## 2.2   *Running and using Mondrian*

Mondrian is an analytic engine rather than an application or server, so it needs to run inside of another application or server. This makes Mondrian highly flexible in that it can be reused within a wide variety of applications and scenarios, depending on the business needs.

Adventure Works has several high-level functional requirements that dictate the approach they can take:

- Use a thin-client interface for user access.
- Provide users with predefined analytical reports.
- Allow users to do their own interactive analysis.
- Easily scale the system as the number of users grows.
- Provide data security based on users and their roles.
- Provide good support and examples for using the tools and system.
- Allow for expansion in the future.

Adventure Works investigated a number of different business analytics solutions and decided to use Pentaho Community Edition (CE). It provides a thin-client interface for users. There are open source tools that their analysts can use to create reports and dashboards based on Mondrian. There are also open source plugins for user-driven analysis. Because Pentaho CE is a web application, it can be scaled through standard web application scaling techniques, and it also has support for data security through the use of users and roles. Pentaho has good online documentation, a global community of users, and a number of companies that provide support and services. Finally, Pentaho is a framework that easily supports customization and expansion.

Pentaho comes in two flavors, Community Edition (CE) and Enterprise Edition (EE). CE is free to download and run; EE requires the purchase of licenses but comes with additional features and support. This early in the process, Adventure Works feels that they don't need the enterprise features yet, and they're willing to provide the technical support with help from the Pentaho and Mondrian online communities as needed. As their use of Pentaho grows, they know they may want to switch to EE, but they also know that anything they do in CE will migrate smoothly to EE.

In the rest of this section, you'll see how to run Pentaho CE with Mondrian and Saiku, an open source analysis tool that works with Mondrian. You'll get some hands-on experience with reports and analysis. We'll start with some simple, predefined reports and dashboards that Adventure Works has created in advance, and move on to user-driven, visual analysis that lets you, the user, do your own data analysis. Finally, we'll introduce you to some advanced analysis capabilities through the use of MDX queries.

### 2.2.1   Getting and running the software

To get you up and running quickly with Mondrian, we've created a virtual machine using VirtualBox, an open source, free solution from Oracle. Appendix A has instructions on how to download and run the virtual machine. The operating system is Ubuntu 12, a popular open source Linux distribution. If you don't know Ubuntu, don't worry. It probably looks a lot like whatever operating system you currently use, and we'll provide instructions as we go along.

Once you have the virtual machine up and running, you need to start the server if it isn't already. Open the terminal window by clicking on the icon on the left that looks like a black computer monitor with >_. A terminal window with a prompt should open.

To make working with Pentaho a little easier, a few commands have been created. Table 2.2 shows each command, what it does, and when to use it. To run the command, simply type it on the command line.

**Table 2.2  Pentaho convenience commands**

| Command | Description | When to use |
| --- | --- | --- |
| `ispentahorunning` | Responds with a message indicating whether or not Pentaho is running. | Use when you want to easily know if the Pentaho process is running. |
| `start_pentaho` | Starts the Pentaho BA server if it isn't running. | Use to start Pentaho when it isn't running. |
| `stop_pentaho` | Stops the Pentaho BA server if it is running. | Use to stop the Pentaho server. |
| `kill_pentaho` | Kills the Pentaho process. | Use as a last resort if `stop_pentaho` won't stop the process. |

Once Pentaho is running, open Firefox and go to http://localhost:8080/. You should see the login page shown in figure 2.2. Pentaho has some predefined users and passwords to make evaluation and experimentation easy, and you'll want to change these before deploying Pentaho for your organization, but for now just use Pentaho's users. Enter a username of joe and a password of password.

**Figure 2.2  Pentaho login page**

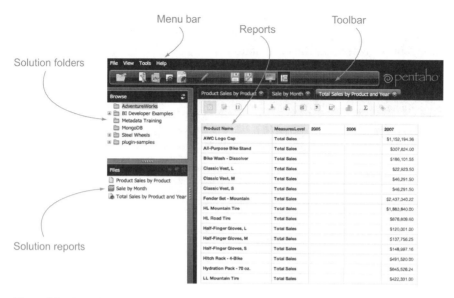

**Figure 2.3   Pentaho User Console (PUC)**

The Pentaho User Console, also known as the PUC, is the main screen for users (see figure 2.3). You can think of the PUC as the command console for business analytics. The PUC contains five main areas that you'll want to be familiar with:

1. The menu bar provides access to a variety of actions related to managing content.
2. The toolbar provides shortcuts to commonly used actions.
3. The solution browser shows all of the top-level solution folders and lets you browse into subfolders.
4. The list of solution reports shows the available objects for the selected folder in the solution browser.
5. Finally, the reports area is where you view and edit analysis and reports.

### 2.2.2   Navigation and viewing reports

Many users aren't interested in doing their own analysis, but just want to see the state of the data. The Adventure Works analysts have created a number of reports and dashboards that users can run by selecting them from the solutions pane. To open an existing report, simply click on the AdventureWorks folder in the solution browser and then double-click the solution object you want to view.

Figure 2.4 shows a report that Adventure Works has created for users to see product sales. The report was created with Pentaho Report Designer using Mondrian data as a source. Figure 2.5 shows a dashboard chart created using Community Dashboard Framework (CDF) using Mondrian as a data source. Finally, figure 2.6 shows a Saiku report that was previously created and saved. Users can open this report and edit it or simply view the latest data. The creation of reports, CDF dashboards, and other Pentaho content will be covered in a later chapter.

Product Sales as of July 27, 2012

| Product | Quantity Ordered | Unit Price | Total Sales |
|---|---|---|---|
| AWC Logo Cap | 2,190 | $ 19,688.10 | $ 43,116,939.00 |
| All-Purpose Bike Stand | 249 | $ 39,591.00 | $ 9,858,159.00 |
| Bike Wash - Dissolver | 908 | $ 7,218.60 | $ 6,554,488.80 |
| Classic Vest, L | 195 | $ 12,382.50 | $ 2,414,587.50 |
| Classic Vest, M | 199 | $ 12,636.50 | $ 2,514,663.50 |
| Classic Vest, S | 168 | $ 10,668.00 | $ 1,792,224.00 |
| Fender Set - Mountain | 2,121 | $ 46,619.58 | $ 98,880,129.18 |
| HL Mountain Tire | 1,396 | $ 48,860.00 | $ 68,208,560.00 |
| HL Road Tire | 858 | $ 27,970.80 | $ 23,998,946.40 |
| Half-Finger Gloves, L | 443 | $ 10,849.07 | $ 4,806,138.01 |
| Half-Finger Gloves, M | 499 | $ 12,220.51 | $ 6,098,034.49 |

**Figure 2.4   A Pentaho report: Product Sales Report**

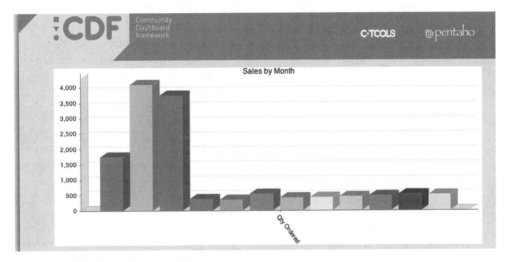

**Figure 2.5   CDF: Product Sales by Month**

| Product Name | MeasuresLevel | 2005 | 2006 | 2007 |
|---|---|---|---|---|
| AWC Logo Cap | Total Sales | | | $1,152,194.36 |
| All-Purpose Bike Stand | Total Sales | | | $307,824.00 |
| Bike Wash - Dissolver | Total Sales | | | $186,101.55 |
| Classic Vest, L | Total Sales | | | $22,923.50 |
| Classic Vest, M | Total Sales | | | $46,291.50 |
| Classic Vest, S | Total Sales | | | $46,291.50 |
| Fender Set - Mountain | Total Sales | | | $2,437,340.22 |
| HL Mountain Tire | Total Sales | | | $1,883,840.00 |
| HL Road Tire | Total Sales | | | $876,809.60 |
| Half-Finger Gloves, L | Total Sales | | | $120,001.00 |
| Half-Finger Gloves, M | Total Sales | | | $137,756.25 |

**Figure 2.6   Saiku: Product Sales by Year**

### 2.2.3 Interactive analytics

Reports are convenient for standard, recurring questions, but many other tools support reporting. Where Mondrian really shines is by providing fast interactive analytics. This capability allows users to ask questions and discover information that's not obvious from a static report. For example, a marketing manager may want to know the impact of promotions by gender. Mondrian with an analysis UI, such as Analyzer or Saiku, allows the manager to do this kind of analysis interactively without the need for technical support.

Initially, Adventure Works has chosen to use the Saiku plugin with Pentaho. Saiku is a popular open source graphical analysis tool for Mondrian that can be run standalone or as a Pentaho plugin. Pentaho CE comes with JPivot preinstalled, but Adventure Works likes the more elegant and intuitive interface provided by Saiku. Pentaho also provides a more advanced analysis plugin called Analyzer in the Enterprise Edition, but it requires purchasing a license, and Adventure Works feels Saiku will meet all of their initial needs. Figure 2.7 shows the Saiku editor.

The Saiku editor is made up of several related sections. Across the top of the screen is the Saiku toolbar, which lets you control the screen, enter advanced commands, drill down, export data, and even create charts. Below the toolbar is where you drag the dimensions and measures for analysis and add any filters to restrict the data. Along the left side are the cubes, dimensions, and measures. The canvas shows the current results of analysis. In this example, people with some college or a bachelor's degree appear to be the best customers. More analysis is required, but perhaps this calls for more advertising on college campuses or research into why people without college degrees don't buy as much.

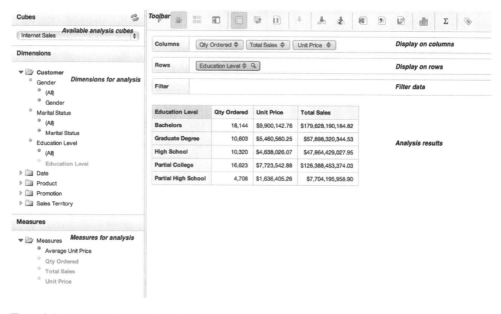

**Figure 2.7  Interactive analysis with Saiku**

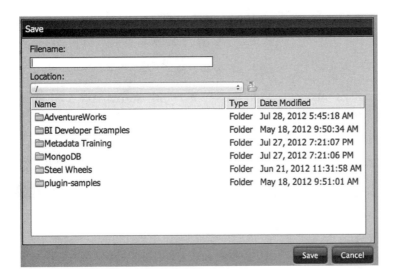

**Figure 2.8 Save a report**

To try it yourself, select a cube from the drop-down list—the form automatically populates the dimensions and measures. We'll describe dimensions in more detail shortly and in the next couple of chapters, but they're basically the attributes for analysis, such as territory, date, customer info, and so on. The measures are the values used for the analysis, such as quantity ordered, sales, inventory, number of website visits, and the like. Next, drag the dimensions and measures you want to use to the rows and columns. Saiku will automatically update the report with the results of your analysis.

Often you might want the values to be shown visually rather than as a table of values. To see a chart, click on the chart icon, and the values are converted to a chart. You can now click on the different types of charts to see the data displayed in different ways.

One of the challenges of charts is that they can quickly become overloaded with data and hard to read and interpret. Typically charts should only have a few values on each axis. Experiment to find the type of chart that best represents your data.

Once you have an analysis or chart you like, you can save it for future use either as it is or in a dashboard. Click on the disk icon on the main toolbar to get the Save dialog box (see figure 2.8). If you double-click on the saved file in the solution list, it will open up the saved analysis in the Saiku plugin.

### 2.2.4 *MDX analysis with Saiku*

Drag-and-drop analysis provides a lot of power and insight to business users—they can rapidly perform a wide variety of analyses without knowing a query language or understanding the details of the underlying database. But experienced analysts might want to perform advanced analyses that aren't supported directly by drag and drop, such as comparing to a previous period or doing linear regression.

Saiku lets you go beyond drag and drop and perform advanced analysis using MDX queries. Multidimensional Expressions (MDX) is a query language for OLAP that allows you to use advanced techniques, such ratio to reported, parallel period comparisons, period over period growth, traffic lighting, and so forth. Mondrian will support virtually all standard MDX queries that you write.

**LEARNING MDX**   Multidimensional Expressions (MDX) is a large topic. We'll cover some of the basics of MDX and the expressions you'll likely find useful, but covering all of MDX is beyond the scope of this book. MDX is covered in detail in a number of other books as well as the Microsoft website.

For example, suppose you want to be able to compare the current sales quarter to the same quarter of the previous year. The following MDX query would allow you to do that.

**Listing 2.1   Comparing quarters across years**

```
WITH MEMBER [Measures].[Previous Year Sales]
AS (
  [Measures].[Total Sales],
  PARALLELPERIOD([Order Date].[Monthly].[Quarter].CurrentMember, 4)
)
SELECT
NON EMPTY {[Measures].[Total Sales],
          [Measures].[Previous Year Sales]} ON COLUMNS,
NON EMPTY {{[Order Date].[Monthly].[Year].Members},
          {[Order Date].[Monthly].[Quarter].Members}} ON ROWS
FROM [Internet Sales]
```

To enter this query, click the button to switch into MDX mode. Saiku will show you the MDX for the current query. You can modify that query or create one from scratch. Enter the preceding MDX command and click the Run Query button. You should get a table with the results of the query, as in figure 2.9.

Now that you've seen what you can do with Mondrian, let's look at the underlying data and schemas that are used to support Mondrian. The next section will introduce multidimensional modeling. Then we'll introduce the data warehouse that supplies Mondrian with analytics data.

| Year | Quarter | Total Sales | Previous Year Sales |
|------|---------|-------------|---------------------|
| 2005 | 3 | $651,178,252.66 | |
| | 4 | $1,024,260,685.73 | |
| 2006 | 1 | $999,767,736.77 | |
| | 2 | $1,278,897,705.22 | |
| | 3 | $1,022,482,207.64 | $651,178,252.66 |
| | 4 | $998,505,090.29 | $1,024,260,685.73 |
| 2007 | 1 | $1,113,861,876.16 | $999,767,736.77 |
| | 2 | $1,542,772,505.10 | $1,278,897,705.22 |
| | 3 | $23,425,778,506.39 | $1,022,482,207.64 |

**Figure 2.9   Results showing comparison to same quarter a year ago**

### Errors in MDX queries

MDX can get complex, and it's picky about syntax. If you have an error in your query, you usually get an error message, particularly for syntax errors. Unfortunately, many other errors result in no data being returned with no indication of the problem. When beginning with MDX, we recommend that you build a query one piece at a time, checking after each change to make sure the query still works.

> **(continued)**
> You can often get a more detailed error message from the tomcat log files. These files are found in the .../tomcat/logs directory. On Unix-like systems, such as the sample VM discussed in appendix A the filename is catalina.out.

## 2.3 *Multidimensional modeling*

Now that you've seen how Adventure Works users use Mondrian for analysis, it's time to talk about what you need to do to make it possible. Mondrian, as an OLAP engine, presents data multidimensionally: the content are data facts that the business analysts want to know about, such as sales and inventory, and the dimensions are attributes about the data for analysis, such as warehouse, geography, customer demographics, and so on.

In this section, we'll introduce modeling via cubes and look at how these models are derived. In chapter 4, we'll explore defining the Mondrian schema in detail.

### 2.3.1 *A simple report*

A senior manager walks into an analyst's office with a question. "I'd like to know more about the demographics of our customers. Can you tell me whether we are selling more to customers who have a college education this year than last year?"

"Sure, I'll build a Sales cube and show you the results this afternoon."

The analyst builds the schema shown in figure 2.10.

The schema, named `Sales`, contains a cube, also named `Sales`. The cube has two measures, `Units` and `Store Sales`, and two dimensions, `Time` and `Customer`. The `Time` dimension has the attributes `Year`, `Month`, and `Day`, and the `Customer` dimension has the attributes `Education` and `Name`.

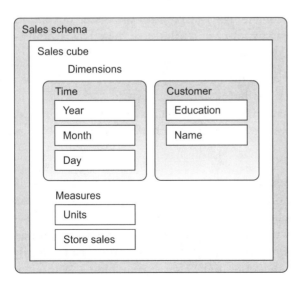

**Figure 2.10  Sales schema**

**VIEWING THE ADVENTURE WORKS SCHEMA**   If you're using the virtual machine, you can find the Adventure Works schema in a file called adventure _works.mondrian.xml in the /opt/pentaho/biserver-ce-4.5/biserver-ce/ pentaho-solutions/adventure_work folder.

What a schema contains and how you define it are described in chapter 4, but for the purposes of building a report, you only need to know the logical elements. There's also sufficient information in the schema to map these dimensions, attributes, and measures onto the tables and columns of the database, so the analyst is able to write an MDX query:

```
SELECT {[Measures].[Units],
       [Measures].[Store Sales]} ON COLUMNS,
   Crossjoin([Time].[Year].Members,
          [Customer].[Education].Members) ON ROWS
FROM [Sales]
```

And the query produces the desired result:

```
Year Education            Unit Sales Store Sales
==== =================== ========== ===========
2011 All Educations          66,291  139,628.35
     Bachelors Degree        17,066   35,699.43
     Graduate Degree          3,637    7,583.71
     High School Degree      19,755   41,945.65
     Partial College          6,309   13,336.92
     Partial High School     19,524   41,062.64
2012 All Educations          62,610  132,666.27
     Bachelors Degree        16,175   34,552.11
     Graduate Degree          3,880    8,096.90
     High School Degree      17,907   37,797.71
     Partial College          5,852   12,389.92
     Partial High School     18,796   39,829.63
```

**HIERARCHIES AND ATTRIBUTES**   Actually, MDX uses *hierarchies*, not *attributes*. Mondrian generates a hierarchy for each attribute, so the effect is almost the same. See section 4.3.3 for the full story.

Note that almost all of these elements (the Sales cube, Customer and Time dimensions, the Year and Education attributes, and the Units and Store Sales measures) are referenced in the MDX query. Because Mondrian is a query engine, the purpose of a Mondrian schema is basically to define elements that can be used in MDX queries.

### 2.3.2   *Modeling business questions*

How do you convert a business question into a dimensional model? In this section, we'll look at how the abstractions of dimensional modeling—cubes, dimensions, attributes, and measures—can model the running of an enterprise.

   In the previous example, the process of designing a schema was instigated by a question from a business user. It was then possible to construct just the attributes and measures necessary to answer that question. This is as it should be. Without a business question to provide focus, the natural inclination would be to pull in every piece of information in the operational schema and produce an over-complicated analytic schema. A specific question helps you to focus on what is important.

**EVOLVING A SCHEMA** Mondrian makes it easy to evolve a schema by adding attributes, dimensions, measures, and calculations when you need them. This allows you to take an agile approach, just building what you need today.

The dimensional model can be gleaned by listening to the business user's question. Each of the key concepts will likely turn into a cube, an attribute, a dimension, or a measure. Attributes correspond to nouns, and attributes that are related (because they describe the same entity in the business) are grouped into dimensions. Quantifiable values are measures. Cubes describe business processes, so they tend to appear as verbs. If the business user says "compare based on ..." or "break down by ...", the next noun will likely be something that will become an attribute in the dimensional model.

For example, the manager might say "Can you break the report down by quarter?" and the analyst would infer that a `[Quarter]` attribute should be added to the `[Time]` dimension.

Sometimes it's not so obvious what dimension the attribute belongs to. For example, if the manager says, "Can you compare based on discount levels?" the analyst can ask a follow-up question: "Does each customer always get the same discount level?" If the manager says, "Yes," the analyst is pleased. This means that `[Discount Level]` should be an attribute of the `[Customer]` dimension. Life is simple.

But suppose the manager's reply was, "Yes and no. Each customer's discount level depends on whether they are a gold or silver customer, and we decide that each quarter. Plus, our sales managers can use their discretion to increase the discount level for really large orders." Here's how the analyst should decode this reply. Discount Level should be a new dimension, so that it can vary for each transaction. The business rule to populate the Discount Level is complicated, and would probably lead to unacceptable SQL performance if performed at runtime. The pragmatic solution is to make Discount Level a column in the fact table, populate it using the business rule when the data is populated in the data warehouse, and build a dimension on top of that column. This keeps the runtime schema simple, and simple schemas perform much better than complicated ones.

Cubes (and the fine-grained events of which they are composed) often appear as verbs. In the original question in section 2.3.1, the manager asked, "Are we selling more ...?" The verb "selling" or sales can become a cube.

Facts within the cube are occurrences of a business process; examples of business processes include sales, shipments of orders, inventory entering or leaving a warehouse, calls arriving at a call center, clicks on a company's website, and mentions of a company's name or products in social media.

If you're familiar with entity-relationship modeling, you're probably wondering whether business processes are a kind of entity. Despite the fact that they're stored as rows in a database, they're not entities. Business processes happen on their own schedule, often outside the company and its information systems, and often don't have a natural unique identifier. Without a unique identifier, they don't qualify as entities in the classical sense of entity-relationship modeling. Consider an HR system: an employee is an entity, but every update to that employee (hiring, firing or resignation, promotion, pay raise, transfer to a different department) is an instance of a business process. Although these business processes involve the same entity, they're different business processes and should be in different cubes. This is why the business question, to motivate the design of the dimensional model, is so important. The cubes you'll need to build, such as [Employee Hires] and [Employee Transfers], are not obvious if you only look at the tables and columns of the operational database.

In the language of traditional modeling, instances of a business process are more like events. Events can be so multitudinous that it's not practical to consider them individually. Instead you should look at the aggregate properties of events that occurred in a similar context. These properties are called *measures*.

Measures are powerful because they apply not only to individual events but to collections of events that occurred in a similar context (time, place, and so forth). For example, you can look at the sum of all sales that occurred in a particular month and region. This is much more powerful than simply generating a report of sales.

In summary,

- *Measures* are the quantities you use to analyze a business process.
- *Attributes* are how you slice the set of measurements into regions that you can compare.
- *Dimensions* are convenient collections of attributes.
- *Cubes* contain the measures, attributes, and dimensions necessary to answer a particular business question.

The Mondrian schema describes the data and organizes it dimensionally. But you need actual data for your analysis. The next section describes how to get the data and organize it for analysis.

## 2.4 *Getting and organizing the data*

So far we've explored the dashboards, reports, and on-demand analysis available to Adventure Works users. We've also looked at how you can organize that information into measures, dimensions, cubes, and schemas. Now we'll dive a bit deeper to see what an analyst needs to do to enable this capability.

The basic process for getting data to the analyst is shown in figure 2.11. Data is typically extracted from the transactional business system (OLTP) into an OLAP database, via a process known as extract, transform, and load (ETL). Mondrian then uses data source definitions to find the data and Mondrian schemas to interpret the data. Mondrian converts MDX queries to SQL queries to get data for users via an analytics tool such as Analyzer or Saiku. In the remainder of this chapter, we'll show how you can

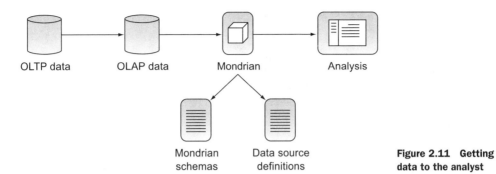

**Figure 2.11  Getting data to the analyst**

get and organize the data, and then describe and expose it for Mondrian's use. Then, in the next few chapters, we'll go deeper into each topic.

### 2.4.1  *The data warehouse: physically storing the data*

As you saw in the previous section, Mondrian presents data as cubes with multiple dimensions for analysis. But Mondrian doesn't store the data; it simply provides a logical view of the physical data. Mondrian is a relational OLAP (ROLAP) engine, meaning that the data is stored in a relational database and Mondrian translates MDX queries into SQL queries for the particular RDBMS you use for storage. This has a number of advantages from a technical perspective:

- You can choose a database that's optimized for the types of queries analysts will typically perform.
- You get all of the backup, failover, and clustering capabilities of an RDBMS system that DBAs are already used to.
- ROLAP engines don't precalculate intersections of dimensions, so the data is available to analysts as soon as it's updated in the database.
- You can switch to a different database in the future and still use Mondrian (assuming the new database is supported).

Mondrian allows you to store your data in a wide variety of ways and expose it for analytic use, but some ways of organizing the data are better than others. The data warehousing industry discovered years ago that organizing data into "star schemas" allows for fast analysis of large amounts of data. This is because the relationships between the data are simplified, and the number of joins needed to connect data is minimized.

Figure 2.12 shows a normalized database schema versus a star schema. In the normalized data, to get information about where orders for a particular product originate, you'd have to join the Product, Line Items, Purchase Order, Customer, City-State, State-Country, and Country-Territory tables. The star schema eliminates these complex multiple joins, and it's easy to understand how the data is related. Using a star schema, the joins are reduced to the Purchase, Geography, and Products tables. Reducing the number of joins simplifies the schema and typically increases performance.

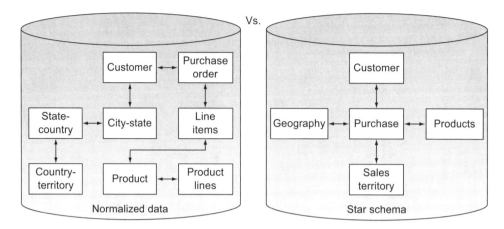

**Figure 2.12** **Normalized data vs. star schemas**

The star schema is simplified by combining related data into single, denormalized tables. For example, the City-State, State-Country, Country-Territory tables are all combined into a Geography table. This means that there are multiple copies of a state to country mapping, increasing data storage and possibly requiring the update of multiple records should a mapping change (for example, if a country splits into multiple countries). In chapter 3, we'll talk about ways to avoid the redundancy, but the choice is generally to pay for additional storage to get faster analysis. The time of a business analyst is usually worth much more than the cost of additional storage space.

### 2.4.2 *Examining the Adventure Works data*

To see how the Adventure Works data is stored, you can use any MySQL tool to view the data. From the command line, type mysql -u root -p. You should be presented with a mysql> prompt. At the prompt, type use adventure_works_dw;. This will change to using the Adventure Works database. To see the tables in the database, type show tables;. We're using a common convention of starting dimension tables with dim_.

   Let's take a quick look at a couple of tables. Type describe internet_sales;. You'll see a bunch of key fields and other values. The values are the facts that we're measuring, and the key fields are the foreign keys to the dimension tables. For example, the ProductKey field is the key into the dim_product table.

   If you now type describe dim_product;, you'll see all of the values that you can use in the dimension. For example, we use EnglishProductName as the product name attribute in the dimension. Because we have a product name and a link between the sales and product tables, we're able to do analysis of facts by product. Note that the fields in the dim_product table can be used as levels in the dimension or as attributes. How they're used depends on the relationship between the fields and the types of questions you want to answer.

### 2.4.3   *Populating the data*

The data in the warehouse is populated via a process known as extract, transform, and load (ETL), illustrated in figure 2.13. The name describes the process. First the data is extracted from the source system, which is usually one or more transactional, relational databases that have normalized database schemas, but big data systems, such as Hadoop, and NoSQL systems, such as MongoDB, are also becoming more common. The data is then transformed to fit into the data warehouse schema. This can include steps such as data cleansing and changing the data so it's easier for business users to understand. Finally the data is loaded into the data warehouse, organized as a star schema where it can be used by Mondrian.

An additional benefit of moving data from transactional systems to analytics systems is that the multiple data sources can be combined into a single data warehouse. Businesses, particularly large enterprises, often have many complex operational databases. For example, they may have a system for inventory and warehouses, a CRM system for customer information, an HR system for employee information, and so on. Combining this information into a unified data warehouse enables more sophisticated analysis, such as viewing changes in inventory (from the inventory system) based on sales in a particular region (from the CRM system) by individual salespeople (from the HR system).

In the past, ETL was done via custom software and scripts, and the source data was typically stored in a relational database. With the growth of the web and the huge amounts of data being created, important data needed for analysis often resides in multiple databases, text files, NoSQL databases, and Hadoop. Writing custom software to perform the ETL step is a huge undertaking, both to develop and to maintain.

Fortunately, Pentaho also provides an open source tool called Kettle (a.k.a. Pentaho Data Integration, or PDI) that makes ETL much easier. Kettle provides a graphical interface, called Spoon, that allows users to graphically create sequences of steps to manipulate data. A series of steps is called a *transformation* because it "transforms" data from the input source to the format that's needed for analysis. For example, a transformation might read some measures from multiple tables in the operational database. The measures might then be manipulated, such as performing calculations or converting cryptic codes to user-readable values. Then dimension keys are looked up to associate the fact (numeric) data with dimension members, such as dates or geography. Finally, the data is put into the analytics database. At no point in the process does a user have to write code.

Kettle provides support for a wide variety of data sources and conversions that would be difficult to write by hand. Kettle allows you to access non-relational data

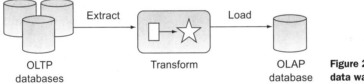

OLTP                    Transform                    OLAP          **Figure 2.13   Loading the**
databases                                            database      **data warehouse using ETL**

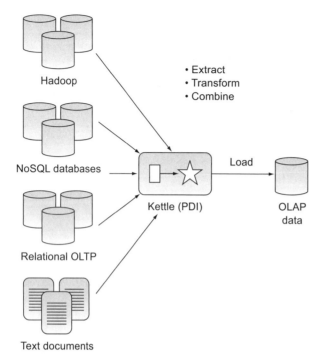

Hadoop

NoSQL databases

Relational OLTP

Text documents

• Extract
• Transform
• Combine

Kettle (PDI)

Load

OLAP
data

**Figure 2.14   Using Kettle for ETL**

and "big data" from systems such as Hadoop and MongoDB without the often difficult coding that has traditionally been required. Finally, Kettle jobs can be sched-
uled, allowing data to be updated regularly so that analysts have the most recent
numbers to work with. Figure 2.14 shows how Kettle fits into the previously defined
ETL process.

## 2.5    Summary

In this chapter, you got an introduction to how Mondrian is used to provide analytics
services in a business setting. We discussed how Mondrian fits into the architecture of
Pentaho. You also saw some of the things Adventure Works is doing with Mondrian. In
particular, you learned the following:

- Mondrian is an engine that's run inside a server or application, such as Pentaho
  Business Analytics.
- Mondrian can be used to generate predefined reports and dashboards.
- Through the use of plugins, such as Saiku and Pentaho Analyzer, business users
  can do their own interactive analysis.
- Advanced power-users can create complex analysis queries using MDX.
- Mondrian uses a logical schema to map from physical data to a multidimen-
  sional cube.

- For efficient work, it helps to denormalize data into a star schema.
- The process of migrating data is called ETL, and it can be simplified through the use of tools such as Pentaho Data Integration (PDI).

In the next chapter, we'll dive deeper into the structure and logic of the data warehouse. Then we'll cover the major portions of the Mondrian schema before moving on to more advanced topics. These chapters will give you enough information to begin creating your own data warehouse and providing analytics solutions based on Mondrian.

# *Creating the data mart* 3

Mondrian makes it easy for users to do analysis, but behind the scenes it requires data organized in a way that's convenient for analysis. Historically data has been organized for operational use in third normal form (3NF), but Mondrian has adopted the use of star schema structures based on industry best practices.

In this chapter, we'll cover the general architecture of an analytic solution and then explore star schemas, the "best practice" database modeling technique for analytic systems. We'll dig into their specifics, understanding that Mondrian is expecting to perform its analytic magic on top of a star schema. We'll compare this with third normal form modeling and examine some of the high-level benefits of the star schema for an analytic system.

We'll conclude with a few additional aspects of the star schema technique, including how to manage changes to data over time, modeling the all-important time dimensions.

By the end of this chapter, you'll understand how data is structured to make analysis with Mondrian possible. This chapter is primarily aimed at the data architect, but other readers will likely find understanding the data architecture useful as well.

## 3.1 Structuring data for analytics

Before we can get into the details of how to build the underlying physical architecture, it's helpful to understand what we're trying to accomplish and the high-level architecture required to meet these goals. In this section, you'll learn why a particular database architecture is needed and how it aids in analysis. By the end of the section, you should understand what a star schema is and how it supports the goals of online analytic processing.

### 3.1.1 Characteristics of analytic systems

As the data warehouse (DW) or business intelligence (BI) architect or developer for Adventure Works, you're charged with making sure the analytics presented to your users exhibit the following three characteristics:

- *Fast*—Users expect results at the "speed of thought," and the fact that your database is scanning millions of transactions to build these results is irrelevant to them. If you haven't presented them with the results quickly enough for them to continue asking questions, refining their results, and exploring, you've lost them.

   **FAST RULE OF THUMB**  If the reporting results take long enough that the user considers going to refill their coffee, your solution isn't fast enough.

- *Consistent and accurate*—Nothing drives users more insane than running two reports in a system and getting results that don't match. For instance, if your OLAP system produces reports on sales by quarter and by year, and the quarterly totals don't add up to the yearly total (as in table 3.1), your users will lose confidence in how accurate the analytics presented by your system are. Your solution must never present results like these.

Table 3.1  Inconsistent and inaccurate results are bad

| Year | Quarter | USD sales |
|------|---------|-----------|
| 2012 | Quarter 1 | $50 |
| 2012 | Quarter 2 | $50 |
| 2012 | Quarter 3 | $100 |
| 2012 | Quarter 4 | $100 |
| 2012 | All Quarters | $350—Different! |

- *Information focused*—Users don't care that the SKU for the product is contained in the column UNIQUE_RESOURCE_LOCATOR in their ERP source system and that it's in the PLU_BASE_UNIT column in the CRM tool. The analytics you present in your OLAP system must focus on the *information subjects,* such as sales and customers, that are analytically significant to your users. Users want to see the customer name "Bob" and the state "California" instead of the transactional IDs for the values (100, 22CA1, and so on).

ERP and CRM systems use IDs and codes, but users think in names and labels. Additionally, transactional (OLTP) systems, like your CRM and ERP, change over time. The OLAP system needs to handle data changes with grace, and delivering reports in terms of information subjects insulates you somewhat from these inevitable changes. Your company may someday move from Oracle Applications to Salesforce.com, but if your analytic system is just sales and customers, this change need not affect the reports.

> ### Desired characteristics of analytic systems
> - Fast
> - Consistent and accurate
> - Information focused

If you've worked with technology for any period of time, you're likely thinking that the fast, consistent, and information-focused objectives aren't implemented easily. These objectives are not the low-hanging fruit that the installation of a single piece of software can achieve. Let's look at the architectures that will help you achieve these characteristics.

### 3.1.2  *Data architecture for analytics*

Fortunately for all of us, building analytic systems to meet the objectives outlined in the previous section is not new. Many thousands of professionals—numerous authors, experts in the industry, and vendors—have spent years refining the tools, techniques, and best practices for implementing analytic systems that are fast, consistent, and information focused.

This collective wisdom boils down to two almost universally accepted tenets of building analytic systems:

- *Copy data to systems dedicated for analytics*—Data, unlike physical assets, can be duplicated with relative ease. Your transaction systems require advanced security and high availability, and they're designed to be fully available to run your company. They are, generally speaking, ill-suited to performing aggregations across many areas, such as multitable joins, and typically include analytic reporting as a bolt-on piece of the primary application. Doing analytics on these systems is a common source of poor system availability and high system loads. If you're reading this, there's a decent chance that you've received an email from a DBA or system administrator complaining about a running query that's slowing down the whole system.

- *Transform, clean, and enrich data for analytics*—While these transactional systems tend to be flexible, they speak a foreign language of codes, effective dates, keys, composite keys, and joins. Data is what transactional systems are built to manage, but that's not what matters to the analytic users. The industry knows that in order for the data to be useful, it must undergo a transformation from data (in the form of CSV files or raw tables in a database) into information subjects such as sales or customers. Often, the data necessary to do an analysis isn't even present in the original data stream, and integrating, matching, and enriching this data in the analytic system is necessary to present certain analytics. The act of moving data from the source system to the analytics system is referred to as extract, transform, and load (ETL).

### Two tenets of OLAP

- Copy data to systems dedicated for analytics.
- Transform, clean, and enrich data for analytics.

Whether you're working with a data warehouse that serves as the long-term storage of company data, a single analysis area commonly called a data mart, or an interdependent set of data marts, the industry has determined that *analytics should be done on separate computer resources and include data that has been cleaned, transformed, and enriched from multiple source systems.* Figure 3.1 shows an overview of a typical analytic environment with separate source systems and analytic systems. Data is copied to the analytic environment via ETL, and users access their reports and data in the analytic environment rather than working directly against the source systems.

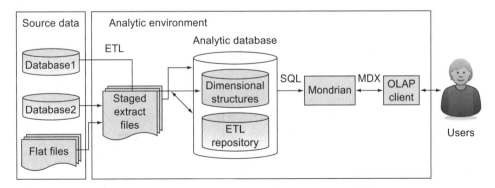

**Figure 3.1** **Analytic architecture overview: data is copied (and enriched) from the source systems to a dedicated analytic environment, which is where users (via Mondrian) access analytic data.**

### 3.1.3   *Star schemas*

The common need for analytic systems that are fast, consistent, and information focused has led the industry to a widely accepted best practice of *dimensional modeling* based on the physical star schema methods. We'll briefly explain the basics of the star schema and how it meets these goals, and compare it with third normal form modeling (3NF).

The star schema is an industry best-practice modeling technique optimized for massive, dynamic aggregations. 3NF modeling is the industry best practice for modeling transactional systems (OLTP), but star schemas are the best practice for analytics (OLAP). The concepts and specifics are outlined comprehensively in the authoritative book on the topic by Ralph Kimball and his colleagues, *The Data Warehouse Lifecycle Toolkit, 2nd edition* (Wiley, 2008). If you're looking for more advanced techniques or greater detail on any concepts introduced and intentionally kept brief in this chapter, we encourage you to refer to that book. We'll cover, later in this chapter, some of the reasons a star schema is a best practice and its numerous benefits.

For all intents and purposes, Mondrian expects your data to be in a relational database, in the star schema format (or one of its closely related permutations). The star schema, as a set of relational database tables, is what Mondrian uses as the basis to perform aggregations and analytics.

We're going to cover the general structure of a star schema, but it's worth noting that the specifics of each individual business model are driven by the analysis needs of that particular company, department, or user. In chapter 2, we noted that the desired analytics and model for Mondrian cubes drive the design of both the Mondrian schema and the star schema that supports it. To understand how the analytic needs of users drive the actual implementation model, we'll use Adventure Works as an example.

Adventure Works managers want to understand how much revenue they're selling to which types of customers. They're looking to understand, first, their sales by customer state. They'll eventually wish to look at additional attributes, such as sales over time, but for our first foray into star schemas, the basic request for sales by customer state will suffice.

> **MONDRIAN AND STAR SCHEMAS**   Mondrian expects your data to be in a relational database, in a star schema which is an industry best-practice modeling technique for OLAP systems.

A star schema consists of a *fact* table surrounded by multiple *dimension* tables. The shape of a fact surrounded by dimensions is how the star schema gets its name.

*Fact* tables contain the stuff you're trying to aggregate, total, and measure. The numbers that are added together to create the total sales number are contained in the fact table and are referred to as the *measures* in the cubes (more on this in chapter 4). The measures are the *what* you're trying to measure and analyze. In our example and figure 3.2, sales is the *what* we're trying to measure.

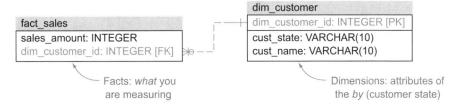

**Figure 3.2** **Star schema. The *fact* contains the *what* you're trying to measure—sales, and more specifically the column that has the data to be aggregated, sales_amount. The dimensions are the *by* attributes that you're trying to segment and allocate the data to—customer, and more specifically the state the customer is from, customer_state.**

*Dimension* tables contain the qualifying attributes that you want to split out those numbers (the measures) by. In our example and figure 3.2, the users wish to split out the total sales (in the fact table) by customer state, so that you can see the total sales for each state individually, along with the total sales for all states. Customer state is the *by* that you are trying to use for comparison and filtering.

*What* you are trying to measure (revenue, web impressions, customer calls, and so on) is in the *fact* table. The things you are trying to split it out *by* (product, geography, and the like) are in the *dimension* tables.

When looking at the physical database model, a star schema consists of the following:

- *Dimension tables* that contain rows, independent of the transactions that have the attributes. For instance, a product dimension would contain a row per product and contain information on product categories, vendors, departments, and the like. Typically this foreign key is also non-nullable, so that you can aggregate the table at any combination of dimensions and always get the same sum total. Remember, consistency is one of the goals, and this ability to aggregate at any combination of dimensions helps keep the sum totals consistent, avoiding the results in table 3.1.

  **SIMPLE EXAMPLE WITHOUT HISTORY** This design, with a single row per product, is a simple example for a Type I dimension. Please see section 3.2.1 on Slowly Changing Dimensions later in this chapter for more detailed discussion of keeping history for dimensions.

  Dimension tables are highly denormalized with many columns when compared to their original source system tables. Your source system may have included information about departments in a table separate from employees, but in the star schema the department name is now a column in the employee dimension.

- A *single fact table* that contains a row for the individual transactions (order line items, individual clicks) matching the grain of the table (see Kimball's book for more information on "grain"). The fact table contains a set of surrogate integer keys that easily join to the dimension tables for the attributes associated. Additionally, it will usually have one or more columns that contain the values to be aggregated, associated with that single transaction.

The other thing to note is that using this technique means that *fact tables typically contain at least 10 times, but more commonly at least 1000 times, more records than the dimension tables.* Fact tables contain millions to billions of rows, and dimension tables typically contain thousands to just a few million. This has important performance benefits, and it's a key reason why this modeling technique can deliver speedy results even when millions of facts are involved.

---

**Star schema: facts and dimensions**

Facts

- Are the *what* you are trying to measure
- Are usually numeric, and are aggregated (sum, count, or avg)
- Contain millions (or more) of "skinny" records, typically only integers and numbers
- Uses many non-nullable foreign keys to dimension records

Dimensions

- Are the *by* you use to allocate or split your numerics
- Contain thousands (sometimes more) of "fat" records, typically with many varchar and descriptive attributes
- Are highly denormalized, often containing typically separate items (such as customer and state names) together in a single table

---

### 3.1.4   *Comparing star schemas with 3NF*

Given that you're reading this book, you've likely either designed, built, maintained, or optimized a database schema for an application. We'll review the technique and then examine why we'll depart from it and use the star schema.

As a brief refresher, 3NF is a modeling technique in which redundancy is reduced, and foreign keys are introduced so that additional attributes (such as the name of the state) are located in a different location and must be accessed in another table.

The 3NF model has been blessed as the "correct" database modeling technique with little discussion or questioning. 3NF is, for the most part, the best model for transactional systems like an ERP or CRM. The 3NF modeling techniques are ideal in the following situations:

- *Lots of concurrent users reading and modifying data*—Keeping similar data together, and factoring out and normalizing repetitive data (such as department names, locations, and the like) allows lots of users to operate on smaller sections of the dataset independently and without conflicts (or locks).

- *Subprograms and people are accessing small slices of data*—Typically users of an HR system are not going to update the last name of every employee in the company. They will, more likely, access a single employee and update the last name of a single record.

- *Source systems usually access smaller slices of data joined together with a foreign key—* These joins are inexpensive with a relatively small amount of data. Databases, to reassemble a complete order with line items, typically need to do two small indexed reads into two tables (for example, retrieving the orders from one table and line items from another). Reading two different locations is a small amount of overhead when dealing with a single order.

The 3NF technique is not, however, a good model for a few users doing large aggregations touching entire sets of data. Joining a single record to others (a small amount of data) tends to be efficient. Joining many tables, to include all the attributes used for qualification (large numbers of database rows) requires much more work by the database. You've likely written a few SQL statements for your reports that are a page or two themselves, and their database EXPLAIN is a small chapter of a book; these queries tend to perform poorly as the dataset grows in size. We certainly wrote our share of these expensive, poorly performing queries before embarking on our OLAP adventures.

If you're accustomed to 3NF modeling, the first star schemas you design will not feel "right." They'll leave you with a strange, lingering feeling that you've just built a terrible data model. Over time, though, as the fit between the star schemas and the use cases becomes increasingly apparent, the modeling technique won't feel quite so strange.

### 3.1.5 Star schema benefits

We can't cover all the benefits of the star schema in this book, but at a top level, the star schema has the following benefits:

- *Star schemas require at most one pass through the table.* There's no need to look over millions of records time and again; the database will simply make one pass aggregating the dataset. The single remaining join path is centered on the largest table. Database planners typically produce efficient executions when cardinality differences between tables are large. Identifying which tables will be expensive (and drive the single-pass approach) and which tables are smaller lookup tables makes the planner's job straightforward.

- *Missing join keys don't cause sum-total issues in star schemas.* Consider the difficulty in balancing sum totals if some products are not assigned to categories. If you join via a key that isn't present, and the join condition in SQL isn't satisfied, you typically lose records before doing the aggregations. In this situation, it's possible to do an aggregation without a GROUP BY statement and get one figure, and then to get different totals if you join to a table. With a star schema, you can mix and match and do aggregations at the intersection of any attributes and always come up with the same exact sum total of revenue. You can probably think back to a SQL report you've written that joins to an extra table for an additional reporting field. All of a sudden, the users' sum totals are missing due to missing join keys. Star schemas help you avoid this pitfall; you must include a dimension record that serves as the star schema equivalent of NULL so that fact records that don't have the attribute always join to every dimension.

- *Many databases have physical optimizations for star schemas.* The star schema eliminates multitable joins, which are extremely inefficient and costly to perform on large sets of data. A single, easy to optimize physical structure (one large table, and single-key joins to surrounding smaller tables) is something that nearly every database can perform effectively. Further, expecting this particular modeling technique and seeing the physical tables organized as a star schema, some databases have features that provide even greater efficiencies and query speed improvements. Bitmap indexes, parallel query and partitioning, and sharded fact tables are just a few of the techniques. In fact, there's an entire class of column storage databases that are purposely built to handle such schemas/workloads and provide blazing fast performance on top of star schemas.

- *Star schemas are the preferred structure for Mondrian, but they're also easier for anyone writing SQL.* Although the primary consumer for a star schema is an OLAP engine like Mondrian, the database and tables themselves represent an information-focused, easy-to-understand view of the data for reporting. A star schema reduces the complexity and knowledge necessary to write plain old SQL reports against the data. Analysts who typically needed to remember complicated join rules (such as remembering to include an effective date in the SQL join so you don't get too many records and double-count your sales) have a simplified information-focused model to report against.

Now that we've looked at the basic structure and benefits of star schema design and compared it to 3NF techniques, it's time to delve into some further techniques that will almost certainly be required with a star schema of any real complexity.

## 3.2    *Additional star schema modeling techniques*

You've learned what star schemas are and why they're useful. In this section, we'll cover some additional aspects of star schema modeling. These additional techniques and patterns fall into two different categories:

- *Techniques for handling changes to dimension data over time*—Products change categories, stores change attributes, and so on. You need to be able to handle changes to your dimensions over time using Slowly Changing Dimension techniques.

- *Performance enhancements*—We'll cover some techniques for improving the overall performance of the system.

### 3.2.1    *Slowly Changing Dimensions (SCDs)*

Slowly Changing Dimensions (SCDs) are dimensions that change slowly over time, and in this section we'll look at techniques for handling changes to dimensional attributes. The "slowly" need not connote any particular rate of change; data can change frequently throughout a day or change once or twice per year. The key aspect we'll try to model and solve is how to handle these changes to data and ensure that we properly account for changes over time.

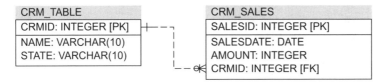

**Figure 3.3 Source data in the CRM system. A single record per customer in CRM_TABLE is uniquely identified by CRMID, with sales transactions related to a customer being referenced through a foreign key in CRM_SALES.**

Industry-standard descriptions of SCD techniques have been developed; they aren't particular to Mondrian but are broadly applicable to star schemas for other OLAP products as well. The three types of SCDs (I, II, and III) were initially outlined in Kimball's definitive and timeless work on dimensional modeling, *The Data Warehouse Lifecycle Toolkit*, 2nd edition (Wiley, 2008), and while some additional permutations of these types exist, the three types cover nearly all use cases.

It's easiest to explain SCDs through an example. We'll examine a customer named Bob, the sales associated with him, and the changes to his data over time. We'll look at how we can manage changes to Bob's data over time.

In the source CRM system, the customer records for Bob are stored in CRM_TABLE (figure 3.3). Bob has a single record in this table, and the table is updated as changes are made (such as by a customer service agent using the CRM software). There is a single, up-to-date version of Bob in the CRM system.

Purchases made by Bob are recorded in the same system, in the CRM_SALES table. Bob lived in California (CA) until June 2002, at which point he moved to Washington (WA). This table contains the date of the sales transaction, foreign key references to Bob's CRM ID (100), and the transaction amount. This is a simplistic (and perhaps a little oversimplified) version of the way data is commonly represented in source systems.

```
-- Before June 2002
select * from CRM_TABLE;
+-------+------+-------+
| CRMID | NAME | STATE |
+-------+------+-------+
|   100 | Bob  | CA    |
+-------+------+-------+

-- After June 2002
select * from CRM_TABLE;
+-------+------+-------+
| CRMID | NAME | STATE |
+-------+------+-------+
|   100 | Bob  | WA    |
+-------+------+-------+

-- All of Bobs sales
select * from CRM_SALES;
```

```
+----------+------------+--------+-------+
| SALESID  | SALESDATE  | AMOUNT | CRMID |
+----------+------------+--------+-------+
|     1001 | 2001-01-01 |    500 |   100 |
|     1002 | 2002-02-01 |    275 |   100 |
|     1003 | 2003-09-01 |    999 |   100 |
+----------+------------+--------+-------+
```

Given your new understanding of star schemas, it's probably clear at this point that because sales are the *what* that you're trying to measure, sales will be a fact table in the star. It would also be common to want to see sales by customer state (the *by*). Reinforcing what you saw earlier in figure 3.3, you know that the *by* attributes (customer state) will be in a dimension table. Now we simply need to address the challenge that arises from Bob moving from CA to WA in June 2002.

The challenge, of course, is determining how to appropriate certain sales amounts in Mondrian and the star schema in keeping with the business requirements. In our example, Bob made two purchases (2001-01-01 and 2002-02-01) while he lived in California. The big question, and the one we can address with one of our SCD techniques, is whether those two sales amounts ($500 and $275) should be totaled in California (where Bob lived when he made those purchases) or in Washington (where Bob resides now). The three SCD techniques give us the ability to achieve the results Adventure Works desires.

### SCD TYPE I

SCD Type I is a dimensional modeling technique that, as in our example source system, keeps a single version of the entity. In our example, Bob just has a single record in a customer dimension table (figure 3.4). As Bob changes attributes (from CA to WA), his record is updated in the table; no history of changes is kept. The fact table records have a reference to the dimension record for Bob.

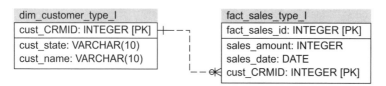

**Figure 3.4   Type I dimension tables. Notice that the foreign key from the fact table to the dimension table is the single-source system identifier CRMID. Given that this is the primary key for the dimension table, it's clear that there's only one record for Bob in the dimension.**

```
-- Dimension Table (Type I).  No History, single version of Bob
select * from dim_customer_type_I;
+------------+------------+-----------+
| cust_CRMID | cust_state | cust_name |
+------------+------------+-----------+
|        100 | WA         | Bob       |
+------------+------------+-----------+
```

```
-- Fact Table (Foreign Key to Customer dimension is cust_CRMID)
select * from fact_sales_type_I;
+---------------+--------------+------------+------------+
| fact_sales_id | sales_amount | sales_date | cust_CRMID |
+---------------+--------------+------------+------------+
|          1001 |          500 | 2001-01-01 |        100 |
|          1002 |          275 | 2002-02-01 |        100 |
|          1003 |          999 | 2003-09-01 |        100 |
+---------------+--------------+------------+------------+

-- Typical Mondrian Star Query (sum measure, group by dimension)
select
  sum(sales_amount) as 'sales',
  cust_state
from
  fact_sales_type_I f,
  dim_customer_type_I d
where
  f.cust_CRMID = d.cust_CRMID
group by
  cust_state;
+-------+------------+
| sales | cust_state |
+-------+------------+
|  1774 | WA         |
+-------+------------+
```

In the preceding code example, notice the query to the star schema that Mondrian will issue to present the total sales by state view. You'll notice that since there's a single record for Bob, and his state is current, indicating that he's living in WA, *all* of Bob's sales are now considered to be WA sales. This is the key attribute of Type I SCD dimensions; changes are made to the single record, and all previous transactions are now included in the new value totals. Even though Bob lived in CA for his first two purchases ($500 and $275), they don't show up in CA; the entire amount of $1,774 is included in WA.

Type I dimensions are often used for items that don't change frequently (country names, area codes, and the like), and when they do change, they represent a true update or correction of the data. For instance, if the name of a country changes ("Suessville" to "Democratic Peoples Republic of North Suessville"), it's unlikely that business users will want to see two different figures (old name and new name) and two different names. For such an update, all records (old transactions and new ones) should be included in the new name.

### SCD TYPE II

SCD Type II dimensions keep a history of changes to the attributes of the dimension. In our example, Bob would have two records in the customer dimension. One record represents the period from when he became a customer in 1980 up until he moved to Washington—in this record his state is CA. The second record covers his time living in Washington. These versioned records of Bob represent him at particular points in time.

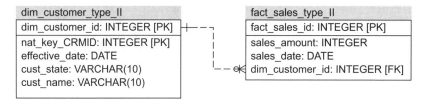

**Figure 3.5    Type II dimension tables.**

For Type II dimensions, a surrogate key is created to uniquely identify a particular version (such as 8888 or 8889) of the natural key (Bob, CRMID 100). For Type II dimensions, the surrogate key is meaningless and it's used only as a simple, single-key join from the fact table.

There is a new unique key that's normally omitted from the physical database schema but is a logical constraint: a combination of the natural key (CRMID) and the effective date identifies unique records in a dimension (figure 3.5).

When loading the fact table, the ETL system examines the date of the sale (sales_date) and chooses which version of the dimension key to use. In our example, two of Bob's transactions use the record where he lived in CA (8888) for a foreign key, and his last transaction uses his current effective record (8889) as a foreign key. It is this versioning, and the ability of the fact table to join to different versions of the same entity, that give SCD Type II dimensions the ability to attribute historical transactions to the correct attributes.

```
-- Bob now has TWO records in the dimension, and when the new record was
-- effective.  Notice the surrogate key is now the PK for the table
select * from dim_customer_type_II;
+-----------------+-----------------+-----------------+-------+------+
| dim_customer_id | nat_key_CRMID   | effective_date  | state | name |
+-----------------+-----------------+-----------------+-------+------+
|            8888 |             100 | 1980-01-01      | CA    | Bob  |
|            8889 |             100 | 2002-06-01      | WA    | Bob  |
+-----------------+-----------------+-----------------+-------+------+

-- Now, Bob's sales point to one of his two different dimension versions
-- The two records before June 2002, point to his first record (8888)
-- The record AFTER he moved, point to his second record (8889)
select * from fact_sales_type_II;
+---------------+--------------+------------+-----------------+
| fact_sales_id | sales_amount | sales_date | dim_customer_id |
+---------------+--------------+------------+-----------------+
|          1001 |          500 | 2001-01-01 |            8888 |
|          1002 |          275 | 2002-02-01 |            8888 |
|          1003 |          999 | 2003-09-01 |            8889 |
+---------------+--------------+------------+-----------------+

-- Now, when creating the sales Star query, the results put Bobs
-- sales when he lived in CA into CA, and when he lived in WA
-- into WA.  Notice the query has no date management; this has
```

```
-- already been done when choosing which version of Bob from
-- the dimension table (8888 or 8889).
select
  sum(sales_amount) as 'sales',
  cust_state
from
  fact_sales_type_II f,
  dim_customer_type_II d
where
  f.dim_customer_id = d.dim_customer_id
group by
  cust_state;
+-------+------------+
| sales | cust_state |
+-------+------------+
|   775 | CA         |
|   999 | WA         |
+-------+------------+
```

Notice that the same SQL query to sum sales now returns totals that put Bob's purchases into the state he was living in when he made the purchase. His $500 and $275 sales in CA are totaled in CA ($775), and his $999 purchase after he moved is attributed to WA.

SCD Type II dimensions are used when a history of changes and attributes is needed. This is very common, and Type II dimensions are used much of the time. You can understand the rationale; business users want accurate per-state sales. They dislike when reports magically move historical data from one line to another; historical data should be settled, finished data.

Type II dimensions often include additional columns for easy management and lookups, even if they aren't required. It's common to see an expiration date, in addition to an effective date, so that the SQL that looks up the dimension can use a straightforward BETWEEN clause rather doing a MIN(effective) where date is greater than effective. It's also not uncommon for a version identifier to be present (1, 2, 3, ...); it's superfluous, but it makes it easy to numerically identify versions of the entity.

### SCD TYPE III

Type III dimensions are somewhat rare; we'll cover them briefly, and you can look into online resources or other books to dig into the details and some examples. Our example of Bob's purchase history doesn't fit with a classic Type III use case.

Type III dimensions are used when you want to keep both attributes around and be able to use either to classify the results. Type III dimensions are often used when you bring in a second classification system, and you don't think of it as a "change" so much as an additional method of bucketing or classifying.

Take, for instance, a sales organization that's reorganizing. Perhaps they were split into four regions before the reorganization (West, Central, East, and International) and they're moving to another system (North, South, International Europe, International Asia). For a while, given that commissions, sales bonuses, and other key company metrics will need to be determined using the old system while the new system is being rolled out, you'll need to be able to use both methods. You'll need to roll up your sales by both the new sales regions and the old sales regions.

This is typically accomplished by adding a column to an existing dimension (Type I or Type II) that retains both sets of regions. In our continuing example, there'd be two columns in the dimension: NEW_REGION would contain the new region names for that salesperson, and OLD_REGION would contain the old region names. This enables a type of dual taxonomy analysis, allowing the user to explore either region.

### SCD SUMMARY

All three types of dimensions can be used, depending on the particular business needs associated with the dimension. A single star schema can mix and match different types of dimension tables, so choosing a Type I for a particular dimension doesn't mean that for another dimension for the same fact table you can't use Type II.

As a general rule, most dimension tables use Type II dimensions, probably followed by Type I. Type III dimensions are rare and represent a small number of use cases. If you're new to dimensional modeling and your experience doesn't automatically tell you how to model the dimension you're adding, start by assuming it'll be a Type II dimension, and then adjust it only if you see the telltale signs that it's a Type I or Type III.

Having covered the methods available for addressing business needs for data changing over time, let's move on to discuss other modeling techniques for performance and enhanced functionality.

### 3.2.2  *Time dimensions*

Time dimensions are critically important to OLAP systems; almost every single system has some sort of time component associated with it, and it's very rare for watching metrics over time to not be a key requirement. It's almost a foregone conclusion that for whatever system you build using Mondrian, you'll have some sort of time dimension. Time dimensions are, for the most part, like any other dimension. In fact, with the exception of a single configuration in Mondrian to enable some powerful time-centric MDX shortcuts (such as year-to-date aggregations or current period versus prior period, and the like), time dimensions are exactly like any other dimension table. We'll look at how you can make Mondrian aware of your time dimension in chapter 4.

Time dimensions are denormalized Type I dimensions where the natural (and usually the primary) key is the date. Type I is almost always appropriate because the attributes rarely change. For instance, July 01 2005 will always be a Friday. Its attributes (the fact it was Friday, was in July, and so on) won't ever change, so managing changes for time dimensions is usually not necessary.

All of the relevant pieces of the date, such as the month name, quarter, and day of the week, are denormalized and included as columns in the table. If you've created SQL reports before, you might be wondering why this is done. After all, extracting the month number from a date is a straightforward function. Usually something like `select month(date) from table` can quickly and easily extract the information. But

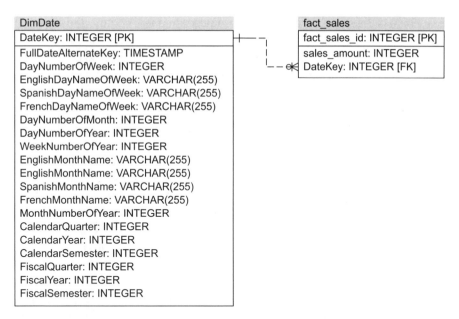

**Figure 3.6** Time dimension: all the attributes of a date are denormalized and presented as real textual values. Even though extracting the month number from the date is possible, a denormalized and repetitive column (MonthNumberOfYear) is created for easy and high-performance grouping and filtering for star queries.

there's a good reason to denormalize it: performing the same calculation, extracting the same exact integer (7 for our July example) from the date (July 01 2005) millions of times with every query, means performing a lot of unnecessary work in the database. Also, some database optimizers can optimize, group by, and filter clauses on straight integer columns (such as MonthNumberOfYear) but have a much harder time optimizing and grouping or filtering on a function, such as `month(date)`. See figure 3.6.

```
+-----------+---------------+-------------+-------------+----------------+
| DateKey   | CalendarYear  | MonthName   | FiscalYear  | FiscalQuarter  |
+-----------+---------------+-------------+-------------+----------------+
| 20050701  |          2005 | July        |        2006 |              1 |
| 20050702  |          2005 | July        |        2006 |              1 |
| 20050703  |          2005 | July        |        2006 |              1 |
| 20050704  |          2005 | July        |        2006 |              1 |
| 20050705  |          2005 | July        |        2006 |              1 |
| 20050706  |          2005 | July        |        2006 |              1 |
| 20050707  |          2005 | July        |        2006 |              1 |
| 20050708  |          2005 | July        |        2006 |              1 |
| 20050709  |          2005 | July        |        2006 |              1 |
| 20050710  |          2005 | July        |        2006 |              1 |
+-----------+---------------+-------------+-------------+----------------+
```

In addition to the performance benefits of having all the regular pieces of the time dimension denormalized, there's another benefit. It's very common for organizations to have additional columns and attributes that need to be used for analysis just as frequently as the standard calendar attributes. The most common of these is the fiscal calendar in use by a company, which is typically offset a few months from the Gregorian calendar. Fiscal attributes (such as fiscal year, quarter, and so on) can be added as additional columns to the time dimension.

In some ways, the time dimension is a very effective part of the solution. When a fact table joins to a single date in the time dimension, a wide variety of time-based aggregations involving different categories, calendars, retail schedules, and so on, are all possible without any additional work. In other words, a well-designed time dimension means the fact table designers and ETL developers don't have to worry about how to roll up these transactions by fiscal and Gregorian calendar attributes.

Notice in figure 3.6 that the primary key for the time dimension is an integer—a coded version of the date. July 01 2005 is the integer 20050701. This is a common trick, so that when loading a fact table you don't have to do a table lookup to find the time dimension record that matches your date. A little date munging, and you can determine the integer for your desired date, without ever having to ask the database for that information. When you're loading millions of rows, this is a helpful little optimization.

Notice that the time dimension has only a day portion but does not include any intra-day attributes (such as hour, minute, and so on). Including down to the minute or second values would make the dimension table much bigger and reduce some of the performance benefits of having dimension tables with fewer records joined to fact tables that have large numbers of records. If intra-day analysis is needed, this is commonly addressed by adding a separate time of day dimension that's separate from the time dimension and that has attributes for the intra-day divisions (hour, minute, and the like).

In section 11.1.3, we'll cover some of the very powerful MDX extensions available for time dimensions. Once these extensions are configured in Mondrian, common analytic questions (this year to date versus last year to date at the same point) become very easy in MDX. Additionally, most ETL products have some sort of time dimension generator, and there are even websites where you can get fully baked time dimensions (data and database table definitions). PDI includes a time dimension generator in its sample directory, and Mondrian 4 has added the ability to create time dimensions automatically.

### 3.2.3    *Snowflake design*

Using a star schema is considered a best practice, and this design should be used for Mondrian in almost all cases. But as usual, there are some use cases where it's appropriate to break the rules; you can use one level of normalization on dimensions (an additional join) for various operational and performance reasons. In this approach, an additional table and join are introduced, creating a fanning-out shape that resembles a snowflake (hence the name).

But a word of caution. Although there are sometimes good reasons to use a snowflake design with Mondrian, more often the design is used as a normalization crutch

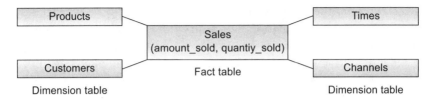

**Figure 3.7  Sales fact as a star. All supplier attributes are included as additional columns in the products dimension. All country information is included in the customers dimension as additional columns. The database only needs to optimize one join for the relevant information.**

**Figure 3.8  Sales fact as a snowflake. The relevant supplier information has been normalized out of products. The database needs to join to the suppliers table from the products table to be able to aggregate and group by supplier attributes.**

for people new to dimensional modeling. Our advice is to try using a star schema first (even if the snowflake looks or feels better), and to only use a snowflake when you clearly have a reason for doing so. As we mentioned earlier, joins amongst millions of records are costly and difficult to optimize, so it's best to avoid them if possible. See figures 3.7 and 3.8.

When is using a snowflake design a good idea? There are typically two use cases where snowflakes make good sense:

- *To reduce the size of dimension tables by factoring out seldom used but really big columns*—Most product data, such as categories and types, are small 10- to 250-character fields, but what if there's a very large (CLOB or LARGETEXT) field that includes a very long product description? It's possible that this needs to be included in Mondrian for some reports but that it's not a commonly used column. Keeping it in the same table, for a row-store database, means the database may be doing a bunch of unnecessary I/O. In short, you might be able to speed up the most common queries that don't use that column by factoring out a handful of columns into a separate table.
- *To more easily manage a Type I type attribute in an otherwise Type II dimension*—Consider the snowflake design in figure 3.8, where we've factored out countries from customer. It's likely that many customer attributes will change over time (including

which country the customer lives in) and will need to be managed as Type II dimensions. The attributes of the country, however, such as its name, tend to be Type I changes when they happen (updates, without any history). Using a snowflake design to separate out a table with update instead of change-tracking attributes allows for easy Type I updates in an otherwise Type II dimension.

### 3.2.4   *Degenerate and combination/junk dimensions*

There are times when creating a whole separate dimension table, including a foreign key reference, and then grouping by attribute just doesn't make sense for performance reasons. For instance, when the dimension only has a single attribute (such as order type or channel), it's overkill to create another join path, a separate table for housekeeping, and so on for simple attributes. There are also times when you'd like to include attributes that aren't really analytically significant, but that are nice for drilling and for including on some drill-through reports. For example, the original order ID for an order would be nice to keep around, so that you could include it on a report to find exceptions or to look up outliers in the original source system. Again, including that as a standard dimension would be impractical because the number of rows in the original order ID dimension would grow close to the same millions of records in the fact table. We'll cover the common techniques for addressing these challenges: degenerate dimensions and combination (or junk) dimensions.

Consider our sales fact example, which includes a few low ordinality items. We have a sales type attribute that has very low ordinality (two different values), indicating what type of sale record this is: NEW or RETURN. We also have a channel type (INTERNET or RETAIL) that is similar. We also want to keep track of an order ID, which will cause a *very* large dimension (nearly as large as the fact). (See figure 3.9.)

For the single attribute dimensions (channel and sales type) it seems overkill to maintain entire dimensions with only single-attribute, low-ordinality dimensions. We

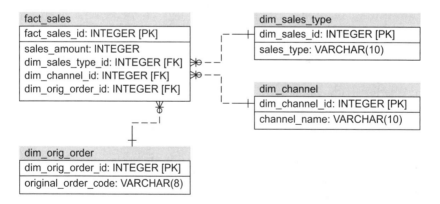

**Figure 3.9   Modeled as standard dimensions using surrogate foreign key references and joins. The sales type dimension includes only two records, as does channel dimension. The original order dimension includes nearly as many rows as the fact table does because every new order also needs a new record in the order dimension.**

can include these attributes as columns directly in the fact table, eliminating the separate table and additional join entirely. This is the ultimate in denormalizing, where the attribute is kept directly with the fact. Mondrian can be configured so that columns in the fact table still show as a separate dimension, but will use the columns directly from the fact table without doing any additional joins (figure 3.10).

| fact_sales_deg |
| --- |
| fact_sales_id: INTEGER [PK] |
| sales_type: VARCHAR(10)<br>sales_amount: INTEGER<br>channel_name: VARCHAR(10)<br>original_order_code: VARCHAR(8) |

**Figure 3.10  Channel, sales type, and original order included as degenerate dimensions in the fact table. This makes sense for small, single-attribute dimensions, where it's beneficial to eliminate management for a separate dimension and eliminate unnecessary joins to very small (or very large in the case of the original order) dimensions.**

We can eliminate the joins and manage the attributes for those dimensions directly in the fact table. This only works for small, low-ordinality columns or very large high-growth attributes that grow with the fact table.

What happens when you've included a bunch of these low-ordinality, single- attribute dimensions in the fact table? A couple of attributes are usually OK, but when you have a bunch of longer (10- to 50-VARCHAR) fields, your fact table size will likely be growing more than you'd like (compared to just using dimension integer surrogate keys). There's another technique for taking lots of single-attribute degenerate dimensions, and putting them back into a standard dimension of unrelated attributes. This type of dimension is referred to as a *combination dimension*, or commonly as a *junk dimension*. It should be noted that the only reason to do this is for performance; from Mondrian's perspective, assuming it's been configured properly, there's no logical difference between consolidating multiple degenerate dimensions into a junk or combination dimension and leaving them as degenerate dimensions in the fact table (figure 3.11).

Junk dimensions are created in a unique way: a Cartesian product of all possible combinations of attributes is created, along with a surrogate key. Then, when you're loading the fact table, the loading process looks into the junk dimensions to grab the record with the correct set of attributes (for example NEW, INTERNET is record 100), which is guaranteed to be in the dimension because all possible combinations are present.

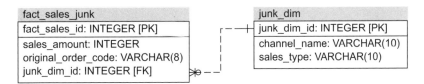

**Figure 3.11  Multiple unrelated degenerate dimensions (channel, sales type) can be consolidated into a junk dimension. This provides the performance benefits of a small, single integer in the fact table and reduces the size of the fact table. Note that the high-ordinality degenerate dimension (original order) isn't moved into the junk dimension because to do so doesn't make sense.**

```
-- All possible combinations of attributes (Channel/Sales Type)
-- are created, along with a surrogate
select * from junk_dim;
+-------------+--------------+------------+
| junk_dim_id | channel_name | sales_type |
+-------------+--------------+------------+
|         100 | INTERNET     | NEW        |
|         101 | INTERNET     | RETURN     |
|         102 | RETAIL       | NEW        |
|         103 | RETAIL       | RETURN     |
+-------------+--------------+------------+
```

## 3.3    *Summary*

In this chapter, we looked at how data should be structured for use by Mondrian in analysis. You saw how and why data is extracted from operational, normalized databases, enriched, and put into a star schema. We also discussed some of the architectural characteristics of an analysis database. Finally, we took a look at some advanced concepts in dimensional modeling.

Now that we've covered the basics of the star schema, some of its ins and outs, and the overall architecture, we're ready to configure Mondrian on top of the star schema. The next chapter will show you how to bring together the physical star schema and the logical analytic structures to create a complete solution. You really should have a good sense of the basics of star schema design, and most importantly the splitting of attributes into facts and dimensions, along with the foreign key patterns we outlined in this chapter, before continuing.

# Multidimensional modeling: making analytics data accessible

In chapter 2, you saw how business questions could be described by creating cubes, dimensions, attributes, and measures, and how a schema contains those logical elements. Then, in chapter 3, you saw how to design and populate the data warehouse.

Mondrian uses the concept of a *schema* to map from the logical data structure used for analysis to the physical structure used in the data warehouse. A completed schema provides cubes that can be used for data analysis. In this chapter, you'll see how to build a schema. (It's a long chapter, because no matter how you slice it, multi-dimensional modeling is a dense topic. We suggest you read the first section, and then take a break before you proceed with section 4.2.)

This chapter describes the XML grammar of Mondrian schemas and the key XML elements and attributes. You'll see in detail not only how to define the logical elements (cubes, dimensions, attributes, and measures) used in analytics, but also how to map them onto physical data structures (tables and columns) so that Mondrian knows how to get the data from the data mart.

You'll see how to create a simple cube with a couple of dimensions and measures, and then you'll see how that cube can be extended, adding more dimensions, navigation hierarchies, and calculations. In chapter 5, we'll cover some more advanced topics in schema design, building on the material in this chapter.

This chapter is essential if you're an architect designing a Mondrian schema. It assumes that you're familiar with XML, as well as the material covered in the previous chapters. If you'll be using prebuilt Mondrian cubes, however, and you're an analyst defining reports and dashboards, you can probably skip this chapter and the next one.

We'll start with a simple example showing the absolutely essential elements: Schema, Cube, Dimension, Attribute, and Measure. Later in this chapter, and continuing on in chapter 5, we'll describe other important schema elements, interspersed with explanations and examples. We'll cover almost all XML elements and their important attributes, but these chapters are not meant to be exhaustive. The online Mondrian documentation contains the definitive reference to all 80 XML elements in a Mondrian schema.

A brief word about how names appear in the text. As we discuss various schema features and define example schemas, we shall refer in the text to the objects in those schemas, and their names appear in code font with the parts of the name enclosed in brackets, as if you were using the object in an MDX query. For instance, a measure named "Unit Sales" would appear like this: [Measures].[Unit Sales]. The MDX language does not require brackets if the parts of the name contain only letters, but we use brackets throughout for consistency.

## 4.1    *A simple schema*

Section 2.3 described a company building a report to improve its sales process. The report compared sales to customers with a college education this year to last year. In order for Mondrian to run that report, you need to define the cube that the report is based on, and how that cube is mapped onto the data mart. A schema is what provides those definitions.

Figure 4.1 shows the elements defined in that schema and an outline of the XML schema file. Listing 4.1 shows the XML schema in full. Don't be concerned with understanding each of the elements in the schema at this point; rather, focus on the overall composite of information contained within a typical Mondrian schema.

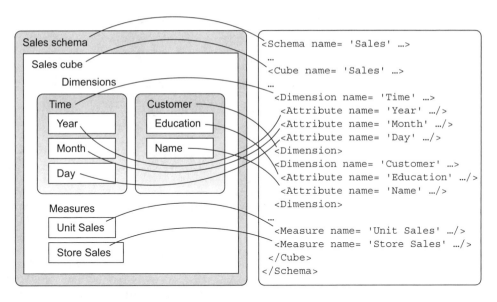

**Figure 4.1  Sales schema mapped to an XML schema outline**

---

**Listing 4.1  Sales schema**

```
<?xml version='1.0'?>
<Schema name='Sales'>                           ←— Sales schema
  <PhysicalSchema>
    <Table name='customer'>
      <Key>
        <Column name='customer_id'/>
      </Key>
    </Table>
    <Table name='time_by_day'>
      <Key>
        <Column name='time_id'/>
      </Key>
    </Table>
    <Table name='sales_fact'/>
  </PhysicalSchema>

  <Cube name='Sales'>                           ←— Sales cube
    <Dimensions>
      <Dimension name='Time' table='time_by_day'
          type='TimeDimension' key='Id'>        ←— Time dimension
        <Attribute name='Year' keyColumn='the_year
            levelType='TimeYears'/>             ←— Year attribute
        <Attribute name='Id' keyColumn='time_id'/>
      </Dimension>
      <Dimension name='Customer' key='Name'>     ←⌐ Customer
        <Attribute name='Name' keyColumn='customer_id  ⌐ dimension
            nameColumn='full_name'/>
```

Id
attribute ⌐→

Name ⌐→
attribute

```
Education   ┌─▷    <Attribute name='Education' keyColumn='education'/>
attribute   │      </Dimension>
                 </Dimensions>

                 <MeasureGroups>
                   <MeasureGroup table='sales_fact'>
     Units   │       <Measures>
   measure   └─▷        <Measure name='Unit sales' column='unit_sales'/>
                          <Measure name='Store Sales' column='store_sales'/>    ◁────┐
                       </Measures>                                                    │
                       <DimensionLinks>                                        Store Sales
                          <ForeignKeyLink dimension='Customer'                   measure
                             foreignKeyColumn='customer_id'/>
                          <ForeignKeyLink dimension='Time'
                             foreignKeyColumn='time_id'/>
                       </DimensionLinks>
                     </MeasureGroup>
                   </MeasureGroups>
                 </Cube>
               </Schema>
```

Because this is the first schema in this book, we've listed it in its entirety. There are quite a few XML elements, but it's not important to understand them all right now. At first, we'll only cover the key elements: Schema, Cube, Attribute, Dimension, Measure, and PhysicalSchema. The following sections will discuss each of these elements.

The other elements will be described later in the chapter: MeasureGroups, MeasureGroup, Measures, DimensionLinks, and ForeignKeyLink.

### 4.1.1   *Schema element*

The Schema XML element is the top-level element of a Mondrian schema. There is one, and only one, Schema element in a Mondrian schema XML file, and it represents the container for all the pieces the schema contains. An analyst would first create a schema and then fill in all the attributes, dimensions, and cubes that together address the business questions.

```
<Schema name="Sales"
  caption="Sales"
  description="Optimizing the Sales process at Two Wheels Cycles"
  metamodelVersion="4.0" measuresCaption="Measures"
  defaultRole="Associate" missingLink="warning">
```

Each schema must have a name attribute (although Mondrian doesn't do anything important with that name), and we recommend that you also provide a description.

We also recommend that you specify metamodelVersion="4.0", because it helps with schema versioning ("4.0" is the current version of Mondrian, and likely the version for which you'll be writing your schema).

Because Schema is the sole root element in the XML document, it contains all of the top-level elements that constitute the schema. A schema always includes a PhysicalSchema element, and it generally includes one or more Cube elements. Other common elements include `Dimension` (to define public dimensions—dimensions shared between cubes), and `Role` for access control.

> **ORDERING OF XML ELEMENTS** In previous versions of Mondrian, the schema parser was extremely sensitive about the order of child elements. If you got child elements in the wrong order (for example, a cube after a role, instead of before as Mondrian was expecting), Mondrian would silently ignore the cube. This situation has been fixed in Mondrian version 4.0. If you've used previous versions of Mondrian, this is one thing you can stop worrying about!

### 4.1.2  Cube element

A cube, defined by a `Cube` XML element, is the context for a report or interactive analysis session. It represents a collection of events, describing the occurrences of a particular business process over the lifetime of the data warehouse. The collection may contain a large number of events—thousands, millions, or even billions—but the events are not presented individually.

Cubes tend to be a complete set of measures and attributes for doing an analysis on the set of events. For instance, if you're interested in sales by customer attributes, you might want to look at sales amounts (events or measures) by customer geography (attributes). A cube collects these things into one place, ready for analysis and querying.

A cube has little configuration itself, but is instead mostly an element that holds the more important measure groups and dimensions. There is usually, but not always, a one-to-one relationship between a star schema (a single fact table and dimension tables outlined in chapter 3) and a cube (measures and dimensions). (For instance, the analyst in chapter 2 would likely have built a star schema containing a `sales` fact table and `customer` dimension table to store the data for the [Sales] cube and its [Customer] dimension.)

```
<Cube name="Sales">
  <Dimensions>
    ...
  </Dimensions>
  <MeasureGroups>
    ...
  </MeasureGroups>
</Cube>
```

Recall from chapter 2 that a cube is a collection of measures and attributes. The measures quantitatively describe events or collections of events, and the attributes represent the context in which the events occurred. By choosing appropriate measures and attributes, a business user can focus on the part of the history that answers their question. Each combination of attributes and measures is effectively a new report that can be created in seconds using a point-and-click interface, and there's an exponential number of such combinations.

In the XML syntax, there are intervening XML elements between the cube and its constituent attributes and measures. `Attribute` elements occur within `Dimension` elements, and all dimensions in a cube are within a `Dimensions` element. `Measure` elements occur within a `MeasureGroup` element, and this is inside a `MeasureGroups` element. Cubes that contain multiple measure groups are a fairly advanced topic that we'll revisit later in section 5.1.5); we'll explain dimensions shortly (in section 4.1.4).

### 4.1.3   *Attribute element*

An `Attribute` XML element describes a data value. If you're familiar with modeling relational database schemas, an attribute is the nearest equivalent in the Mondrian schema to a column. In practice, nearly all of the columns in your dimension tables (see section 3.1.3) will be configured via attribute elements.

In the `[Sales]` cube (see figure 2.10) one of the attributes to be analyzed is the education of the customer. This will likely be a column (`education`) in a dimension table (`customers`) in the database star schema, and also a configured XML `Attribute` element.

```
<Attribute name="Education" caption="Education level"
    description="The education level of this customer"
    keyColumn="education"/>
<Attribute name="Name" keyColumn="customer_id" nameColumn="full_name"/>
```

The preceding example shows the `[Name]` and `[Education]` attributes from the `[Customer]` dimension. Every attribute must have a name. The `[Education]` attribute has, in addition, `caption` and `description` attributes.

#### NAME, CAPTION, AND DESCRIPTION

Captions are similar to names, and people often confuse the two. The purpose of a caption is to be displayed on the screen to a business user, whereas the name is intended to be used in code, particularly in an MDX statement.

Often the name and caption are the same (and the caption defaults to the name if a caption is not explicitly specified). But they have different localization behavior: captions can be localized, but the name is the same in all languages. This makes sense, when you consider that your business users will expect to see captions on the screen in their own language, whereas the underlying MDX code needs to be the same regardless of the language the client is using.

For example, here's an attribute whose caption and description have been localized into French:

```
<Attribute name="Marital Status" caption="Etat civil"
    description="L'état civil de ce client" keyColumn="marital_status"/>
```

You use its name, `[Marital Status]`, when writing MDX:

```
SELECT ... ON COLUMNS,
    [Customer].[Marital Status] ... ON ROWS
FROM [Sales]
```

but as figure 4.2 shows, the attribute is labeled in French ("Etat Civil") when the query results appear in a user interface.

| Etat civil | Country | Unit sales | Store sales |
|---|---|---|---|
| M | Germany | 38 | 3833 |
| | France | 12 | 1297 |
| | Belgium | 5 | 523 |
| S | Germany | 38 | 2864 |
| | Belgium | 5 | 257 |

**Figure 4.2  Report showing localized caption**

Descriptions are quite straightforward. Many user interfaces (such as Pentaho Analyzer and Saiku) display descriptions as tooltips when you move the mouse over an element. Descriptions can help business users find their way around a cube that they're unfamiliar with. Like captions, descriptions can be localized.

Name, caption, and description are not unique to attributes; the other elements that may appear on business user's screen also have them, including Schema, Cube, Measure, and Dimension. They also have a visible attribute, which tells the user interface to hide the element but doesn't affect its behavior in MDX queries. To see which elements have name, caption, description, and visible attributes, consult the Mondrian online documentation. (Appendix B lists all online resources.) The same localization rules apply: caption and description can be localized; name can't be, and is therefore the same for all locales.

### MAPPING ATTRIBUTES ONTO COLUMNS

We said that an attribute is like a column, but because attributes are part of a dimensional model intended for business users, the behavior is richer. Every attribute is based upon at least one database column. For example, [Education] is a simple attribute that's mapped, via the keyColumn attribute, onto the education column of the customers table.

For each property of an attribute, you can specify the property using an XML attribute, or there's an equivalent nested XML element. Table 4.1 shows the elements and attributes available.

**Table 4.1  XML elements and attributes that map dimensional attributes onto columns**

| XML attribute | Equivalent nested XML element | May be composite? | Description |
|---|---|---|---|
| keyColumn | Key | Yes | Required. Specifies the column that holds the key for members of this attribute. The key must be unique. |
| nameColumn | Name | No | Optional. Specifies the column that holds the name of members of this attribute. If not specified, it defaults to the key (or the last key column if the key is composite). |

**Table 4.1   XML elements and attributes that map dimensional attributes onto columns *(continued)***

| XML attribute | Equivalent nested XML element | May be composite? | Description |
|---|---|---|---|
| `orderByColumn` | `OrderBy` | Yes | Optional. Specifies sort order. If not specified, attribute is sorted by key. |
| `captionColumn` | `Caption` | Yes | Optional. Defaults to name, which in turn defaults to last column of key. |

Table 4.2 shows example attributes, illustrating cases where it makes sense for the attribute's name, caption, and ordinal to be different from the attribute's key.

**Table 4.2   Example attributes**

| Dimension | Attribute | Key | Name | Caption | Ordinal | Comments |
|---|---|---|---|---|---|---|
| Time | Year | 2012 | 2012 | 2012 | 2012 | Same value for all properties. |
| Time | Month | [2012, 1] | 1 | January | [2012, 1] | Composite key ensures that January 2012 is distinct from January 2011. Name is distinct from caption; thus the unique name is `[Time].[2012].[1]`, but "January" is displayed on the screen (in applications running in the English locale). |
| Customer | Name | 13874 | Bob Arctor | Bob Arctor | [Arctor, Bob] | Numeric key ensures uniqueness if there happen to be two Bob Arctors. Caption is same as name, because attribute is not localized. (It is unusual for attributes with large numbers of distinct values to be localized.) Composite ordinal sorts customers by their last name. |
| Customer | State | [USA, CA] | CA | CA | [USA, CA] | Key is composite, because the same state name may occur in different nations. |

### 4.1.4 *Dimension element*

A Dimension is a collection of logically related attributes. If, as we said earlier, an attribute is the dimensional equivalent of a column, then a dimension is the equivalent of a table. (And, in fact, many dimensions map directly to a dimension table in the star schema.)

What do we mean by logically related? [Gender], [Zipcode], and [State Population] belong in the [Customer] dimension because they are all properties associated with the customer who made a particular purchase. [Day of Week] belongs in the [Time] dimension, not the [Customer] dimension, because it does not depend on the customer: a customer might have one purchase on a Monday in their history and another on a Thursday.

There's also a more down-to-earth reason to group attributes into dimensions. If a cube contains a large number of attributes, dimensions are a convenient way of grouping them on the screen, in the same way that folders make large numbers of files easier to manage.

### 4.1.5 *Measure element*

The Measure XML element defines a measure. A measure is a value, almost always numeric, that appears in a cell. If the cell represents many rows in the fact table, then the cell's value is the measure aggregated (usually summed) over all of those rows. Measures are the aggregated values from columns in the fact tables described in chapter 3; they represent the *what* you're trying to measure.

Consider the cell showing the [Unit Sales] measure in the second row of figure 4.2, with a value of 12. This means that 12 units were sold to customers whose country was France and whose marital status was M. There happen to have been three sales transactions, therefore three rows in the fact table, with those criteria, and their values in the unit_sales column are 3, 1, and 8. The cell value, 12, is the sum of these values.

Strictly speaking, the XML Measure element defines a *stored* measure. Mondrian also supports *calculated measures*, which are calculated from other measures using an MDX formula. Though stored and calculated measures are defined and evaluated differently, they appear the same to a business user running a report. Calculated measures, and more generally calculated members, are described in section 5.4.2.

Here are some measures:

```
<Measure name='Unit Sales' aggregator='sum' column='unit_sales' />
<Measure name='Store Sales' aggregator='sum' column='store_sales' />
<Measure name='Sales Count' aggregator='count' />
```

Each measure has a name and an aggregator, describing how to roll up values. Table 4.3 shows the available aggregators. A column attribute describes which column's values are to be aggregated; it's required for all aggregators except count. A count measure without a column, such as the [Sales Count] measure in this example, counts rows.

**AGGREGATE FUNCTIONS IN MONDRIAN AND SQL**    If you're familiar with aggregate functions in SQL, then Mondrian's aggregate functions will look familiar. Each aggregator maps to a SQL aggregate function in an obvious way. For instance, the [Unit Sales] measure becomes SUM(unit_sales) in generated SQL, and [Sales Count] becomes COUNT(*).

**Table 4.3   Aggregators**

| Aggregator | Comments |
|---|---|
| sum | Sums numeric values. The most common aggregator. |
| count | Counts the number of rows for which a column is not null; if column isn't specified, counts the number of rows. |
| distinct-count | Computes the number of distinct values of the column. Nulls are not counted. |
| max | Finds the maximum value of a column. |
| min | Finds the minimum value of a column. |
| avg | Computes the average value of a numeric column. |

Like other elements that appear in a report, a measure definition also includes caption, description, and visible attributes.

### 4.1.6   *PhysicalSchema element*

The PhysicalSchema XML element describes which tables and columns in the data mart provide the data for the dimensions and cubes in the schema. The physical schema is not something that the business user is aware of; the business user interacts only with the logical model (cubes and dimensions).

The physical schema is a close representation of the physical star schema, with the fact table and dimension tables, their columns, data types, and relationships. You'd expect most of the columns, including the surrogate IDs for Slowly Changing Dimensions (covered in section 3.2.1) and foreign keys in your fact table, to be defined in your physical schema.

The purpose of the physical schema is to provide a foundation for building the logical model. As figure 4.3 shows, the physical schema is a bridge between the logical model and the actual database. It presents a simple model of tables, columns, and links between tables, where the reality may be more complex. For example, a "table" in the physical schema may really be a view or a SQL query. Two tables with different names might be uses of the same database table, or may inhabit different schemas or different database instances. A column with data type "integer" might actually have a data type of NUMBER(10, 0) when stored in Oracle.

The physical schema also allows the structure of the data mart to change over time. For instance, suppose that a table you need as a fact or dimension table doesn't exist in the schema but can be computed using a SQL query. You can create a placeholder

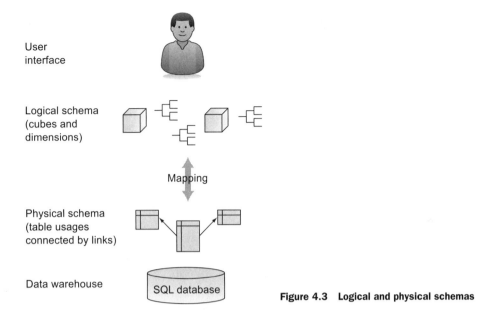

User
interface

Logical schema
(cubes and
dimensions)

Mapping

Physical schema
(table usages
connected by links)

Data warehouse

**Figure 4.3   Logical and physical schemas**

"table" in the physical schema and run queries against it. Tomorrow, when you have fixed the ETL process to create and populate a real table, you can change the physical schema to use the real table; you won't have to change the logical schema, because the physical schema has insulated rest of the model from changes to table structure.

The physical schema shown in figure 4.4 and in listing 4.2 declares tables `customer`, `time_by_day`, and `sales_fact`. It declares primary keys for `customer` and `time_by_day`, which are needed because these tables will contain dimensions; `sales_fact` is a fact table, so it doesn't require a primary key. No columns are defined, so Mondrian reads each table's column definitions from JDBC.

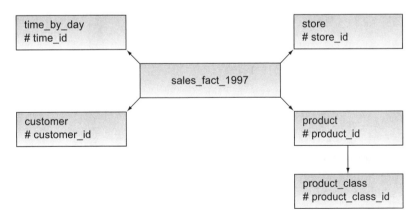

**Figure 4.4   Physical schema of the Sales data mart**

---

**Listing 4.2   Physical schema**

```
<PhysicalSchema>
  <Table name="customer">                          customer table has
    <Key>                                          key customer_id
      <Column name="customer_id"/>
    </Key>
  </Table>
  <Table name="time_by_day">                       time_by_day table
    <Key>                                          has key time_id
      <Column name="time_id"/>
    </Key>
  </Table>
  <Table name="sales_fact"/>                        sales_fact table has
</PhysicalSchema>                                   no primary key
```

Inside each table, you can list the columns explicitly. As well as serving as a check that the columns your schema needs still exist in the database, this allows you to specify a precise type. You can also define calculated columns.

Listing 4.3 includes three columns customer_id, fname, and lname, and it defines a calculated column, full_name, by concatenating first name and last name. Note that when the fname and lname columns are used in the expression for full_name, we use the <Column> element, because we're using, not defining, a column.

---

**Listing 4.3   Physical schema with columns**

```
        <Table name='customer' ... />              customer table
          <Key ... />
          <ColumnDefs>
            <ColumnDef name='customer_id' type='Integer'/>   customer_id column
fname
column      <ColumnDef name='fname' type='String'/>
            <ColumnDef name='lname' type='String'/>
full_name   <CalculatedColumnDef name='full_name' type='String'>
column is     <ExpressionView>                               lname
calculated by  <SQL>                                         column
concatenating    <Column name='fname'/> ||
fname and        ' ' ||
lname in SQL     <Column name='lname'/>
               </SQL>
             </ExpressionView>
           </CalculatedColumnDef>
         </ColumnDefs>
       </Table>
```

When Mondrian generates a SQL query to retrieve data from the database, it'll generate an expression based on the formula within the SQL element, replacing the Column elements with references to other columns.

One problem with SQL is that database dialects tend to differ significantly. The schema we just wrote will work on Oracle and PostgreSQL, which use the conventional || operator for concatenating strings, but it will fail on MySQL, which uses the CONCAT()

function. Is it possible to write one Mondrian schema that will work against multiple SQL databases?

Yes! The `ExpressionView` element allows multiple SQL child elements, with a dialect attribute to distinguish them. When you add support for MySQL, a fragment of the previous listing becomes what's shown in listing 4.4.

**Listing 4.4  Calculated column with expressions for multiple SQL dialects**

```
<CalculatedColumnDef name='full_name' type='String'>
    <ExpressionView>
        <SQL dialect='mysql'>
            CONCAT(<Column name='fname'/>,
                ' ',
                    <Column name='lname'/>)
        </SQL>
        <SQL dialect='generic'>
            <Column name='fname'/>  ||
            ' ' ||
            <Column name='lname'/>
        </SQL>
    </ExpressionView>
</CalculatedColumnDef>
```

- ◁ **SQL expression to use when running against MySQL database**
- ◁ **Expression to use for all other SQL dialects**

Each table in a physical schema has a unique alias, and the alias defaults to the table name. Usually you don't need to assign a table an alias, but the following listing shows some exceptions.

**Listing 4.5  Table alias examples**

```
            <Table schema='sales'
                name='customer'/>
            <Table schema='marketing'
                name='customer'
                alias='marketing_customer'/>
            <Table schema='sales'
                name='customer'
                alias='customer2'/>
            <Query alias='canadian_customer'>
              <SQL>
                SELECT *
                FROM sales.customer
                WHERE country = 'Canada'
              </SQL>
            </Query>
```

- ◁ **Alias is "customer", from table name**
- **Explicit alias, to avoid clash with sales.customer** ▷
- ◁ **Second use of sales.customer table**
- **Every query needs an explicit alias, because there is no default** ▷

Why would you want to create more than one use of the same table? Usually to avoid ambiguities in join paths. For example, consider a movie database where a film has both a language and an original language; the language is usually the same as the original language, but it will be different if the film is dubbed. The `Film` dimension has one use of the `film` table and two uses of the `language` table, via different foreign keys. When defining the physical schema, you'd create a link between the `film` table and each use of the `language` table, as shown in listing 4.6.

**Listing 4.6   Multiple uses of the same table**

```
                    <Table name='film' ... />
language table      <Table name='language' ... />          ◁──┐ Alias is implicitly
used again, as                                                 │ "language"
original_language ┌▷ <Table name='language'
                      alias='original_language' ... />

                    <Link source='language' target='film'>  ◁──┐ Link to film's (maybe
                      <ForeignKey>                                │ dubbed) language
                        <Column name='language_id'/>
                      </ForeignKey>
                    </Link>
                    <Link source='original_language' target='film'>  ◁──┐ Link to film's
                      <ForeignKey>                                         │ original
                        <Column name='original_language_id'/>             │ language
                      </ForeignKey>
                    </Link>
```

When you base an attribute on a column in either the `language` or `original_language` table in the physical schema, it's clear which join path is intended.

**PUTTING IT TOGETHER**

`PhysicalSchema` is the last of the elements you need to build a simple multidimensional schema. It defines the tables and relationships between them. Upon these, you can build a cube, which contains dimensions, attributes, and measures. A cube is the unifying concept that allows business users to analyze their own data.

In this section, you've seen how to build a simple cube. Next, we'll look at the overall structure of a schema file, and at some of the more advanced concepts it supports.

## 4.2   Anatomy of a schema

Now you've seen an example of a schema file and some background on its structure and purpose. Why are schema files defined in XML? What tools can be used to author a schema? What are the valid contents of a schema? That's what we'll look at in this section.

### 4.2.1   XML schema files

Why does Mondrian use XML as the language to define schemas? By design, Mondrian gives people a choice about whether they'll author schemas with a tool (such as Schema Workbench) or with a text editor. XML is a language that can be written and read by both humans and computers, and the particular dialect of XML used is designed to be concise to type and forgiving of errors.

XML also improves interoperability between tools. For example, the Pentaho Aggregate Designer generates fragments of XML and inserts them into a schema. And, you can achieve some powerful effects by writing a dynamic schema processor, which is invoked as a connection is being created, reads the source XML schema, and transforms it to another piece of XML. Dynamic schema processors are used for applications such as localization and access control in a multi-tenant environment. They're described in section 8.2.

Mondrian schemas can be processed with standard text-processing tools such as grep and diff. Authoring tools are encouraged not to make wholesale changes to the XML, because this makes it difficult to store schemas in a version-control system, such as Subversion or git.

XML elements typically have quite a few attributes and subelements, but we won't describe all of them here. This chapter aims to describe the general purpose of each XML element, but the definitive description of each element is in Mondrian's online schema reference, as described in appendix B. We sometimes describe attributes separate from their parent element, where it makes logical sense. For example, we discuss the Schema element's defaultRole attribute when we discuss roles and access control in chapter 6.

### 4.2.2  Structure of a schema

Figure 4.5 shows the elements allowed in a Mondrian schema and their hierarchical structure.

As you've seen, Schema is always the root element. In the simple schema, its children were a PhysicalSchema and a Cube; children can also include more Cube elements and also Dimension, Role, NamedSet, UserDefinedFunction, Parameter, and Annotations elements.

Some elements can occur in more than one context. For instance, Dimension may occur within a cube (when defining a private dimension), or it can be a child of a schema (when defining a shared dimension, as you'll see in section 5.1.2, in the next chapter).

Some elements exist to hold a collection of child elements of the same type. These are called *holder elements*. A holder element doesn't have attributes, and its name is the plural of the name of the element it contains. For example, the Dimensions element contains a list of Dimension elements. Other examples include Columns, Dimensions, Hierarchies, and Attributes.

Some holder elements' children have types that are similar but not identical. For example, DimensionLinks has children ForeignKeyLink, FactLink, ReferenceLink, and NoLink. These elements have a similar purpose—to create a link between a dimension and a measure group—and several attributes in common.

### 4.2.3  Schema versioning and upgrading

We recommended earlier that you include the metamodelVersion="4.0" attribute in your Schema element. This is necessary because Mondrian's schema language changes over time. Each Mondrian release introduces new concepts, and these are manifested as new XML elements and attributes. The version number allows the Mondrian engine to decide whether to run the schema as is, or to try to upgrade automatically.

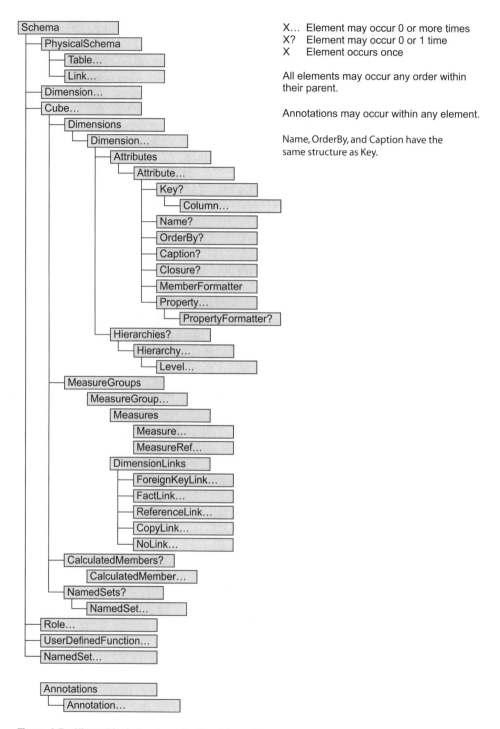

X...  Element may occur 0 or more times
X?   Element may occur 0 or 1 time
X    Element occurs once

All elements may occur any order within their parent.

Annotations may occur within any element.

Name, OrderBy, and Caption have the same structure as Key.

**Figure 4.5  Hierarchical structure of a Mondrian schema**

The version number is particularly important in the version 4.0 release because there was a major change in the schema metamodel between Mondrian versions 3.x and 4.0. The Mondrian 4.0 engine is able to upgrade most 3.x schemas automatically. For example, Mondrian 3.x virtual cubes became obsolete in Mondrian 4.0, and Mondrian automatically converts each `VirtualCube` element to a cube that has multiple `MeasureGroup` elements.

The `metamodelVersion` attribute was only introduced in version 3.4.2, and using it is strongly recommended from version 4.0 onward. If the attribute is missing, Mondrian will do its best to guess the intended target version. (If there's a `PhysicalSchema` element, Mondrian assumes that the schema was intended for version 4.0 but the author forgot the version attribute; otherwise Mondrian assumes that the schema is in 3.x format.)

The `metamodelVersion` attribute will allow future versions of Mondrian to upgrade schemas, and will also allow Mondrian to detect a schema that is too recent. For example, if there are significant changes to the schema in Mondrian 5.0, a schema written for that engine will be stamped with `metamodelVersion="5.0"` and the Mondrian 4.0 engine will refuse to run it.

Now you've seen a simple schema and we've covered the overall structure of a schema file. For the remainder of the chapter, we'll look at the elements that allow you to slice and dice data: dimensions and attributes, hierarchies and levels.

## 4.3 Dimensions, hierarchies, and levels

Multidimensional analysis is a top-down technique. Rather than looking at individual rows, an analyst often starts off by looking at a single row that summarizes the entire dataset, and then zooming in on the data of interest. You saw already how attributes allow you to subdivide the dataset into groups, or to winnow the data into a smaller group. Now we'll look at how organizing attributes into hierarchies and levels allows a business user to navigate more intuitively and efficiently.

Each analyst knows that their business users naturally arrange data into these hierarchies; a year is composed of four quarters, and quarters are composed of three months. And the users want to examine their measures up and down different levels of aggregations. This section will help make your schema reflect the reality of these relationships that your users already know and want.

Then we'll look more closely at the most familiar dimension of them all, the time dimension. You'll see that there are some deep unifying patterns within the dimensional model, that measures are members of their own special dimension, and that every attribute has its own hierarchy, whether or not it is organized into a multi-level hierarchy.

### 4.3.1 Hierarchies and levels

You've seen how you can use attributes to qualify the data shown in a report, and how attributes are organized into dimensions. The attributes of a dimension can always be used independently, but some attributes are so closely related that most users will want to use them together. To do this, you can define a hierarchy.

Listing 4.7 builds a hierarchy called [Customers] from the attributes [Country], [State], and [City]. These attributes form the three levels of the hierarchy.

**Listing 4.7  Customers hierarchy**

```
<Dimension name='Customer'>
  <Attributes>
    <Attribute name='Country' ... />
    <Attribute name='State' .../>
    <Attribute name='City' .../>
  </Attributes>
  <Hierarchies>
    <Hierarchy name='Customers'>
      <Level attribute='Country'/>
      <Level attribute='State'/>
      <Level attribute='City'/>
    </Hierarchy>
  </Hierarchies>
</Dimension>
```

Figure 4.6 shows some of the members of the hierarchy.

Hierarchies allow for a better experience in the user interface. For example, the members of a hierarchy can be displayed in a single column, rather than with one column for each level; each member is preceded by a "+" or "-" icon, allowing it to be expanded or collapsed. Several navigation actions are possible if a member belongs to a multilevel hierarchy. Double-clicking on the [California] member might drill down, so that the axis now consists of just the cities in California. Another action supported by many user interfaces is drilling up: [California] would be replaced by the nations [Canada], [Mexico], and [USA].

That said, sometimes a hierarchy is too restrictive. For a particular analysis, the business user might wish to show only certain levels of the hierarchy, or to put one level on the col-

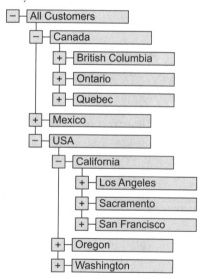

**Figure 4.6   Members of the Customers hierarchy**

umns axis and another on the rows. The best practice is to design a schema with just the attributes at first; then create hierarchies to optimize common navigation paths between attributes, but leave the attributes visible so that business users can work with the raw attributes if they prefer.

The attribute of each level of a hierarchy must have a strict one-to-many relationship with the attribute of the next level. In the [Customers] hierarchy, each state belongs to only one country, and each city belongs to only one state. The net effect is that each level down has more members than the last.

If your attributes don't have this structure, you probably shouldn't be creating a hierarchy on them. Consider, for example, the [Month] and [Week] attributes of a [Time] dimension, as shown in table 4.4.

**Table 4.4   Month and Week attribute values**

| Year | Month | Week | Day of week | Day |
|------|-------|------|-------------|-----|
| 2012 | January | 4 | Saturday | 28 |
| 2012 | January | 5 | Sunday | 29 |
| 2012 | January | 5 | Monday | 30 |
| 2012 | January | 5 | Tuesday | 31 |
| 2012 | February | 5 | Wednesday | 1 |
| 2012 | February | 5 | Thursday | 2 |
| 2012 | February | 5 | Friday | 3 |
| 2012 | February | 5 | Saturday | 4 |
| 2012 | February | 6 | Sunday | 5 |

Week 5 of 2012 straddles both January and February of 2012. The relationship between [Month] and [Week] is therefore many-to-many, not one-to-many as required for a hierarchy. The member for week 5 of 2012 does not have a well-defined parent, so you can't define a hierarchy where [Month] is the parent level of [Week].

> **KEEPING WEEKS FROM CROSSING YEAR BOUNDARIES**   Time dimensions often have two time hierarchies defined: Year-Month-Day and Year-Week-Day. To prevent weeks from crossing year boundaries, years often start with a shortened week 1 and end with a shortened week 53.

But hold on! Both January and February contain a member whose [Day] value is 1. Surely this breaks the rule that a member can have only one parent. No, because January 1, 2012, and February 1, 2012, are different members. They may both have the name [1], but their keys are different (Julian dates 2455927 and 2455958, respectively). The short-form name is more convenient to display, and it's unique provided that the member is shown in the context of its parent month. (The concise name is, in fact, another good reason to use a hierarchy.)

Note what has happened here. Organizing attributes into a hierarchy doesn't affect the number of instances of that attribute. The [Day] attribute has 365 (or 366) distinct values for each year covered by the [Time] dimension, and the resulting [Day] level has the same number.

So, when defining an attribute, you need to define a key that gives the attribute enough distinct values. The attributes of the [Time] dimension show the various approaches:

```
<Attribute name='Year' keyColumn='year'/>
    <Attribute name='Month'>
      <Key>
        <Column name='year'/>
        <Column name='month_of_year'/>
      </Key>
    </Attribute>
    <Attribute name='Week'>
      <Key>
        <Column name='year'/>
        <Column name='week_of_year'/>
      </Key>
    </Attribute>
    <Attribute name='Day' keyColumn='date_id'
        nameColumn='day_of_month'/>
```

**SCHEMA SHORTHANDS**

The previous example used them, so now is a good time to discuss the topic of schema shorthands. XML can be quite a verbose language, which is fine if a machine is generating the XML (in order to save the state of a graphical schema design tool, for instance), but it's not as good if you're writing the XML by hand in a text editor. Mondrian allows common constructs to be expressed more concisely.

In the previous example, the [Year] attribute could have been written as follows:

```
<Attribute name='Year'>
  <Key>
    <Column name='year'/>
  </Key>
  <Name>
    <Column name='year'/>
  </Name>
</Attribute>
```

But we abbreviated that to keyColumn='year' because the key has just one column and the name is the same as the key.

The [Month] attribute in the previous example is equivalent to the following:

```
<Attribute name='Month'>
  <Key>
    <Column name='year'/>
    <Column name='month_of_year'/>
  </Key>
  <Name>
    <Column name='month_name'/>
  </Name>
</Attribute>
```

That's because the name of a composite key is by default the last component of that key (the month_of_year column in this case).

There are other shorthands. If you're writing XML by hand, learn the available shorthands and save yourself some typing! The full set of schema shorthands is in the online Mondrian documentation.

**DISCONNECTED ATTRIBUTES**

We just described how to ensure that the [Month] attribute has 12 values per year (120 values if your time dimension contains 10 years), but what if you wanted to compare sales that happened from any January to any December? You'd want a version of the month attribute that has 12 values; January would contain sales that happened in any January, and so forth.

In this case, you'd define an attribute for which the year column is not part of the key:

```
<Attribute name='Month of Year' keyColumn='month_of_year'
    nameColumn='month_name'/>
```

There is no formal relationship between this [Month of Year] and the [Month] attribute defined previously, but because the attributes are grouped into the [Time] dimension and are similarly named, your users will figure it out.

### 4.3.2 Time dimension

Cubes almost invariably have a time dimension. In section 3.2.2, you saw why it was a good idea to model time dimensions as Type I dimensions: a time dimension table containing one row for each day in the dataset, a surrogate key (usually an integer) containing the day ID, and a foreign key column in the fact table referencing that key. One of the advantages of that approach is that the time dimension is modeled much like any other dimension: there's a collection of attributes that can be used individually or organized into hierarchies.

MDX contains a number of operators specific to the time dimension (see table 4.5). For example, the YTD (year-to-date) function generates a range of members between the start of the year and the current time member; summing over these members yields a running total:

```
WITH MEMBER [Measures].[Unit Sales to Date] AS
  Aggregate(YTD(), [Measures].[Unit Sales])
SELECT {[Measures].[Unit Sales],
        [Measures].[Unit Sales to Date]} ON COLUMNS,
  [Time].[1997].Children ON ROWS
FROM [Sales];
```

```
|      |    | Unit Sales | Unit Sales to Date |
+------+----+------------+--------------------+
| 1997 | Q1 |     66,291 |             66,291 |
|      | Q2 |     62,610 |            128,901 |
|      | Q3 |     65,848 |            194,749 |
|      | Q4 |     72,024 |            266,773 |
```

**Table 4.5   MDX time operators**

| Function | Description |
|---|---|
| `YTD()` or `YTD(member)` | Year to date |
| `QTD()` or `QTD(member)` | Quarter to date |
| `MTD()` or `MTD(member)` | Month to date |
| `WTD()` or `WTD(member)` | Week to date |

To enable these operators, you need to tell Mondrian which attributes represent which kind of time period using `Dimension`'s type attribute and `Attribute`'s `level-Type` attribute. Listing 4.8 shows how these attributes are used.

**Listing 4.8   Labeling a time dimension and its attributes**

```
<Dimension name='Time' table='time_by_day' key='Time Id'
    type='TimeDimension'>                              ◁—— Time dimension
  <Attributes>
    <Attribute name='Year' keyColumn='the_year'
        levelType='TimeYears'/>                        ◁—— Year level
    <Attribute name='Quarter' levelType='TimeQuarters'>  ◁
      <Key>
        <Column name='the_year'/>                          Month level
        <Column name='quarter'/>
      </Key>
    </Attribute>
    ...
```

**TIME DIMENSION TABLE GENERATOR**

The most common way to generate a time dimension table is through an ETL tool. Pentaho Data Integration, for instance, includes a Time Dimension generator in its examples directory that can be used piecemeal or can be enhanced to build time dimension tables. But sometimes a tool like this isn't available, such as when you're running Mondrian against an operational schema. Mondrian provides a neat way to generate and populate a time dimension the first time you need it.

Recall how you declare a regular time dimension table:

```
<PhysicalSchema>
    <Table name='time_by_day'/>
    <!-- Other tables... -->
</PhysicalSchema>
```

Mondrian sees the table name, `time_by_day`, checks that it exists, and finds the column definitions from the JDBC catalog. The table can then be used in various dimensions in the schema. An auto-generated time dimension is similar:

```
<PhysicalSchema>
    <AutoGeneratedDateTable name='time_by_day_generated'
        startDate='2012-01-01' endDate='2014-01-31'/>
    <!-- Other tables... -->
</PhysicalSchema>
```

The first time Mondrian reads the schema, it notices that the table isn't present in the schema, and it creates and populates the table. Here's the DDL:

```
CREATE TABLE `time_by_day_generated` (
  `time_id` Integer NOT NULL PRIMARY KEY,
  `yymmdd` Integer NOT NULL,
  `yyyymmdd` Integer NOT NULL,
  `the_date` Date NOT NULL,
  `the_day` VARCHAR(20) NOT NULL,
  `the_month` VARCHAR(20) NOT NULL,
  `the_year` Integer NOT NULL,
  `day_of_month` Integer NOT NULL,
  `week_of_year` Integer NOT NULL,
  `month_of_year` Integer NOT NULL,
  `quarter` VARCHAR(20) NOT NULL);
```

The table contains one column for each time domain (shown in table 4.6). Table 4.7 shows the first few rows generated.

**Table 4.6   Time domains recognized by `<AutoGeneratedDateTable>`**

| Role | Default column name | Default data type | Example | Description |
|------|---------------------|-------------------|---------|-------------|
| JULIAN | time_id | Integer | 2454115 | Julian day number (0 = January 1, 4713 BC). An additional attribute, epoch, if specified, changes the date at which the value is 0. |
| YYMMDD | yymmdd | Integer | 120219 | Decimal date with two-digit year. |
| YYYYMMDD | yyyymmdd | Integer | 20120219 | Decimal date with four-digit year. |
| DATE | the_date | Date | 2012-12-31 | Date literal. |
| DAY_OF_WEEK | day_of_week | Integer | 2 | Ordinal of the day of the week: a value from 1 to 7. The first day of the week varies by locale. In the U.S. it's Sunday; in France it's Monday. |
| DAY_OF_WEEK_NAME | the_day | String | Friday | Name of day of week. |

**Table 4.6   Time domains recognized by `<AutoGeneratedDateTable>` *(continued)***

| Role | Default column name | Default data type | Example | Description |
|------|---------------------|-------------------|---------|-------------|
| DAY_OF_WEEK_IN_MONTH | day_of_week_in_month | Integer | 1 | Ordinal number of the day of the week within the current month. For example, the third Friday of the month will have the value 3. Unlike DAY_OF_WEEK, the value is the same in all locales. Days 1 through 7 of a month have the value 1, days 8 through 14 are 2, and so forth. |
| MONTH_NAME | the_month | String | December | Name of month. |
| YEAR | the_year | Integer | 2012 | Year. |
| DAY_OF_MONTH | day_of_month | Integer | 31 | Day ordinal within month. |
| WEEK_OF_YEAR | week_of_year | Integer | 53 | Week ordinal within year. |
| MONTH | month_of_year | Integer | 12 | Month ordinal within year. |
| QUARTER | quarter | String | Q4 | Name of quarter. |

**Table 4.7   Contents of `time_by_day_generated` table**

| JULIAN | YYMMDD | YYYYMMDD | DATE | DAY_OF_WEEK | DAY_OF_WEEK_NAME | DAY_OF_WEEK_IN_MONTH |
|--------|--------|----------|------|-------------|------------------|----------------------|
| 2455928 | 120101 | 20120101 | 2012-01-01 | 1 | Sunday | 1 |
| 2455929 | 120102 | 20120102 | 2012-01-02 | 2 | Monday | 1 |
| 2455930 | 120103 | 20120103 | 2012-01-03 | 3 | Tuesday | 1 |

| MONTH_NAME | YEAR | DAY_OF_MONTH | WEEK_OF_YEAR | MONTH | QUARTER |
|------------|------|--------------|--------------|-------|---------|
| January | 2012 | 1 | 1 | 1 | Q1 |
| January | 2012 | 2 | 1 | 1 | Q1 |
| January | 2012 | 3 | 1 | 1 | Q1 |

Suppose you wish to choose specific column names, or to have more control over how values are generated. You can do that by including a `<ColumnDefs>` element within the table, and <ColumnDef> elements within that—just like a regular <Table> element. Here's an example:

```
<PhysicalSchema>
  <AutoGeneratedDateTable name='time_by_day_generated'
      startDate='2008-01-01 endDate='2020-01-31'>
    <ColumnDefs>
      <ColumnDef name='time_id'>
        <TimeDomain role='JULIAN' epoch='1996-01-01'/>
      </ColumnDef>
      <ColumnDef name='my_year'>
        <TimeDomain role='YEAR'/>
      </ColumnDef>
      <ColumnDef name='my_month'>
        <TimeDomain role='MONTH'/>
      </ColumnDef>
      <ColumnDef name='quarter'/>
      <ColumnDef name='month_of_year'/>
      <ColumnDef name='week_of_year'/>
      <ColumnDef name='day_of_month'/>
      <ColumnDef name='the_month'/>
      <ColumnDef name='the_date'/>
    </ColumnDefs>
    <Key>
      <Column name='time_id'/>
    </Key>
  </AutoGeneratedDateTable>
  <!-- Other tables... -->
</PhysicalSchema>
```

The first three columns have nested <TimeDomain> elements that tell the generator how to populate them. The other columns have the standard column name for a particular time domain, so the <TimeDomain> element can be omitted. For instance,

```
<ColumnDef name='month_of_year'/>
```

is shorthand for

```
<ColumnDef name='month_of_year' type='int'>
  <TimeDomain role="month"/>
</ColumnDef>
```

The nested <Key> element makes that column valid as the target of a link (from a foreign key in the fact table, for instance), and it also declares the column as a primary key in the CREATE TABLE statement. This has the pleasant side effect, on all databases I know of, of creating an index. If you need other indexes on the generated table, you can create them manually.

### 4.3.3  Attribute hierarchies

Earlier we suggested that you should build dimensions and attributes first, and defer building hierarchies. This advice is valid, but it oversimplifies what's happening.

Actually, the MDX language can't see attributes at all. It can only see dimensions, hierarchies, and levels. So, given the following schema,

```
<Dimension name='Customers' ...>
  <Attributes>
    <Attribute name='Gender' .../>
  </Attributes>
</Dimension>
```

how can this query possibly work:

```
SELECT [Customers].[Gender].Members ON ROWS FROM [Sales]
```

The answer is that Mondrian implicitly creates attribute hierarchies.

An *attribute hierarchy* is a hierarchy that's implicitly created for an attribute. It has the same name as the attribute, a single level, and optionally an `all` member. The effect is the same as if you had added the following code to the definition of the [Customer] dimension:

```
<Hierarchy name='Gender'>
  <Level attribute='Gender'/>
</Hierarchy>
```

As a result, [Customer].[Gender] is actually referring to the attribute hierarchy. The query yields three members:

```
SELECT [Measures].[Unit Sales] ON COLUMNS,
    [Customer].[Gender].Members ON ROWS
FROM [Sales];
```

| Gender     | Unit Sales |
|------------|------------|
| All Gender |    266,273 |
| F          |    131,558 |
| M          |    135,215 |

[Customer].[Gender].[Gender] refers to the main level of the attribute hierarchy. It yields two members (omitting the `All Gender` member, which is in the [(All)] level):

```
SELECT [Measures].[Unit Sales] ON COLUMNS,
    [Customer].[Gender].[Gender].Members ON ROWS
FROM [Sales];
```

| Gender | Unit Sales |
|--------|------------|
| F      |    131,558 |
| M      |    135,215 |

An attribute hierarchy is created by default for each attribute, but you can disable it using the hasHierarchy attribute:

```
<Attribute name='Marital Status' hasHierarchy='false'/>
```

Such an attribute would only be useful if you explicitly include it in a hierarchy.

Mondrian's MDX validator allows you to omit the name of the hierarchy from an MDX expression if the dimension includes only one hierarchy. Then you could write [Customer].Members as shorthand for [Customer].[Customer].Members. But the hierarchy list includes attribute hierarchies; you would have to set hasHierarchy='false' for each attribute. In practice, the rule is most useful in schemas that have been automatically upgraded from version 3 format.

### 4.3.4 *The measures dimension*

We'll end this introduction to the structure of a schema with a word about the idiosyncratic measures dimension. The fact that measures belong to a dimension—the same kind of structure that years, months, customers, and products belong to—is one of the characteristic features of the dimensional model. (Contrast that with the relational model, where every value has precisely two coordinates, a row and a column, and rows and columns behave very differently.) In the dimensional model, a cell can have a large number of coordinates (one for each hierarchy in the cube, in fact), and every coordinate is a member of some hierarchy. And because every cube has a measures dimension, one of those coordinates is always a measure.

The [Measures] dimension is implicit. Every cube has one, and it's illegal to even try to declare the measures dimension using a <Dimension> element. The [Measures] dimension has a single hierarchy, called [Measures], which has a single level, also called [Measures].

> **CHANGING THE CAPTION OF THE MEASURES DIMENSION** If you wish to localize, since the measures dimension has is no Dimension element, you can change the caption of the measures dimension using the measuresCaption attribute of the Schema element.

When you define a measure using a <Measure> element (inside a measure group), it becomes a top-level member. For example, the measure defined in figure 4.1 with the name "Store Sales" becomes [Measures].[Store Sales]. (You can follow the usual "dimension.hierarchy.member" naming convention and write [Measures].[Measures].[Store Sales] if you like, but qualifying with a hierarchy name is unnecessary because the [Measures] dimension contains only one hierarchy.)

Some user interfaces, such as Pentaho Analyzer, allow measures to be displayed hierarchically. The [Measures] hierarchy has just one level, so no measure has a parent member. By convention, the hierarchical structure is created using an annotation called AnalyzerBusinessGroup:

```
<Measure name='Parent' column='column0'>
    <Annotations>
        <Annotation name='AnalyzerBusinessGroup'>Numbers</Annotation>
    </Annotations>
</Measure>
<Measure name='Child' column='column1'>
    <Annotations>
        <Annotation name='AnalyzerBusinessGroup'>
```

```
        Numbers/Sub group
    </Annotation>
  </Annotations>
</Measure>
<Measure name='Grandchild' column='column2'>
    <Annotations>
        <Annotation name='AnalyzerBusinessGroup'>
          Numbers/Sub group/Sub sub group
        </Annotation>
    </Annotations>
</Measure>
```

Then the user interface displays members in a hierarchy. When referenced from MDX, the members are still in one flat level: [Measures].[Parent], [Measures].[Child], and [Measures].[Grandchild].

> **ANNOTATIONS**  Because Mondrian's schema didn't natively allow measures to be displayed hierarchically, Analyzer's developers defined them using an extension mechanism called *annotations*. Annotations are a way to add arbitrary extra information to a Mondrian schema. Mondrian doesn't try to "understand" the annotations, but it makes them available to tools via its API. Section 9.1.4 describes some further annotations used by Analyzer.

Measures can also be calculated. We'll cover the various ways to create calculated measures (and members) in section 5.4.2 in the next chapter, but for now a simple example will suffice.

> **DON'T FORGET ABOUT CALCULATED MEMBERS**  Because "measure" sounds like "member," many people hear about calculated members and forget that you can define them for dimensions other than the measures dimension. Thus one of the dimensional model's most powerful features, the ability to define calculations on several dimensions simultaneously, is often ignored.

This schema fragment,

```
<CalculatedMember name='Profit' hierarchy='Measures'>
    <Formula>
        [Measures].[Store Sales] - [Measures].[Store Cost]
    </Formula>
</CalculatedMember>
```

creates a calculated measure that can be referenced in MDX as [Measures].[Profit]. Its value doesn't come directly from a column in the database; whenever its value is needed, Mondrian evaluates the given expression.

## 4.4    Summary

In this chapter you learned a lot about Mondrian schemas. These are the main points you should keep in mind:

- Mondrian schemas are represented in XML, and they can be written by hand or with authoring tools.
- The most important XML elements are `<Schema>`, `<PhysicalSchema>`, `<Cube>`, `<Dimension>`, `<Attribute>`, and `<Measure>`. With just these elements (and a few supporting elements), you can create a cube to do analysis.
- Dimensions are collections of logically related attributes, and hierarchies and levels make it easier to navigate among related attributes.
- Mondrian has special support for time dimensions. Just about every cube has one.
- Measures belong to their own dimension, and every attribute has its own hierarchy.

The full definitions of XML elements and their attributes can be found in Mondrian's online documentation, a link to which appears in appendix B.

The next chapter continues the description of Mondrian schema elements, covering some advanced topics that may not be required for every cube and many of the XML element types we didn't discuss in this chapter. A few other schema elements are so tied to particular subject areas that they're discussed in the chapters that cover those subject areas: roles are covered in chapter 8, which covers security; and aggregate tables are described in chapter 7.

# How schemas grow

5

---

In chapter 4, you learned how to write a Mondrian schema that contains a simple cube. Even a basic cube can support countless analyses; each analysis answers some questions and raises new ones. If that first cube is successful, your business users will come back and ask for more dimensions, more attributes, and more powerful ways to model and analyze the data.

This chapter is about how dimensional models tend to evolve in the real world. Much of that evolution is "more of the same": adding cubes, dimensions, and measures. A small addition to the model can allow a significant new area of the business to be analyzed. For example, a business user might ask you to add a `Referrer` dimension to the `Sales` cube so that they can analyze the effectiveness of social media campaigns.

Mondrian has features that keep schemas manageable as they grow. We'll look at how you can create and use shared dimensions, and how you can use measure groups to build a cube based on more than one fact table.

There are also some new, advanced concepts that will allow you to model richer kinds of data. For example, a parent-child hierarchy would allow you to model the organizational structure of your sales organization, and by using a hanger dimension you could compare target sales with actual sales, starting with each salesperson and propagating to each group in the sales organization. Using a calculation, you could project the sales for the current quarter based on sales over the last few weeks, and using another calculation, you could compare the performance of any salesperson with the top five salespeople in their region.

We'll start by looking at how schemas evolve.

## 5.1 *Schema evolution*

There's an old saying in the software industry: bad products have no bugs. Of course, all software has bugs, but if a piece of software is no good, the users won't stick around long enough to find very many. If software is good, users will employ it in ways that the designers didn't expect. Of course they will find bugs, but they'll patiently stick around until those bugs are fixed, and they'll offer suggestions to the developers about ways to make the software better.

So it is with an analysis model. You'll know that your model is being used, because you'll receive a stream of requests to make it better. Remember how, in the last chapter, we said not to build too many hierarchies; just build attributes. Your users will ask for the hierarchies they need, along with extra cubes, dimensions, measures, and attributes. You, as the schema designer, need to translate their requirements into changes to the analysis schema. You may also need to load additional data from the operational system into the data mart.

Here are a few ways that a schema can evolve:

- Change the caption, description, or format string of any element
- Add an attribute to a dimension
- Add a hierarchy to a dimension
- Add a level to a hierarchy
- Add a measure that's the same granularity or dimensionality as existing measures
- Add a measure of different granularity or dimensionality than existing measures
- Create a calculated column and use it in an attribute or measure
- Add a calculated member to a cube
- Add a named set to a cube

In this chapter, we'll discuss these and other ways that schemas can grow to address business requirements. Some are straightforward, whereas others require structural changes to the underlying schema, and sometimes require changes to the ETL process that populates it. As you'll see, Mondrian's schema is designed to make evolution as straightforward as possible.

### 5.1.1   *Multiple cubes in a schema*

Suppose you've built a `[Sales]` cube to analyze the process of taking and shipping orders in your business, and now you wish to analyze the process of receiving products into your warehouses, storing them as inventory, and shipping them to fulfill orders.

In chapter 4, we defined a cube as a collection of data over time that describes a business process. In order to analyze a new process, we therefore need a new cube. Listing 5.1 shows the `[Warehouse]` cube.

**Listing 5.1   Schema containing `Sales` and `Warehouse` cubes**

```
                  <Schema name='Sales and Warehouse'>
  Physical  ▷      <PhysicalSchema .../>
   schema
 shared by        <Cube name='Sales'>                        ◁—— Sales cube
 both cubes         <Dimensions>
                      <Dimension name='Time' .../>           ◁⌐ Time, Customer,
                      <Dimension name='Customer' .../>         │ Product, Promotion
                      <Dimension name='Product' .../>          │ dimensions
                      <Dimension name='Promotion' .../>
                    </Dimensions>
                    <MeasureGroups .../>
                  </Cube>

 Warehouse  ▷     <Cube name='Warehouse'>
    cube           <Dimensions>
                      <Dimension name='Time' .../>            ◁⌐ Time, Product,
                      <Dimension name='Product' .../>           │ Warehouse
                      <Dimension name='Warehouse' .../>         │ dimensions
                    </Dimensions>
                    <MeasureGroups .../>
                  </Cube>
                </Schema>
```

You can add as many cubes as you need. Mondrian allows an unlimited number of cubes in a schema.

Each cube is a starting point for an analysis. In Saiku or other similar tools, the user can choose the cube that's the best fit for the area of the business to be analyzed.

Most of the time, each cube you build will be on a new set of data. But there are a couple of reasons why you might want to create more than one cube on the same set of data, so we'll briefly mention them here.

If you've designed a cube that's daunting to some business users, you may wish to implement what user-interface experts call *information hiding*. You can create a simplified version of the cube for beginner users that contains only the most important measures and dimensions. As the users get to feel more confident with the system, they can start using the full cube.

*Access control* is very similar to information hiding, but it has a different goal. You can create cubes that display different combinations of dimensions and measures, and give access to these cubes to just the groups of users who are allowed to see them. More access-control techniques, including how to control access to individual dimensions, measures, and members, are described in chapter 6.

## 5.1.2 Shared dimensions

Take a look again at listing 5.1, and specifically at the dimensions that occur within each cube. The [Sales] and [Warehouse] cubes both have [Time] and [Product] dimensions, and then there are one or two dimensions specific to each cube.

This is a common pattern: cubes describing different areas of a business have common dimensions where those areas have overlapping concepts, such as products, time, or customers.

Let's assume for a minute that these dimensions have the same definitions. (We'll look at some reasons why they might not when we discuss conformed dimensions in the next section.)

It would seem to be a waste to have identical definitions of the [Time] and [Product] dimensions in each cube. Even if it doesn't affect the end user, it's more code to maintain and there's a greater opportunity for inconsistencies and errors to creep in. Luckily, Mondrian allows you to create *shared dimensions* at the schema level. These can be incorporated by any cube in the schema by using a <Dimension source=...> element.

Listing 5.2 shows the structure of the schema after the [Time] and [Product] dimensions have been factored into shared dimensions. The definitions of the [Time] and [Product] dimensions in each cube, previously dozens of lines of XML each, are now just a single line of XML.

**Listing 5.2  Sales and Warehouse cubes using shared dimensions**

```
<Schema name='Sales and Warehouse'>
  <PhysicalSchema .../>

  <Dimension name='Time' .../>           ⟵── Shared Time dimension

  <Dimension name='Product' .../>        ⟵── Shared Product dimension

  <Cube name='Sales'>
    <Dimensions>
      <Dimension source='Time'/>           Time and Product dimensions based
      <Dimension name='Customer' .../>     on shared dimensions; private
      <Dimension source='Product'/>        Customer and Promotion dimensions
      <Dimension name='Promotion' .../>
    </Dimensions>
    <MeasureGroups .../>
  </Cube>

  <Cube name='Warehouse'>               Time and Product dimensions
    <Dimensions>                        based on shared dimensions;
                                        private Warehouse dimension
```

```
      <Dimension source='Time'/>
      <Dimension source='Product'/>
      <Dimension name='Warehouse' .../>
    </Dimensions>
    <MeasureGroups .../>
  </Cube>
</Schema>
```

### 5.1.3   *Conformed dimensions*

What happens if, say, the Product dimension has different definitions in the two cubes? First, let's look at why they might be different. Unless there's a good reason to do otherwise, similar dimensions should have the same definitions. These are technically known as conformed dimensions.

*Conformed dimensions* are dimensions with the same set of attributes and hierarchies, and are stored in the same underlying table structure. (Ralph Kimball coined the term when talking about star schemas, and specifically dimension tables that could be referenced by multiple fact tables, but it naturally extends to cube design.)

Conformed dimensions are desirable for several reasons. They allow different parts of the business to be compared using the same terms, and they may allow cross-departmental optimizations. As a bonus, they save disk space, because you only need one copy of the table.

Mondrian doesn't have a feature called "conformed dimensions," but if two cube dimensions conform, you very likely should model them as uses of a single shared dimension.

Now back to that question of why two product dimensions might not conform. If the dimensions have different definitions by accident (say, because they were created by different developers), then it's worth spending the effort to make them conform. Once they conform, defining them as shared dimensions in the Mondrian schema will ensure that their definitions stay the same from that point on.

But sometimes the difference arises for political reasons. These kinds of problems are much more difficult to solve than mere technology problems. Suppose that the departments that own the Sales and Warehouse fact data have different definitions of "product" and manage their data in different operational databases. To create a conformed dimension, the business owners would need to agree on the definition of a product, and the ETL process that populates the data warehouse from the operational systems would need to be changed to use the same product dimension table.

To create a conformed dimension that meets several departments' needs, several people will need to agree on the solution, and several systems will need to be changed. It may not be practical or cost-effective to fully solve the problem, at least at first. A pragmatic approach might be to start with a partial solution, such as agreeing on a common key and a few core attributes for analysis purposes. Use that partial solution to demonstrate a business benefit, and then maybe you can convince the stakeholders to support a better solution.

Assuming that the dimensions already conform, when should dimensions be shared? We recommend creating shared dimensions for key business concepts like time, customer, and product, which are very likely to appear in multiple cubes. Other dimensions can be created as private at first; it's straightforward to promote them to shared (and conformed) when they're needed in another cube.

### 5.1.4 Using a dimension twice in the same cube

Shared dimensions aren't always used in different cubes—you can use a shared dimension more than once in the same cube. These are called *role-playing dimensions*.

Suppose you wish to record and analyze the dates on which an order was received and shipped. You can create dimensions called [Ship Time] and [Order Time]; since they're conformed, you can base them on the shared [Time] dimension, as follows.

```
<Dimension source='Time' name='Order Time'/>
<Dimension source='Time' name='Ship Time'/>
```

Note how the name attribute has been called into service to give the two uses of the [Time] dimension different names. When a shared dimension is used only once in a cube, usually the name is the same as the source dimension, so you can omit the name attribute.

[Ship Time] and [Order Time] are independent dimensions. This means that the value of one dimension can vary without affecting the other. You could, for example, select [Order Time].[Yearly].[2011].[Q4].[12] on the columns axis and [Ship Time].[Yearly].[2012].[Q1] on the rows axis to see which orders were made in December but not shipped until Q1.

Because the dimensions are independent, you need to wire them both up to the fact table using different foreign key columns:

```
<DimensionLinks>
   <ForeignKeyLink dimension='Order Time'
                   foreignKeyColumn='order_time_id'/>
   <ForeignKeyLink dimension='Ship Time'
                   foreignKeyColumn='ship_time_id'/>
   ...
</DimensionLinks>
```

We'll look at further examples of the ForeignKeyLink element and other kinds of dimension links in the following sections.

### 5.1.5 Measures across multiple fact tables

Adding a *measure* is straightforward when it's based on an existing column in the fact table. You can apply a new aggregate function to a column already used by another measure, or use a column that has not been used before.

If the measure column doesn't exist, you need to ask whether it belongs in the current fact table. It may if the measure has the same dimensionality and granularity as the fact table, but if not, you'll need to put the measure in a new fact table, and that requires something called a measure group.

**Before measure groups**

Measure groups are a new feature, introduced in Mondrian version 4.

In previous versions of Mondrian, cubes had only one fact table. If you wanted to create a cube that had multiple fact tables, you had to create a "virtual cube" that combined several regular cubes. Virtual cubes are no longer supported, but Mondrian migrates them automatically to cubes that have multiple measure groups if it sees a schema in version 3 format.

A *measure group* is the logical equivalent of a fact table, just as a dimension is the logical equivalent of a dimension table. It's a collection of measures that have the same dimensionality and granularity and that are therefore stored together.

Let's define dimensionality and granularity, and look at the various ways that measure groups are used in practice.

### DIMENSIONALITY AND GRANULARITY OF MEASURES

First some definitions:

- The *dimensionality* of a measure is the set of dimensions that determine its value.
- The *granularity* of a measure concerns the exact attributes of the dimensions that it depends upon.

Dimensionality and granularity are best explained using examples. Consider the following measures:

- [Unit Sales] depends on dimensions [Product], [Time], [Customer], and [Promotion], and it's stored in the sales_fact_1997 fact table.
- [Store Sales] depends on dimensions [Product], [Time], [Customer], and [Promotion], and it's stored in the sales_fact_1997 fact table.
- [Forecast Sales] depends on dimensions [Product], [Time] (at the [Quarter] level), [Customer] (at the [Region] level), and [Promotion], and it's stored in the sales_forecast fact table.
- [Inventory Count] depends on dimensions [Product], [Time], and [Warehouse], and it's stored in the inventory_fact fact table.

The [Unit Sales] and [Store Sales] measures have identical dimensionality and granularity. [Forecast Sales] has a coarser granularity: forecasts are made for whole months, not down to the day level, and for a state, not individual customers. [Inventory Count] has a different dimensionality: it still depends on the [Time] and [Product] dimensions, but it depends on the new dimension [Warehouse] and doesn't depend on [Customer] or [Promotion] at all.

Figure 5.1 shows the star schema that stores these four measures.

We've been talking about dimensions and measures, but a star schema is physical, so figure 5.1 shows tables and columns. Still, it is fairly clear what's what from the names of the tables and columns. The three fact tables are in the center of the diagram, their

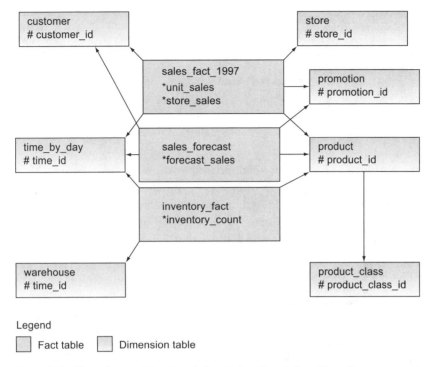

**Legend**

☐ Fact table  ☐ Dimension table

**Figure 5.1  Star schema with unit and store Sales, Forecast, and Inventory measure groups**

arrows pointing outward to dimension tables at the sides. Measures of the same granularity are stored in the same fact table: the [Unit Sales] and [Store Sales] measures are stored as the unit_sales and store_sales columns in sales_fact_1997, [Forecast Sales] as forecast_sales in sales_forecast, and [Inventory Count] as inventory_count in inventory_fact. This makes a lot of sense from a data normalization standpoint.

### FINE-GRAINED MEASURE GROUPS

The sales_fact_1997 and inventory_fact fact tables both contain data at a fine level of granularity. Their contents are different because they have different dimensionality: they cover different areas of the business.

Now let's define a cube that has a measure group for each fact table. Listing 5.3 shows the Sales cube with these measure groups.

**Listing 5.3   Sales cube with multiple measure groups**

```
<Cube name='Sales'>
  <Dimensions .../>
  <MeasureGroups>
    <MeasureGroup name='Sales' table='sales_fact_1997'>    ◁──┐ Measure group based
      <Measures>                                               on sales_fact_1997
        <Measure name='Unit Sales' .../>                      fact table
        <Measure name='Store Sales' .../>
```

```
      </Measures>
      <DimensionLinks .../>
    </MeasureGroup>
    <MeasureGroup name='Inventory' table='inventory_fact'>
      <Measures>
        <Measure name='Inventory Count' .../>
      </Measures>
      <DimensionLinks .../>
    </MeasureGroup>
  </MeasureGroups>
</Cube>
```

Measure group based
on inventory_fact
fact table

Each measure group has a source table (which you must have previously defined in the physical schema), a collection of measures, and a collection of dimension links.

Mondrian needs to know which dimensions a measure group depends upon, and, if it depends on a particular dimension, how to join to that dimension's table and at which level. Dimension links convey all of that information; in short, they define dimensionality and granularity. Table 5.1 shows the dimensionality of the `Sales` and `Inventory` measure groups.

**Table 5.1   Dimensionality of the `Sales` and `Inventory` measure groups**

| Dimension | Sales | Inventory |
|---|---|---|
| Time | `time_id` foreign key | `time_id` foreign key |
| Product | `product_id` foreign key | `product_id` foreign key |
| Customer | `customer_id` foreign key | no link |
| Warehouse | no link | `warehouse_id` foreign key |

Now let's consider a measure group that has the same dimensionality as the `Sales` measure group but coarser granularity.

**COARSE-GRAINED MEASURE GROUPS**

There's a step between using and not using a dimension in a measure group: a measure group can use a dimension at a coarse granularity. Consider the `Forecast` measure group, whose dimensionality is shown in table 5.2.

**Table 5.2   Dimensionality of the `Forecast` measure group**

| Dimension | Forecast |
|---|---|
| Time | (`time_year_id`, `time_month_id`) composite foreign key |
| Product | `product_id` foreign key |
| Customer | `customer_country_id` foreign key |
| Warehouse | no link |

In terms of dimensionality, the `Forecast` measure group is the same as `Sales`: it depends on the `[Time]`, `[Product]`, and `[Customer]` dimensions, and not on `[Warehouse]`. But the granularity is more coarse. The values of measures in this group are defined by month, not day; a value exists at the day level, but it's inherited. For example, on January 31, 2012, the `[Forecast Sales]` measure for a particular product does have a value, but it's the same as for January 1, 2012. Coarser granularity means fewer distinct values than if the key attribute had been used, but more than if the dimension had been dropped altogether.

Listing 5.4 shows the XML definition of the `Forecast` measure group. The `attribute` attribute in the links for the `[Time]` and `[Customer]` dimensions indicate that they are at lesser granularity. Because the `[Time].[Month]` attribute has a composite key, the foreign key for the `[Time]` dimension matches it, using the `the_year` and `month_of_year` columns from the `sales_forecast` fact table.

**Listing 5.4   The `Forecast` measure group**

```
<MeasureGroup name='Forecast' table='sales_forecast'>
  <Measures>
    <Measure name='Forecast Unit Sales' .../>
  </Measures>
  <DimensionLinks>
    <ForeignKeyLink dimension='Time' attribute='Month'>
      <Column name='the_year'/>
      <Column name='month_of_year'/>
    </ForeignKeyLink>
    <ForeignKeyLink dimension='Product' foreignKeyColumn='product_id'/>
    <ForeignKeyLink dimension='Customer'
                    foreignKeyColumn='customer_country'
                    attribute='Country'/>
    <NoLink dimension='Warehouse'/>
  </DimensionLinks>
</MeasureGroup>
```

*Annotations:* Measure group based on forecast table; Use Month attribute as key, rather than default Day; Composite key matches Month attribute's composite key; Join to Country attribute

That just about concludes our first look at measure groups, but we'll meet them again when we discuss aggregate tables in chapter 7. Aggregate tables are basically coarse-grained measure groups whose measures are rolled-up versions of measures from other finer-grained measure groups. They don't contribute any new measures for the business user to analyze, but they give Mondrian the option of working from highly aggregated data, which can have a stunning effect on performance.

Next, we'll talk about how to decide whether to create cubes that span several measure groups or more targeted cubes, and how many cubes to include in a schema.

### 5.1.6   *Smart evolution: multiple cubes versus single cubes*

Schema designers often ask, "When should I create multiple cubes, as opposed to a single cube with multiple measure groups?" Mondrian supports shared dimensions, so both designs are straightforward and quite similar. As a result, this is primarily a usability question.

> ### Right-sizing cubes and schemas
>
> When designing a schema, it's best to start small and add complexity only if you need it.
>
> - Start off with simple cubes, with fewer dimensions and just one measure group.
> - Create complex cubes with multiple measure groups if you need to answer complex business questions.
> - Even if you build complex cubes, keep the simple cubes around for less advanced users performing simpler analyses.
> - Consider splitting a schema into multiple schemas if it contains many unrelated cubes.

Listen to the business questions your users need to solve. Consider the question, "How much of our revenue comes from products for which we have fewer than two days of inventory in stock?" This involves the sales_fact_1997 fact table (and its revenue measure) and the inventory_fact fact table. To solve the question, you'll need to create a cube based on the two fact tables.

Shared dimensions are another clue: if the measure groups have many dimensions in common, they should probably belong to the same cube.

You can have it both ways. You can use a fact table in a cube with multiple measure groups, and you can also create a more focused cube with just one measure group. If you do this, try to name measures consistently so that your business users know that the data is coming from the same source.

Other typical questions are about the right size for a schema: "I have a dozen cubes. Should they all go in the same schema, or should I create two smaller schemas?" This is partly a usability question. It can be daunting to business users if there are many cubes to choose from. Consider the subject areas that the cubes address and the dimensions in common between cubes. If a schema seems to sprawl over several subject areas, and there is very little in common among the cubes, split them into smaller schemas.

Remember, different Mondrian schemas can share the same database tables, and copying and pasting a dimension definition from one schema to another is not difficult. Another pragmatic reason to split up a schema is to help in the development process: a schema is defined within a single file, so only one developer can edit it at a time.

### 5.1.7   *Other schema evolution patterns*

Let's review a few of the other ways you can modify a schema. We'll focus on the tools you'll use every day, rather than on how to solve particular problems. The right tool for the job is usually clear.

- *Change the caption, description, or format string of an element*—It's always easy to change the caption, description, or format string of an element. Good descriptions, in particular, help to make a schema accessible to business users who haven't used it before. No reports or MDX statements will be broken by making these changes, so it's worth spending a little time getting them right. Think of it as adding a little polish.

- *Change the name of an element*—Changing the name of elements is easy, but you need to take care. If reports are based on those elements, those reports will break. You'll need to find and fix them manually.

- *Add an element*—Adding an attribute is usually benign if the column you need is already in the schema, but you should be careful if you use abbreviations when you write MDX. For example, suppose that you've written [Time].[Day].Members in a report, referring to the [Day] level of the [Yearly] hierarchy in the [Time] dimension. Now you add an attribute called [Day]. Next time you run that report, the expression will return the members of the [Day] attribute hierarchy. Those results look similar to the members of the [Day] level but will include an [All Day] member that wasn't there before. This problem can also occur when adding other elements, such as levels, hierarchies, and dimensions. The best way to avoid it is to use full object references in hand-written MDX.

- *Add a hierarchy to a dimension*—Adding a hierarchy to a dimension is straightforward if you have attributes from which to build its levels.

- *Add a level to a hierarchy*—Adding a level to a hierarchy is also straightforward if you have an attribute of the appropriate cardinality to base it upon. (See the discussion in section 4.1.3 about choosing the right key for attributes that are to become levels.)

- *Add a calculated member to a cube*—You can easily add a calculated member to a cube. Because it's a pure MDX expression, you don't need any changes to the underlying schema. It's usually most convenient to develop a calculated member in the WITH MEMBER clause of a handwritten query, and then paste its MDX expression into the cube definition. Calculated members are explained in more detail in section 5.4.2.

- *Add a named set to a cube*—You can easily add a named set to a cube. Like calculated members, you can develop named sets in a WITH SET clause of a query.

Now that you understand the ways that you can improve and change your schema, let's move on to some of the more advanced ways that Mondrian can map dimensions onto tables.

## 5.2 Alternative ways to store dimensions

Mondrian is very flexible in how dimensions are mapped to tables, and you can use that flexibility to improve performance, optimize the use of disk space, and map them onto structures such as operational tables.

Star, snowflake, and degenerate dimensions are three mapping styles. In this section, we'll cover each style in turn.

### 5.2.1  *Star dimensions*

When we showed you how to define dimensions in chapter 4, we focused on one storage model, which mapped each dimension onto a single table. The [Customer] dimension, for example, was based on the customer table. The dimension had a surrogate key, customer_id, and was linked to the fact table via a ForeignKeyLink referencing that key from the fact table's customer_id foreign key column.

This pattern is called a *star dimension*, and it's so named because a diagram of dimension tables arranged around a central fact table looks like a star. In figure 5.2, time_by_day, customer, and store are all examples of this. But a star dimension is not the only pattern used for storing dimensions.

A *snowflake dimension* consists of two or more tables connected by a chain of many-to-one foreign keys (product and product_class form a two-table snowflake in figure 5.2). A *degenerate dimension* has no table of its own, but stores its attributes in the fact table (the payment_type column in sales_fact_1997).

In the next sections, we'll describe when it makes sense to use snowflake and degenerate dimensions, and how to define them in a schema.

### 5.2.2  *Snowflake dimensions*

A snowflake dimension is a star dimension broken up into two or more tables. If you've designed OLTP database schemas before, you know what it means to convert a database into third normal form (3NF) by splitting up tables that contain redundant information. A snowflake is basically a "more normalized" version of a star dimension. But, as you'll see, it doesn't always make sense to break all your dimensions into snowflakes.

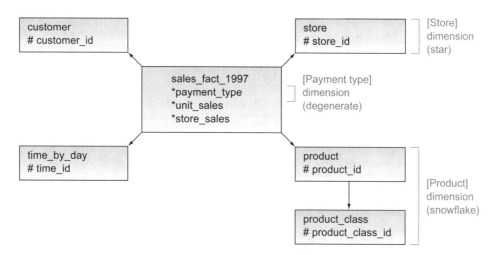

**Figure 5.2  Schema with star, snowflake, and degenerate dimensions**

Consider the [Product] dimension, with levels [Product Family], [Product Department], [Brand Name], and [Product Name], stored as a star dimension in a single product table. Table 5.3 shows the first few rows of the product table.

**Table 5.3**  [Product] **dimension stored in the** product **table**

| product_family | product_department | brand_name | product_name | product_id |
|---|---|---|---|---|
| Food | Snack Foods | Best Choice | Best Choice BBQ Potato Chips | 218 |
| Food | Snack Foods | Best Choice | Best Choice Corn Chips | 219 |
| Food | Snack Foods | Fort West | Fort West Potato Chips | 1474 |
| Food | Snack Foods | Fort West | Fort West Lemon Cookies | 1475 |
| Food | Snack Foods | Fort West | Fort West Graham Crackers | 1476 |
| Food | Baking Goods | Super | Super Pepper | 298 |
| Food | Baking Goods | Super | Super Salt | 300 |

As you can see, there's considerable duplication. Each value of product_family, product_department, and brand_name occurs several times. To reduce the number of duplicate values, you could try normalizing into product_class and product tables (tables 5.4 and 5.5).

**Table 5.4**  **Upper levels of** [Product] **dimension stored in** product_class **table**

| product_family | product_department | brand_name | brand_id |
|---|---|---|---|
| Food | Snack Foods | Best Choice | 45 |
| Food | Snack Foods | Fort West | 12 |
| Food | Baking Goods | Super | 4 |

**Table 5.5**  **Lower levels of** [Product] **dimension stored in** product **table**

| brand_id | product_name | product_id |
|---|---|---|
| 45 | Best Choice BBQ Potato Chips | 218 |
| 45 | Best Choice Corn Chips | 219 |
| 12 | Fort West Potato Chips | 1474 |
| 12 | Fort West Lemon Cookies | 1475 |
| 12 | Fort West Graham Crackers | 1476 |
| 4 | Super Pepper | 298 |
| 4 | Super Salt | 300 |

The [Product] dimension is now based on two tables, so this is a snowflake structure. You need to declare the tables in the physical schema, and a link between them:

```
<Table name='product' keyColumn='product_id'/>
<Table name='product_brand' keyColumn='brand_id'/>
<Link name='product_brand' source='product_brand'
      target='product' foreignKeyColumn='brand_id'/>
```

**Declare product and product_brand tables**

**Declare a join path from product to product_brand**

We first described the <Link> element in chapter 4. Here, there's a direct link from the product table to the product_brand table, but Mondrian will find and use a path over multiple links, as long as there is just one path.

Now you can use these tables' columns when you define the attributes of the [Product] dimension:

```
<Dimension name='Product' key='Product Name'
           table='product_brand'>
  <Attributes>
    <Attribute name='Product Family'
               keyColumn='product_family'/>
    <Attribute name='Product Department'>
      <Key>
        <Column name='product_family'/>
        <Column name='product_department'/>
      </Key>
    </Attribute>
    <Attribute name='Brand Name'
               keyColumn='brand_id' nameColumn='brand_name'/>
    <Attribute name='Product Name'
               table='product'
               keyColumn='product_id'
               nameColumn='product_name'/>
  </Attributes>
</Dimension>
```

**Default table for attributes is product_brand**

**Upper attributes are based on product_brand table**

**Attribute overrides table to product**

What have you achieved? You've reduced the number of duplicated values, and therefore saved some space, and you've simplified the task of maintaining consistency while updating the dimension. But you've introduced a join, which may slow down queries. Snowflake dimensions are a tradeoff.

If you've designed OLTP databases before, you're probably feeling uncomfortable right now. Your inclination is to normalize all tables, so it feels natural to create snowflake dimensions. But remember that normalization was invented chiefly to reduce amount of effort required to maintain consistency when performing updates; this is much less important in a data warehouse, where reads are much more frequent than updates. Normalizing a dimension table into two or more snowflake tables won't save much space on disk (especially in a modern analytic database with column-oriented storage), but it'll incur significantly more effort performing joins.

When are snowflake dimensions useful? If you have a conformed dimension that's used at various granularities, a snowflake dimension may let you join directly to the upper levels of the dimension. In section 5.1.5, the `Forecast` measure group referenced the `[Customer]` dimension at the level of the `[Customer].[Country]` attribute. That required a foreign key from the `sales_forecast` fact table to the `country` column of the `customer` dimension table. Because `country` is not unique, Mondrian has to eliminate duplicates, generating a `(SELECT DISTINCT country FROM customer)` subquery, or something like it, and that's expensive to evaluate.

The same applies if the most of the uses of a dimension are at a high level, using measures rolled up into aggregate tables (see section 7.3). If the dimension is decomposed into a star, the aggregate table can join directly to the table holding the upper levels.

Otherwise, you should consider snowflaking a dimension only if there are space savings and demonstrable performance improvements. One case where this might happen is if the smaller of the resulting tables has a large number of columns and a small number of rows. Then the database may be able to cache the smaller table in memory, and the cost of the extra join will be negligible.

Follow the performance-tuning process outlined in chapter 7 by running representative queries on the star and snowflake forms of the dimension. If the snowflake doesn't perform better, keep the dimension as a star.

### 5.2.3   *Degenerate dimensions*

Whereas a star dimension has one dimension table, and a snowflake dimension has two or more, a degenerate dimension has none. All of the columns that describe the dimension live in the fact table.

Suppose you wish to break down orders by their payment type (cash, credit, debit), and that the payment type is represented by a `payment_type` column in the `sales_fact_1997` fact table. You need to create a dimension with a single attribute based on the `payment_type` column. If you were to model this as a star dimension, you'd create a dimension table with one column and three rows, and you'd use `payment_type` as a foreign key to get ... tada! ... exactly the same value. As you can see, a star dimension would be overkill. A degenerate dimension instead lets the values stand for themselves.

Here's how you could define `[Payment Type]` as a degenerate dimension:

```
<Dimension name='Payment Type' table='sales_fact_1997'>
  <Attributes>
    <Attribute name='Payment Type' keyColumn='payment_type'
            approxRowCount='3'/>
  </Attributes>
</Dimension>
```

The attribute definition includes the `approxRowCount` attribute, saving Mondrian the effort of a full table scan to find out that there are three distinct values. Mondrian treats this value as approximate, but it is nevertheless very useful when Mondrian is making decisions, such as whether to use an aggregate table. Still, the need to do a full scan of the fact table to find its root members is one of the downsides of a degenerate dimension.

In the <DimensionLinks> section of the measure group, instead of the usual <ForeignKeyLink> element, you'd use a <FactLink> element to indicate that the dimension is in the fact table, and therefore no join is required.

```
<MeasureGroup name='Sales' table='sales_fact_1997'>
  <Measures .../>
  <DimensionLinks>
    <FactLink dimension='Payment Type'/>
    ...
  </DimensionLinks>
</MeasureGroup>
```

The other downside to a degenerate dimension is that it can only support a very simple structure. If you find you need to add extra attributes, or even if the attribute's name or ordinal property differs from its key, it's probably time that your degenerate dimension grew up to use a conventional star dimension structure.

We've now covered how to map dimensions onto various table structures. It's time to discuss some data structures that present dimensions to the end user in ways other than ordinary hierarchies.

## 5.3    Advanced hierarchy structures

The previous section described various ways to map hierarchies onto database schemas: star, snowflake, and degenerate dimensions. These decisions affect query performance and the amount of disk space needed for your warehouse, but they don't affect the end user. A dimension looks the same on the screen, regardless of how it's stored.

We'll now consider some structures that affect how dimensions appear to the end user. Parent-child hierarchies and ragged hierarchies let you model dimensions so they look more like the real world.

### 5.3.1    Parent-child hierarchies

Suppose you want to analyze the human resources in an organization: the salary, benefits, days worked, and accrued vacation time of every employee. Employees belong to departments, and each department has a manager, so there's a hierarchical structure.

Unlike the "regular" hierarchies we've seen previously (in section 4.3.1), this hierarchy doesn't have a fixed depth. The deputy assistant janitor might be 11 levels below the CEO, and the system should not prevent the company from hiring a trainee deputy assistant janitor at level 12.

Regular hierarchies, in contrast, have a fixed number of named levels. The [Customers] hierarchy you saw in chapter 4 has levels based on the [Country], [State], and [City] attributes of the [Customer] dimension, and each level is named after its attribute. Members adhere to those strict levels: a member of the [City] level is always a child of a member of the [State] level, which is a child of a member of the [Country] level.

In contrast, the [Employees] parent-child hierarchy has only one named level, but parent and child members can each be at that level. Here's how you would model [Employees] in the schema:

```
<Dimension name='Employee' table='employee' key='Employee Id'>
  <Attributes>
    <Attribute name='Supervisor Id' keyColumn='supervisor_id'/>
    <Attribute name='Employee Id' keyColumn='employee_id'
              nameColumn='full_name' orderByColumn='employee_id'
              parent='Supervisor Id' nullParentValue='0'/>
  </Attributes>
  <Hierarchies>
    <Hierarchy name='Employees'>
      <Level attribute='Employee Id'/>
    </Hierarchy>
  </Hierarchies>
</Dimension>
```

Another thing that is different about parent-child hierarchies is that users expect to see measures rolled up. A manager's salary total should be their personal salary plus the salaries of all employees under them in the organization. The salary shown for the CEO, who is at the root of the tree, would be the total salary for the whole company.

By the way, the MDX language also lets you get at a manager's personal salary, if you want it. Listing 5.5 shows how.

**Listing 5.5   MDX query on parent-child hierarchy**

```
mdx> WITH MEMBER [Measures].[Personal Salary] AS
   >      ([Employees].DataMember,
   >      [Measures].[Salary])
   > SELECT {[Measures].[Salary],
   >      [Measures].[Personal Salary]} ON Columns,
   >      Head([Employees].Members, 10) ON Rows
   > FROM [HR];
```

*Calculation for employee's personal salary* — pointing at the WITH MEMBER lines

*First ten employees* — pointing at the Head line

*Report shows totals with and without underlings' salaries* — pointing at the output below

```
                                        Salary   Personal Salary
================================== ========== ===============
All Employees                      $39,431.67
 + Sheri Nowmer                    $39,431.67          $864.00
  + Derrick Whelply                $36,494.07          $432.00
   + Beverly Baker                  $4,938.83          $324.00
    + Shauna Wyro                     $358.54          $162.00
     + Bunny McCown                   $196.54           $86.40
      + Nancy Miller                   $70.20           $70.20
      + Wanda Hollar                   $39.94           $39.94
    + Jacqueline Wyllie             $4,256.29          $183.60
     + Ralph Mccoy                  $4,072.69          $140.40
```

*Nancy Miller has no underlings, so totals are the same* — pointing at the Nancy Miller row

The first column is the regular [Salary] measure, which is rolled up; the second column is the salary without rollups. How is it computed? Each member of a parent-child hierarchy has a shadow member, called its *data member*, that represents just that member, without implicit rollups. The query accesses it using the DataMember property.

In summary, parent-child hierarchies are a very different model for member data than regular hierarchies. You should use a regular hierarchy if possible, but for certain kinds of nested data, a parent-child hierarchy is the natural organization.

### 5.3.2  *Ragged hierarchies*

Ragged hierarchies are another way to model data that doesn't quite fit into the rigid structure of a conventional hierarchy, but they're closer to regular hierarchies than parent-child hierarchies are. Whereas a parent-child hierarchy throws off the constraint of named levels, a ragged hierarchy has named levels just like a regular hierarchy, but allows them to be skipped. More precisely, a member's parent may be more than one level above it.

Let's consider some examples from geography:

- The city of San Francisco belongs to the state of California, which belongs to the country United States, which belongs to the continent of North America. This is a "normal" sequence of members, with one at each level and each member's parent being one level higher.
- The city of Tel Aviv belongs directly to the country of Israel. Israel does not have states.
- Vatican City belongs directly to the continent of Europe. There is no nation or state.
- The continent of Antarctica has no constituent countries, states, or cities.

You've probably realized that the easiest way to solve these problems is to cheat and create hidden members. For example, Israel can have a single state, to which Tel Aviv and every other Israeli city belongs. You could create a Vatican City nation and state, and for Antarctica you could create a dummy nation, state, and city.

Indeed that's what Mondrian does behind the scenes. But Mondrian's purpose is to provide a data model for end users, and the end users don't want to see dummy values. If you ask [Tel Aviv] for its parent member, it will return the country [Israel]. If you ask the continent [Antarctica] for its children, it will return the empty set.

The members of the hierarchy will look like what's shown in table 5.6.

**Table 5.6  Members of the [Geography] ragged hierarchy**

| Continent | Country | State | City |
|-----------|---------|-------|------|
| Antarctica | (hidden) | (hidden) | (hidden) |
| Asia | Israel | (hidden) | Tel Aviv |
| Europe | (hidden) | (hidden) | Vatican City |
| Europe | France | Bouches-du-Rhône | Marseille |

**Table 5.6**   **Members of the** `[Geography]` **ragged hierarchy** *(continued)*

| Continent | Country | State | City |
|---|---|---|---|
| Europe | France | Rhône | Lyon |
| North America | United States | (hidden) | Washington, D.C. |
| North America | United States | California | San Francisco |
| North America | United States | New York | New York |

When you define a ragged hierarchy, you tell Mondrian when members of a level should be considered "hidden." The `hideMemberIf` attribute, whose values are shown in table 5.7, achieves this:

```
<Dimension name='Geography' table='geography' key='City'>
  <Attributes>
    <Attribute name='Continent' keyColumn='continent'/>
    <Attribute name='Country' keyColumn='country'/>
    <Attribute name='State' keyColumn='state'/>
    <Attribute name='City' keyColumn='city_id' nameColumn='city'/>
  </Attributes>
  <Hierarchies>
    <Hierarchy name='Geography'>
      <Level attribute='Continent' hideMemberIf='Never'/>
      <Level attribute='Country' hideMemberIf='IfBlankName'/>
      <Level attribute='State' hideMemberIf='IfParentsName'/>
      <Level attribute='City' hideMemberIf='IfBlankName'/>
    </Hierarchy>
  </Hierarchies>
</Dimension>
```

**Table 5.7**   **Values for a level's** `hideMemberIf` **attribute**

| Value | Meaning |
|---|---|
| `Never` (default) | Member always appears. |
| `IfBlankName` | A member doesn't appear if its name is null, empty, or all whitespace. |
| `IfParentsName` | A member appears unless its name matches its parent's. |

New York City isn't hidden, but it would have been if the `City` level were flagged `IfParentsName`.

Once a member is hidden, Mondrian will make sure that it stays hidden, even when you evaluate expressions in MDX, such as `<Member>.Parent` and `<Level>.Members`.

> **HIDDEN, INVISIBLE, AND INACCESSIBLE**  Don't confuse *hidden* with *invisible* or *inaccessible*. Missing members in ragged hierarchies are called *hidden*. If an element is *invisible*, this is just a hint to the user interface that it shouldn't display the element on the screen; invisible elements are otherwise normal when

evaluating MDX. An element might also be rendered *inaccessible* to particular users due to access control. Like a hidden element, an inaccessible element doesn't appear in MDX calculations; it may even change the value of other elements in the calculation, if, for instance, the rollup policy says that the values of parent members should only include accessible children.

The link to a measure group works the same way as a link to a regular dimension. It joins at the key attribute of the dimension, even if some instances of that attribute are hidden. The hidden city in Antarctica must exist in the dimension table, and facts pertaining to Antarctica will reference that city's key value.

Next, we'll describe how Mondrian can create something out of nothing: how members and set expressions are defined using MDX calculations.

## 5.4    *Calculations*

Mondrian has been described as a huge, virtual, multidimensional spreadsheet. It's fine for browsing the raw data, but things get interesting when you start to define calculations. Mondrian allows you to define calculations in the schema in SQL and MDX, and to define further calculations in MDX queries. Furthermore, the MDX language allows you to create calculations on top of calculations.

In this section, we'll show you how to create new measures based on SQL expressions using the example of a "bucketing attribute" that converts a continuous quantity, such as age, into ranges that can be analyzed together. Then we'll show you how to create calculated measures and calculated members in other dimensions, such as profitability of a product, growth in time, or comparison to other geographical regions. Finally, we'll introduce hanger dimensions, which are dimensions consisting only of calculated members—they're useful for building advanced analytics.

### 5.4.1    *Bucketing attributes*

Adding an attribute to a dimension is straightforward if its key, name, and other required properties are already columns in the dimension table. If the key values for a new attribute don't already exist as columns, they can sometimes be calculated using a simple SQL expression. A common case is an attribute based on bucketing values.

Suppose you know the age of a customer in years, or their date of birth. Age is a continuous quantity, and you can divide the dataset too finely if you put a particular age value onto the filter axis. You aren't interested in whether customers aged 18 years and 100 days behave differently than customers aged 18 years and 101 days.

The solution is to create an [Age Range] attribute that has members [0 - 19], [20 - 29], [30 - 39] and so on. The most efficient way to do this is to enhance the ETL that populates the customer table to populate a new age_range column.

```
<Table name='customer'>
  <ColumnDefs>
    <CalculatedColumnDef name='age_range'>
      <ExpressionView>
```

**Define calculated age_range column**

```
        <SQL>
          CASE FLOOR(<Column name='age'/> / 10)
          WHEN 0 THEN '0 - 19'
          WHEN 1 THEN '0 - 19'
          WHEN 2 THEN '20 - 29'
          WHEN 3 THEN '30 - 39'
          WHEN 4 THEN '40 - 49'
          WHEN 5 THEN '50 - 59'
          ELSE '60+'
          END
        </SQL>
      </ExpressionView>
    </CalculatedColumnDef>
  </ColumnDefs>
</Table>
```

⟵ **Reduce number of clauses in the CASE expression with integer division**

You can also apply this bucketing approach to convert measure values into attributes. For example, the column sales_fact_1997.store_sales is a measure. But suppose you create a new column in the fact table, order_size, whose value is Small for orders less than $100, Medium for orders less than $1000, and otherwise Large. This column can be used as an attribute. (Technically, it's a degenerate dimension; these are described in section 5.2.)

This is another case where a calculated column is useful while you're developing the formula:

```
<Table name='sales_fact_1997'>
  <ColumnDefs>
    <CalculatedColumnDef name='order_size'>
      <ExpressionView>
        <SQL>
          CASE
          WHEN <Column name='store_sales'/> &lt; 100
              THEN 'Small'
          WHEN <Column name='store_sales'/> &lt; 1000
              THEN 'Medium'
          ELSE 'Large'
          END
        </SQL>
      </ExpressionView>
    </CalculatedColumnDef>
  </ColumnDefs>
</Table>
```

⟵ **Define calculated order_size column**

⟵ **Use &lt; for < because this is XML**

When the formula is correct, you can improve performance by changing your ETL process to make it a real column.

## 5.4.2 Calculated members

You just saw a few ways to enhance a model by writing expressions in SQL, but things get really interesting when you use the MDX language to define calculations. The MDX language allows you to define calculations that depend on the results of other calculations. In this respect, Mondrian is like a spreadsheet.

But in a spreadsheet you define a calculation in each cell you wish to be calculated. Because Mondrian's set of cells is unlimited, and because cells don't come into existence until you ask for them to be calculated in a query, it's not practical to store calculations in cells. Instead, Mondrian defines calculations in the dimensions of the cube as calculated members.

It's as if your spreadsheet allowed you to define a formula on a column (say column C) that applied to all cells in that column, and furthermore allowed you to define a formula on a row (say row 2) that applied to all cells in that row. When you compute cell C2, there are two formulas that need to be applied, in a well-defined order. It's a little confusing at first, but very powerful.

### A CALCULATED MEASURE

Let's consider a simple example first. [Profit] is a calculated member that belongs to the [Measures] dimension, and it's computed with the following formula:

```
[Measures].[Store Sales] - [Measures].[Store Cost]
```

Here it is applied in a query:

```
mdx> SELECT
   >   { [Measures].[Store Cost],
   >     [Measures].[Store Sales],
   >     [Measures].[Profit] } ON Columns,
   >   Descendants(
   >       [Product].[Products].[Drink], 2, SELF_AND_BEFORE) ON Rows
   > FROM [Sales];
```

|  | | Store Cost | Store Sales | Profit |
|---|---|---|---|---|
| Drink | | 19,477.23 | 48,836.21 | $29,358.98 |
| | Alcoholic Beverages | 5,576.79 | 14,029.08 | $8,452.29 |
| | | Beer and Wine | | |
| | | 5,576.79 | 14,029.08 | $8,452.29 |
| | Beverages | 11,069.53 | 27,748.53 | $16,679.00 |
| | | Carbonated Beverages  2,484.60 | 6,236.35 | $3,751.75 |
| | | Drinks  2,247.11 | 5,642.29 | $3,395.18 |
| | | Hot Beverages  3,708.08 | 9,261.74 | $5,553.66 |
| | | Pure Juice Beverages  2,629.73 | 6,608.15 | $3,978.42 |
| | Dairy | 2,830.92 | 7,058.60 | $4,227.68 |
| | | Dairy  2,830.92 | 7,058.60 | $4,227.68 |

When used in a query, the calculated measure works the same way as the stored measures [Store Cost] and [Store Sales].

Calculated members can be defined either in an MDX query or in the schema (specifically, in a cube definition). There are advantages to each. Calculated members in the schema are available to all analytics that use the cube. They're easy to share and maintain. In contrast, calculations in a query can be written on the fly by the user (or tool) writing the query, so they're better for rapid iterations.

Let's look at how you can add a calculated member to the schema definition.

### DEFINING CALCULATED MEMBERS IN THE SCHEMA

Calculated members are defined in a section of the `Cube` element we haven't used before, called `CalculatedMembers`, as shown in listing 5.6.

**Listing 5.6  Calculated member defined in a cube**

```
<Cube name='Sales'>
  ...
  <CalculatedMembers>
    <CalculatedMember name='Profit'
        hierarchy='[Measures].[Measures]'>          [Profit] calculated
                                               ◀─┘  member
      <Formula>
        [Measures].[Store Sales] - [Measures].[Store Cost]   ◀─┐ MDX expression
      </Formula>                                               │ to be evaluated
    </CalculatedMember>
  </CalculatedMembers>
</Cube>
```

Note that we've defined the formula and format string using subelements. If you prefer a more compact notation, you can use the `formula` and `formatString` attributes. Listing 5.7 defines an equivalent calculated member with the `<Formula>` element being replaced by a `formula` attribute.

**Listing 5.7  Calculated member defined in a cube using compact notation**

```
<CalculatedMember name='Profit'
    hierarchy='[Measures].[Measures]' formatString='Currency'
    formula='[Measures].[Store Sales] - [Measures].[Store Cost]'/>
```

**XML CHARACTERS**  You have to take a little care with characters such as the opening angle bracket (<) and the single quote ('), because of slight differences in how XML handles text in attributes versus elements. If you're having trouble with escaping, move to the first format and enclose the text of your formula in a `<![CDATA[ ... ]]>` section.

### DEFINING CALCULATED MEMBERS IN A QUERY

Calculated members can also be defined in queries, using the `WITH MEMBER` clause of an MDX statement. This makes them more flexible for rapid development.

We don't have time in this chapter for a deep dive into MDX syntax, but a simple example should give you the general idea. The query in listing 5.8 defines a calculated member equivalent to the previous examples.

**Listing 5.8  Calculated member defined in an MDX query**

```
mdx> WITH MEMBER [Measures].[Profit] AS
   >      [Measures].[Store Sales] - [Measures].[Store Cost],
   >      FORMAT_STRING = 'Currency'
   > SELECT
   >    { [Measures].[Store Cost],
   >      [Measures].[Store Sales],
   >      [Measures].[Profit] } ON Columns,
```

```
  >      Descendants(
  >          [Product].[Products].[Drink], 2, SELF_AND_BEFORE) ON Rows
  > FROM [Sales];
```

```
                                    Store Cost Store Sales Profit
===== ========= ==================== ========== =========== ==========
Drink                                 19,477.23   48,836.21 $29,358.98
      Alcoholic                        5,576.79   14,029.08  $8,452.29
      Beverages
                Beer and Wine          5,576.79   14,029.08  $8,452.29
      Beverages                       11,069.53   27,748.53 $16,679.00
                Carbonated Beverages   2,484.60    6,236.35  $3,751.75
                Drinks                 2,247.11    5,642.29  $3,395.18
                Hot Beverages          3,708.08    9,261.74  $5,553.66
                Pure Juice Beverages   2,629.73    6,608.15  $3,978.42
      Dairy                            2,830.92    7,058.60  $4,227.68
                Dairy                  2,830.92    7,058.60  $4,227.68
```

Calculated members behave similarly, whether you define them in a query or a cube; which you choose is a matter of convenience. Calculated members in a cube can be used by any report that uses that cube (subject to access control). A query can be edited more easily than a schema, so many people use this approach for development and debugging.

> **DEBUGGING CALCULATIONS**  Develop your calculations in an MDX statement, and paste them into your schema definition when they're correct.

Mondrian uses a very similar trick behind the scenes. While it's loading a schema, it needs to validate the calculated members and named sets in each cube. These calculations can depend on each other and can even be recursive. Mondrian solves the problem by internally generating an MDX statement that contains all calculated members and named sets, so that it can validate them all simultaneously. This monster statement is usually invisible, but it will surface from the depths if you have made an error in one of your calculations.

Let's try adding another calculated member, this time with a subtle error in the schema:

```
<CalculatedMember name='Profit'                    [Profit] calculated
    hierarchy='[Measures].[Measures]'>             member, as before
  <Formula>
    [Measures].[Store Sales] - [Measures].[Store Cost]
  </Formula>
</CalculatedMember>
<CalculatedMember name='Profit Growth'             [Profit Growth]
    hierarchy='[Measures].[Measures]'>             calculated member
  <Formula>
    ([Measures].[Profit], [Time].PreviousMember)       The mistake:
  </Formula>                                           PreviousMember
</CalculatedMember>                                    should be
                                                      PrevMember
```

Mondrian duly fails to create the connection, giving you a nasty-looking error stack:

```
mondrian.olap.MondrianException: Calculated member or named set in cube
            'Sales' has bad formula
    at mondrian.resource.MondrianResource$_Def0.ex
...
Caused by: mondrian.olap.MondrianException: Failed to parse query 'WITH
MEMBER [Measures].[Measures].[Profit]
  AS '[Measures].[Store Sales] - [Measures].[Store Cost]',
[$member_scope] = 'CUBE',
MEMBER_ORDINAL = 3
MEMBER [Measures].[Measures].[Profit Growth]
  AS '([Measures].[Profit], [Time].PreviousMember)',
[$member_scope] = 'CUBE',
MEMBER_ORDINAL = 4
SELECT FROM [Sales]'
    at mondrian.resource.MondrianResource$_Def0.ex
...
Caused by: mondrian.olap.MondrianException: MDX object
            '[Time].PreviousMember' not found in cube 'Sales'
    at mondrian.resource.MondrianResource$_Def1.ex
    at mondrian.olap.Util.lookup
...
```

Buried in the stack, you can see the MDX statement that Mondrian's schema loader has generated, with the formulas of the two calculated members. The next error on the stack comes from Mondrian's MDX validator:

```
MDX object '[Time].PreviousMember' not found in cube 'Sales'
```

This tells you the root cause of the problem: an MDX expression. The built-in property you need is called `PrevMember` not `PreviousMember`. Once you fix the formula, the schema will load successfully and you can run a query:

```
mdx> SELECT {[Measures].[Profit],
    >         [Measures].[Profit Growth]} ON Columns,
    >     CrossJoin(
    >         Descendants(
    >             [Product].[Products].[Drink], 1, SELF_AND_BEFORE),
    >         [Time].[1997].Children) ON Rows
    > FROM [Sales];
```

| | | | | Profit | Profit Growth |
|-------|---------------------|------|----|-----------|---------------|
| Drink | | 1997 | Q1 | $6,964.30 | $6,964.30 |
| | | | Q2 | $7,186.11 | $221.81 |
| | | | Q3 | $7,203.34 | $17.23 |
| | | | Q4 | $8,005.22 | $801.88 |
| | Alcoholic Beverages | 1997 | Q1 | $1,858.19 | $1,858.19 |
| | | | Q2 | $2,117.16 | $258.97 |
| | | | Q3 | $2,086.54 | ($30.62) |
| | | | Q4 | $2,390.40 | $303.85 |
| | Beverages | 1997 | Q1 | $4,069.30 | $4,069.30 |
| | | | Q2 | $4,077.05 | $7.74 |
| | | | Q3 | $4,127.92 | $50.87 |

```
|            |          |      | Q4 | $4,404.73 |      $276.81 |
|            | Dairy    | 1997 | Q1 | $1,036.80 |    $1,036.80 |
|            |          |      | Q2 |   $991.90 |      ($44.90) |
|            |          |      | Q3 |   $988.88 |       ($3.02) |
|            |          |      | Q4 | $1,210.10 |      $221.21 |
```

Calculations are powerful because they can be built out of other calculations (as [Profit Growth] is built from [Profit]) and because they can be applied in a wide variety of contexts. Here, the calculations work on members of the [Product Family] and [Product Department] levels of the [Products] hierarchy, but they would work on any hierarchy.

### CALCULATED MEMBERS ON DIMENSIONS OTHER THAN [MEASURES]

You can create calculations on hierarchies other than [Measures]. Here, for example, is a [Top 10] member in the [Customers] hierarchy.

```
<CalculatedMember name='Top 10'
    hierarchy='[Customer].[Customers]'>
  <Formula>
    Aggregate(
        TopCount([Customer].[Name].[Name].Members,
            10, [Measures].Value))
  </Formula>
</CalculatedMember>
```

[Top 10] can apply to virtually any other hierarchy. (I'll explain what I mean by "virtually" in a moment.) The following example applies it to measures and gender to compute sales and profit based on the top 10 male and female customers. All that from a small formula!

```
mdx> SELECT {[Measures].[Store Sales],
    >          [Measures].[Profit]} ON Columns,
    >      CrossJoin(
    >          [Customer].[Gender].Children,
    >          {[Customers].[All Customers],
    >          [Customers].[Top 10],
    >          [Customers].[USA].[CA]}) ON Rows
    > FROM [Sales];

                        Store Sales Profit
= ============= === == =========== ===========
F All Customers       280,226.21 $168,448.73
  Top 10                7,748.11   $4,659.42
  All Customers USA CA 79,050.79  $47,459.17
M All Customers       285,011.92 $171,162.17
  Top 10                8,603.81   $5,191.79
  All Customers USA CA 80,117.05  $48,178.24
```

You could easily write queries to find the top 10 customers buying beer, or the top 10 customers in Q3 2004, or even the top 10 female customers buying beer in Q3 2004. But you can't find the top 10 customers in Oregon, or Mexico, or Pacific Grove, CA. Here's what I meant by "virtually": the only hierarchy you cannot apply [Top 10] to is its own, [Customers]. That's because only one member of a hierarchy can be current at a time. If [Top 10] is the current member, then all other customers aren't.

### USING HANGER DIMENSIONS TO ALLOW CALCULATION ON ALL DIMENSIONS

If a calculated member can't intersect its own dimension, how can you create a calculated member that can intersect [Customers] as well as all other dimensions? The solution is to move [Top 10] into its own dimension, a dimension reserved for calculations. This kind of dimension is called a *hanger dimension*.

To define a hanger dimension, specify hanger='true' in the dimension definition, and define an attribute. You don't need to map that attribute to any tables or columns; in fact, Mondrian won't let you. Nor will it let you create a ForeignKeyLink to join the dimension to the measure group's fact table. A hanger dimension is disconnected from the star schema; it just hangs out on its own.

```
<Cube name='Sales'>
  <Dimensions>
    ...

    <Dimension name='Top' hanger='true'>        ←──┐ Hanger
      <Attributes>                                 │ dimension
        <Attribute name='Customers'/>         ←──── Attributes in hanger
      </Attributes>                                 dimensions don't
    </Dimension>                                     have columns
  </Dimensions>
  ...
                                              Calculated member in
  <CalculatedMembers>                         Customers hierarchy
    ...                                       of hanger dimension

    <CalculatedMember hierarchy='[Top].[Customers]' name='Top 10'>   ←──┐
      <Formula>
        Aggregate(
            TopCount([Customer].[Customers].[Name].Members,
                10, [Measures].Value)</Formula>
    </CalculatedMember>
  </CalculatedMembers>
</Cube>
```

Using that hanger dimension, you can find the sales for the top 10 customers in California.

```
mdx> SELECT {[Measures].[Unit Sales], [Measures].[Profit]} ON Columns,
   >    CrossJoin(
   >       {[Customer].[Customers].[USA],
   >        [Customer].[Customers].[USA].[CA]},
   >       {[Top].[Customers], [Top].[Customers].[Top 10]}) ON Rows
   > FROM [Sales];

                    Unit Sales Profit
=== == ============= ========== ===========
USA    All Customers    266,773 $339,610.90
       Top 10             4,123   $5,400.41
    CA All Customers     74,748  $95,637.41
       Top 10             4,123   $5,400.41
```

Hanger dimensions also have other uses. You can use them for the "budget versus actual" comparison commonly used by accountants. Create a [Budget vs Actual] hanger dimension with two members, [Budget] and [Actual], and make your measures into formulas that redirect to different base measures (maybe in different measure groups) depending on which is current. For example, the [Sales] measure would be a calculation:

```
Iif([Budget vs Actual].CurrentMember Is [Budget vs Actual].[Budget],
    [Measures].[Budget Sales],
    [Measures].[Actual Sales])
```

You can also use a hanger dimension to create a parameter with a fixed set of values. For instance, when determining investment strategy, you might create an [Interest Rate] dimension with values [2%], [3%], and [4%]. Then you could use those values in other calculations. In many UIs, if you include this dimension in the slicer, the UI will present the values in a drop-down list. If you include the hanger dimension on an axis, you can compare scenarios with different interest rates side by side.

Lastly, Mondrian uses hanger dimensions to implement writeback. The system-generated [Scenario] dimension is, behind the scenes, a hanger dimension. (Scenarios and what-if analysis are described in section 11.2).

## 5.5    *Summary*

In chapter 4 we discussed the elements of a Mondrian schema, and this chapter filled out that knowledge. Using multiple cubes, multiple dimensions, and various kinds of calculations, you should be able to model complex business intelligence applications. We also covered some advanced dimension and hierarchy types: parent-child hierarchies, ragged hierarchies, star and snowflake dimensions, and degenerate and hanger dimensions. You should have a good understanding of the basics now, but if you need more detail about the XML elements and attributes that make up the schema, consult the online Mondrian documentation.

Further chapters of this book will build on what you've learned here and will focus on particular subject areas. In particular, the following chapters introduce further schema elements:

- Chapter 7 describes how to tune a Mondrian system. Some tuning techniques call for aggregate tables (defined using the MeasureGroup element).
- Chapter 10 describes how to extend the capabilities of your Mondrian system using your own and third-party code. Elements such as UserDefinedFunction register these extensions in a Mondrian schema.

First, though, chapter 6 will cover access control and introduce the Role, CubeGrant, and related elements.

# Securing data

6

A key consideration in any organization is limiting access to sensitive data, and Adventure Works is no exception. They want to be able to restrict sensitive sales information to only the sales managers who need it. They also want to make sure that only HR has access to human resource information about employees.

There are a number of ways to limit data access, such as by user ID, roles, or a user's attributes. Mondrian uses an approach called role-based access control (RBAC). In an RBAC data approach, users are assigned roles, and data is restricted by the role assigned to the user. Using RBAC means you don't need to manage permissions for each individual user.

This chapter will show you how to restrict access to specific data items, dimensions, and even the entire schema.

## 6.1  *Use of roles*

The first things to understand are what a role is and how it can be used by Mondrian to restrict access to data. After reading this section, you'll understand what roles are, how they're generally applied to restrict data, and how they're provided via external settings. You'll also see how to set the default role in the schema. Finally, we'll touch on the concept of joint roles, which let you combine multiple roles together to create entirely new roles.

### 6.1.1  *What's a role?*

A role can be thought of as a collection of the rights and responsibilities of a person. For example, one role might be that of sales manager. This person would be interested in the sales of the people under him or her, the level of sales for particular products or services, and who the top customers are. To perform this role, the sales manager would need access to information about products, sales, customers, and so on.

A separate role might be that of inventory manager. This person would be more interested in the sale of items by time period, popular items by region, and similar inventory-related items. The inventory manager doesn't need to know profit margins, top customers, or top salespeople.

By assigning individuals to roles, it's possible to then restrict access to data. Table 6.1 shows a simplified view of which roles should have access to which data. In this case, the fact table contains sales data, and there are four general roles that have access to different parts of the cube.

- The product manager role is given access to the numbers of items being sold, including the locations and dates of the sales. The product manager can use this information to determine popular products and make decisions about what new products to sell or products to discontinue. The product manager isn't given details of the sales, such as customer information and salesperson information.
- The inventory manager cares about the movement of inventory in order to anticipate stock levels in the various warehouses. The inventory manager doesn't require sales details.
- The US sales manager will see almost all information about sales but doesn't know the details of specific item sales. This manager is interested in how sales are going, who the big customers are, and who the top salespeople are.
- State sales manager is a variation of the US sales manager. Adventure Works restricts sales information for state sales managers so they can only see the data from their state.

**Table 6.1** Data access by role

| Data | Product manager | Inventory manager | US sales manager | State sales manager (individual state data only) |
|------|----------------|-------------------|------------------|-------------------------------------------------|
| Warehouse | | ✓ | | |
| Customer | | | ✓ | ✓ |
| State | ✓ | ✓ | ✓ | ✓ |
| Item | ✓ | ✓ | ✓ | ✓ |
| Sale price | | | ✓ | ✓ |
| Qty purchased | ✓ | ✓ | ✓ | ✓ |
| Sales person | | | ✓ | ✓ |

**TOO MANY ROLES?** In the preceding example, you'll notice that Adventure Works had to create 50 different roles for the various state managers. In a global company, there might be thousands if various regions are described. Even more challenging is if each store has a manager who needs their own data restrictions. In chapter 8, we'll show you how to use information from the user session to restrict data access, eliminating the need for so many roles.

You also need to understand the concept of a joint role. A *joint role* is the union of two or more roles into a single role. A user with this role will have rights to see anything that any of the combined roles can see. For example, if the product manager and sales manager are combined, someone with the product and sales manager role would see both inventory and sales information. This can be useful for managers who oversee multiple departments and need access to all data without having to create a completely new role. Note that this means that if something is restricted in one role but allowed in the other, the person with the joint role can see that data.

There are two ways to combine roles. The first is by explicitly declaring a joint role with the Union element, as shown in section 6.1.2. The Union element lists the names of the previously defined roles and then assigns the combined role security into a single role with a new name. This role has the combined privileges of all of the combined roles.

The second way of combining roles is to define them implicitly at connection time by having the user be in two or more existing roles. Because a joint role can see data from both roles, it's important when designing and assigning roles to make sure users in multiple roles will only see the data that they really should. If you're using a lot of roles and complex filters, this can get confusing and hard to manage. In this case, it might be better to create explicit combined roles and have each user assigned to the joint roles.

## 6.1.2 *Declaring roles in the Mondrian schema*

Roles must be defined in the Mondrian schema to which they'll be applied. Listing 6.1 shows the high-level role declarations. The basic declaration of a role is simple; just use the `Role` element and assign a value to the `name` attribute. Later sections will describe the various security grants that can be given. The last role declaration combines the product and sales manager role using the `Union` element.

**Listing 6.1   Declaring roles**

```
<Role name="Inventory Manager">          <──── Inventory manager role
  <grants>...</grants>
</Role
<Role name="Product Manager">            <──── Product manager role
  <grants>...</grants>
</Role>
<Role name="US Sales Manager">           <──── US sales manager role
  <grants>...</grants>
</Role>
<Role name="WA Sales Manager">           <──── WA state sales manager role
  <grants>...</grants>
</Role>
<Role name="OR Sales Manager">
  <grants>...</grants>
</Role>
<Role name="ID Sales Manager">
  <grants>...</grants>
</Role>
<Role name="Product and Sales Manager">  <──── Union role
  <Union>
    <RoleUsage roleName="General Sales Manager"/>
    <RoleUsage roleName="Product Manager"
  </Union>
</Role>
```

## 6.1.3 *Enforcement of roles*

Mondrian allows you to define role-based restrictions for security. For example, if a user is assigned to the role of sales manager, that person can only see data that a sales manager is allowed to see. If sales managers aren't allowed to see information about customers, anyone assigned to this role couldn't see customer information unless they're assigned to a second role that gives access to customer information.

Mondrian schemas define roles, and Mondrian enforces roles, but it's up to the container to provide the role of the user when performing queries. The container does this when it makes a connection to Mondrian. It's important to remember that Mondrian doesn't perform any authentication for incoming requests. Mondrian assumes that the security is handled by the container and that the roles provided are correct. This makes sense, because it means Mondrian can be used in a wide variety of containers and security scenarios without change. But it also means that if the container doesn't properly apply security restrictions, Mondrian will return data that you might want restricted.

How roles are set depends on the container. If you're writing your own application, setting roles must be part of the code. If you're using the Saiku server, you can set the user roles in the users.properties file. Finally, if you're using Mondrian with Pentaho, you have to tell Pentaho to send role information to Mondrian via XML configuration. Because Pentaho is the most common container for Mondrian, we'll explore how to configure security for Pentaho.

Pentaho security is configured by specifying a role mapper, which will then map from Pentaho user roles to Mondrian roles. The configuration is done in the Pentaho Objects.spring.xml file located in the pentaho-solutions/system directory. In chapter 8, you'll see how to programmatically assign custom roles, but for now we'll use the standard role mappings provided.

> **NO ROLE MAPPER MEANS NO SECURITY**  A common mistake with new users to Mondrian security is to forget to assign the role mapper. The default, if no roles are set, is to have *no* security applied. That means that all users will see all data in the schema.

Keep in mind that we're talking about two different roles. The first is the role as understood by the container. Sometimes these are called *groups*, but Pentaho uses the term *role*. The second is the role as defined in the Mondrian schema. Our goal is to map between the Pentaho role and the Mondrian role.

There are three predefined role mappers in Pentaho, and each takes a slightly different approach. By default, no role mappers are defined, which means that Mondrian will not be told to restrict by role, and all users will have access to everything. The bean ID in the configuration file is called `Mondrian-UserRoleMapper`. The following sections describe each of the role mappers, along with their configurations.

### ONE-TO-ONE ROLE MAPPER

The one-to-one role mapper is the simplest of the role mappers. It passes the Pentaho roles of the user to Mondrian, so if a user has a role of "Sales Manager" in Pentaho, then that's passed to Mondrian without changes. Because many companies develop Mondrian schemas for existing users and roles, this is a very common role mapper.

This mapper has an optional parameter called `failOnEmptyRoleList` that will throw an exception if no role matches from user to role are found. This is the default behavior for the mapper, and it's safe. You can, however, set this value to `true`, in which case a user with no role mapping will have all permissions, as if no role mapper was specified. To configure this role mapper, simply uncomment or add the bean declaration shown in listing 6.2

---

**Listing 6.2  One-to-one role mapper configuration**

```
<bean id="Mondrian-UserRoleMapper"
      name="Mondrian-One-To-One-UserRoleMapper"
      class="org.pentaho.platform.plugin.action.
            mondrian.mapper.MondrianOneToOneUserRoleListMapper"
      scope="singleton" />
```

**LONG JAVA CLASS NAMES**   The class for the role mappers is spread over two lines in the text due to formatting limitations. When you're configuring Mondrian, the entire class name will be on one line inside the quotes.

### LOOKUP-MAP ROLE MAPPER

The lookup-map role mapper maps Pentaho roles to Mondrian roles. This might be useful when you're using the same schema for different customers or departments that have different names for the same roles.

The configuration for this mapper is shown in listing 6.3. To add a role mapping, simply enter a key value that represents the role in Pentaho. Then enter a value that the Pentaho role will be mapped to in Mondrian. When Pentaho makes calls to Mondrian, it will look at the user's roles and pass the mapped roles instead.

**Listing 6.3   Lookup-map role mapper configuration**

```
<bean id="Mondrian-UserRoleMapper"
    name="Mondrian-SampleLookupMap-UserRoleMapper"
    class="org.pentaho.platform.plugin.action.
        mondrian.mapper.MondrianLookupMapUserRoleListMapper"
    scope="singleton">
  <property name="lookupMap">
    <map>
      <entry key="sales_manager" value="Sales Manager" />
      <entry key="product_manager" value="Product Manager" />
      <entry key="inventory_manager" value="Inventory Manager" />
    </map>
  </property>
</bean>
```

### USER-SESSION ROLE MAPPER

The user-session role mapper maps from a session attribute of the user to one or more Mondrian roles. When Pentaho makes a connection to Mondrian, it will look at the user session and find the session attribute. The values in this session attribute will then be passed to Mondrian.

The only configuration item you need to provide is the name of the session attribute to use for the roles. In the following listing, the session attribute name is `MondrianUserRoles`.

**Listing 6.4   User-session role mapper configuration**

```
<bean id="Mondrian-UserRoleMapper"
    name="Mondrian-SampleUserSession-UserRoleMapper"
    class="org.pentaho.platform.plugin.action.
        mondrian.mapper.MondrianUserSessionUserRoleListMapper"
    scope="singleton">
  <property name="sessionProperty"
        value="MondrianUserRoles" />              ◁──┐ Session attribute
                                                       that contains roles
</bean>
```

There are a number of ways that the session can be populated, and section 8.1 will explain how to populate session variables when a user session starts. The user-session role mapper will then extract the value from the session and convert it to Mondrian roles.

The conversion that takes place depends on the type of value in the session attribute. Table 6.2 shows the conversion for each recognized type. The conversions are chosen in the order listed.

**Table 6.2   Session attribute to role list conversion process**

| Attribute type | Conversion approach |
|---|---|
| String [] | Each array entry is used as a Mondrian role. |
| java.util.Collection | Each entry in the collection is converted to a string using `Object.toString()`. |
| Object [] | Each object in the array is converted to a string using `Object.toString()`. |
| Anything else | The object is converted to a string using `Object.toString()`. |

**YOUR VERY OWN ROLE MAPPER**

If none of the provided role mappers meets your needs, you can also create your own. The simplest approach is to extend the abstract class `org.pentaho.platform.plugin.action.mondrian.mapper.MondrianAbstractPlatformUserRoleMapper`. This class does most of the heavy lifting and only requires you to implement a single method:

```
    protected abstract String[] mapRoles(String[] mondrianRoles, String[] platformRoles) throws PentahoAccessControlException;
```

> **VIEWING THE PENTAHO MAPPERS**   You can also look at the Pentaho mappers to see how they work. The source code is in a public Subversion repository that anyone can access online. The root for the Mondrian platform extensions is http://source.pentaho.org/viewvc/svnroot/pentaho-platform/trunk/extensions/src/.

The method receives an array of Mondrian roles from the schema and a set of platform roles from Pentaho. It's up to the role mapper to map between the two and return an array of roles for the user to pass to Mondrian. The method is also expected to throw a `PentahoAccessControlException` if the user shouldn't have access to Mondrian for some reason.

To make the concept a bit more concrete, listing 6.5 shows an example of a role mapper. The management of Adventure Works has decided to restrict roles based on state. Rather than create a unique role for each user, however, they'll simply append the two-letter acronym for the state to each role except Authenticated and Admin. This is done by looking up the state for the user and then adding it to the end of each role. The code for getting the state isn't included here. Note that a production version might also check to see if the new role exists in the Mondrian schema, but it's not required.

**Listing 6.5   User-state role mapper**

```
package org.pentaho.mondrian.mapper;

import org.pentaho.platform.api.engine.PentahoAccessControlException;
import org.pentaho.platform.plugin.action.mondrian
        .mapper.MondrianAbstractPlatformUserRoleMapper;

public class UserStateRoleMapper
  extends MondrianAbstractPlatformUserRoleMapper {

  protected String[] mapRoles(String[] mondrianRoles,
                              String[] platformRoles)
    throws PentahoAccessControlException {              ◁── Implement
                                                            abstract method

    String userState = getUserState();
    String [] newRoles = new String[platformRoles.length];
    for (int cnt = 0; cnt < platformRoles.length; cnt++) {   ◁── Add state
      newRoles[cnt] = platformRoles[cnt] + "_" + userState;      to the role
    }

    return newRoles;                ◁── Return array of
  }                                     roles for Mondrian

  private String getUserState() {
    return "WA";                    ◁── Get user's state
  }
}
```

The last step to get this to work is to configure the Pentaho Objects.xml file to use the new class as the role mapper. The following listing shows what this looks like. This declaration can be put in the same area as the commented-out role mappers.

**Listing 6.6   User-state role mapper configuration**

```
<bean id="Mondrian-UserRoleMapper"
      name="Mondrian-One-To-One-UserRoleMapper"
      class="org.pentaho.mondrian.mapper.UserStateRoleMapper"
      scope="singleton" />
```

So far we've explored the concept of roles for restricting data. We've talked about what roles are and how they're mapped. But we still haven't restricted access to any data. The next section will show you how to apply a wide variety of controls to the data based on the roles you've defined.

## 6.2   *Security grants*

Now that you have a few roles, it's time to restrict data, but how do you specify the data to be restricted? Suppose you only want the product manager to see the state, item, and quantity purchased. Next, you want the state sales manager to see all of the same data as the US sales manager, but only for the one state. This section shows how to apply such restrictions.

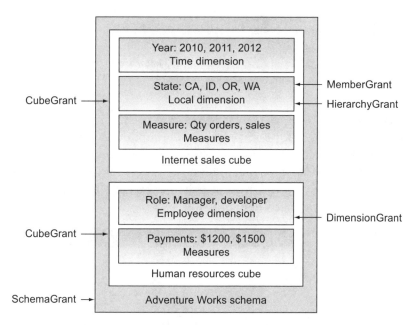

**Figure 6.1 Security grants within security grants**

Mondrian security grants can be thought of as a set of filters on the data, and the role can only see what their filters let through. At each level in the schema, the user can have data explicitly blocked or shown. The nesting of the security grants matches the general nesting of the schema design, as shown in figure 6.1.

The SchemaGrant applies to the entire schema. Nested inside of that, the Cube-Grant controls access to individual cubes. Each cube can have further restrictions through DimensionGrant and HierarchyGrant. Finally, access controls can be applied to individual members via MemberGrant. We'll discuss each of these types of grants in detail in the remainder of this section.

### 6.2.1 *Schema grants*

The first security grant is the SchemaGrant, and it has one attribute, access. There are three options available for SchemaGrant access: all, none, and all_dimensions. The all and none access grants are the most common. The access type of all_dimensions is rarely used; it gives the same results as none and is likely to be removed in the future, so we won't cover it further here. The next few sections explain the use of each of the schema grant types.

#### SCHEMA GRANT ALL
Listing 6.7 shows the use of the all option. It gives the role access to all of the cubes and dimensions in the schema, but you can later limit access to all or parts of the data using finer detailed grants. Other grants are nested within the schema grant.

**Listing 6.7   Granting access to the entire schema**

```
<Role name="Product Manager">
  <SchemaGrant access="all">           ◁──┐  Allow access to
    <!-- other grants -->                  │  entire schema
  </SchemaGrant>
</Role>
```

**SCHEMA GRANT NONE**

Listing 6.8 shows the use of the none option. This option is used when you want to restrict a user from seeing the schema completely. For example, maybe you have a schema completely dedicated to Human Resources and want to limit it from everyone except HR. You can create a role that all users get except HR, and then restrict the schema from this role with a few lines of XML.

**Listing 6.8   Granting access to none of the schema**

```
<Role name="Product Manager">
  <SchemaGrant access="none">          ◁──┐  Deny access to
  </SchemaGrant>                           │  the schema
</Role>
```

The more common use of setting access to none is to then grant access back to users. When a role has no access to the schema, they won't be able to see any of the dimensions or cubes in the schema. If your schema has a lot of different cubes, this is an easy way to initially restrict access to all of the cubes. Then, when specific cubes are to be used by certain roles, you can simply add the cubes back. This also has the advantage that if new cubes are added to the schema, the old roles won't be able to see the new cubes unless permission is explicitly granted, which means you don't need to remember to restrict access to the new cubes.

Note that when a role is granted access to something, it's implicitly given access to the parent. This means that if you use an access type of none for a schema and then grant access to a cube, the role now has access to the schema as well. In this case, an access type of none is a shortcut to taking away access from all other cubes except the one(s) specified.

> **PENTAHO'S AUTHENTICATED ROLE**  When using the default configuration in Pentaho, all logged-in users will have the Authenticated role. This is a convenient role for limiting or granting access to all users of the system. For example, if you create an Authenticated role and use a schema grant access="none", the default behavior is to have no access to the schema unless it's explicitly granted. In cases where data is sensitive and new roles may be created by others, this can be a good security precaution.

### 6.2.2   Cube grants

The next level of detail in security grants below the schema is the CubeGrant. The CubeGrant takes two attributes: the name of the cube that the grant applies to and the access control for the grant. There are only two options for cube grant access: `all` or `none`. Both work similarly to the schema grant, but at the cube level.

**CUBE GRANT ALL**

The `all` option gives the role access to the cube. If a user has no access to the schema, this gives access to the particular cube but no others. As with the previous schema options, you can restrict access to parts of the cube after granting access. A common approach is to restrict access to a role that every user will have, such as Authenticated, and then specifically grant access to the cubes the user should be able to see.

The following listing shows the use of the `all` option at the cube level. In this case, the product manager didn't have access to the schema but is given access to the `Product Sales` cube.

**Listing 6.9  Granting access to the entire cube**

```
<Role name="Product Manager">
  <SchemaGrant access="none">                          ◁─── Deny access to
                                                              entire schema
    <CubeGrant cube="Product Sales" access="all">    ◁─┐
    </CubeGrant>                                        │
  </SchemaGrant>                        Allow access to │
</Role>                               Product Sales cube │
```

**CUBE GRANT NONE**

A cube grant of `none` means that a user who is in the given role is not given access to the cube. Unlike with the schema grant, once access to the cube has been taken away, the user can't see any of the cube data. A cube grant with no access would be used when most users of the system can see many of the things in the schema, but you want to restrict certain cubes for certain roles. Note that unless the restricted cube is for a role that all users are guaranteed to have, there's a higher risk of unintentionally giving access to the cube.

Listing 6.10 shows the use of the `none` option. In this case, the product manager has access to the entire schema but doesn't need access to the `Human Resources` cube that likely contains sensitive information about employees.

**Listing 6.10  Granting access to none of the cube**

```
<Role name="Product Manager">
  <SchemaGrant access="all">                             ◁─── Allow access to entire schema

    <CubeGrant cube="Human Resources" access="none">   ◁─┐ Deny access
    </CubeGrant>                                          │ to HR cube
  </SchemaGrant>
</Role>
```

Cube grants are often all that you need for many cubes. If roles that are allowed to see the cube can see everything in the cube, and those that aren't don't know about the cube, this is enough. But you'll often want to control access to parts of the cube. That's where hierarchy grants are used.

### 6.2.3 *Dimension and hierarchy grants*

If you recall from chapter 4, hierarchies make up the structure of dimensions. Each dimension must have at least one hierarchy and one or more levels. Similarly, within a cube grant you can have dimension and hierarchy grants, and these are both at the same level. The dimension grant restricts access to an entire dimension and all of its hierarchies, whereas a hierarchy grant specifies access to just a single hierarchy within the dimension.

The `DimensionGrant` has two required attributes: `dimension`, the name of the dimension, and `access`, which can be either `all` or `none`. An access of `all` doesn't usually add a lot of value, because it's the default, so you'll typically only use `none`. Dimension grants also can't have any children. If you want finer-grained control over the contents of a dimension, you'll need to use a hierarchy grant.

The following listing shows an example of a dimension grant that gives access to the `Location` dimension and restricts access to the `Customer` dimension.

**Listing 6.11   Granting access to dimensions**

```
            <Role name="Product Manager">
              <SchemaGrant access="none">        <--- Deny access to entire schema
Grant access to   <CubeGrant cube="Product Sales"
Product Sales cube └--->        access="all">

                 <DimensionGrant dimension="[Location]"       Allow access to the
                            access="all"/>              <---- Location dimension

                 <DimensionGrant dimension="[Customer]"
                            access="none"/>             <-- Deny access to the
              </CubeGrant>                                  Customer dimension
              </SchemaGrant>
            </Role>
```

The `HierarchyGrant` has two required attributes: `hierarchy`, the name of the hierarchy, and `access`. The values for each of these attributes are described in the following sections. There are also several optional attributes that we'll discuss in a bit. As you'll also see, there are some special rules for the `HierarchyGrant` if you want to include other grants.

The name of the hierarchy can be either the full name of the hierarchy or, if the hierarchy name follows the conventions of Mondrian and there is only one, just the dimension name. For example, if the dimension is named `[Product]` and the hierarchy is named `[Products]`, it is enough to set the hierarchy name to `[Product]`. But if you have multiple hierarchies, such as `[Org Structure.Financial]` and `[Org Structure.Reporting]`, you'd need to specify the full name for the hierarchy you want to use.

#### HIERARCHY GRANT ACCESS
The hierarchy grant has three types of access: `all`, `none`, and `custom`.

All is used when you want to grant access to the entire hierarchy and all its members. All is the default for hierarchies, so it's rarely explicitly set. The following listing shows how you would explicitly grant an access type of all to the hierarchy.

**Listing 6.12  Granting access to all of the hierarchy**

```
<Role name="Product Manager">
  <SchemaGrant access="none">            ◁—— Deny access to entire schema
    <CubeGrant cube="Product Sales"
               access="all">              ◁—┐ Grant access to
                                             │ Product Sales cube

      <HierarchyGrant hierarchy="[Product].[Products]"
                      access="all"/>       ◁—┐ Allow access to the
    </CubeGrant>                             │ Product hierarchy
    </SchemaGrant>
</Role>
```

The hierarchy access of none restricts a user from seeing a hierarchy, including any of the levels or members in the hierarchy. The none option, shown in the following listing, is useful when you want to allow a role to see all parts of a cube except certain ones.

**Listing 6.13  Granting access to none of the hierarchy**

```
<Role name="Product Manager">
  <SchemaGrant access="all">             ◁—— Allow access to entire schema
    <CubeGrant cube="Product Sales"
               access="all">              ◁—┐ Allow access to
                                             │ Product Sales cube

        <HierarchyGrant hierarchy="[Product].[Products]"
            access="none"/>              ◁—┐ Deny access to the
      </CubeGrant>                         │ Product hierarchy
    </CubeGrant>
    </SchemaGrant>
</Role>
```

The custom access role is only used, and must be used, when you want to specify access to particular members in a level or if you want to specify a top or bottom level. Suppose you want to restrict sales managers at the state level to only see the members in their state. An example of the custom access with a MemberGrant is shown in the next section. Note that if you use an access type of custom and then don't specify any other settings, it behaves like an access type of all.

**TOP AND BOTTOM LEVELS**

In addition to the hierarchy grant's required attributes of name and access, there are two optional attributes, topLevel and bottomLevel. These attributes allow you to grant access to a range of levels within the hierarchy, and they're only used with an access of custom.

The topLevel attribute specifies the highest level in the hierarchy a user is allowed to view data at. For example, you may want to specify that managers can only see up to the business unit level and not the entire organization.

The `bottomLevel` attribute does the exact opposite; it restricts access to details of data below a certain level. This is useful when you want to provide access to the higher-level data but not the details. For example, perhaps you want to let salespeople see how sales in general are doing, but not how individual salespersons have done.

Listing 6.14 shows an example of using the `topLevel` and `bottomLevel` attributes. In this example, you're restricting the product manager to only be able to see sales information up to the country level and down to the city level. The product manager won't be able to see at the territory level above the country, nor will they see details about specific stores.

> **Listing 6.14  Limiting access to certain levels of the hierarchy**

```
<Role name="Product Manager">
  <SchemaGrant access="all">                    ⟵── Allow access to entire schema
    <CubeGrant cube="Product Sales"
              access="all">                     ⟵┐ Allow access to
                                                  │ Product Sales cube
      <HierarchyGrant hierarchy="[Location]"
              access="all"
              topLevel="[Location].[Country]"
              bottomLevel="[Location].[City]"
      />                                          ⟵┐ Only see from city
    </CubeGrant>                                   │ to country levels
  </SchemaGrant>
</Role>
```

Figure 6.2 shows how the `topLevel` and `bottomLevel` attributes restrict access to parts of the hierarchy. In this case, `topLevel` hides the territory level, and `bottomLevel` hides the city level. The user would only have access to the lighter shaded data.

### 6.2.4  Member grants

Member grants provide finer-grained control to dimensions than hierarchy grants. The role has access to the dimension but can only see the specific members that it is given access to. For example, the location hierarchy has a state level that includes as members all of the individual states. Suppose you want to restrict a state sales

| Location | Sales |
|---|---|
| [NA] | 85,000 |
| [NA].[USA] | 27,000 |
| [NA].[USA].[CA] | 8,000 |
| [NA].[USA].[OR] | 1,400 |
| [NA].[USA].[WA] | 1,800 |
| [NA].[USA].[WA].[Seattle] | 1,200 |
| [NA].[USA].[WA].[Spokane] | 600 |
| [NA].[USA].[WA].[Spokane].[Store1] | 200 |
| [NA].[USA].[WA].[Spokane].[Store2] | 400 |

**Figure 6.2  Top- and bottom-level restrictions**

manager to see only the values associated with their state. To do so, you'll want to use a member grant.

**CUSTOM HIERARCHY GRANT**  As mentioned previously, to use member grants, the hierarchy grant for the hierarchy must have an access type of custom.

Member grants have two access levels: all and none. How these are interpreted can be fairly complex, so it's good to understand what's going on. If you have a member grant, no matter what the access, access to all other members is taken away. For example, if you have access of type none on [Location].[Country].[USA], that's equivalent to a hierarchy access of type none. The difference is that instead of the hierarchy being hidden from the user, the report will simply generate no data.

On the other hand, if you grant access of all to a member, you'll see that member, its parents, and all its children. In the case of [Location].[Country].[USA] that means you'd see [North America], [USA], [CA], [WA], and so on. Understanding how each of these works allows you to combine them in a variety of ways.

Listing 6.15 shows an example of limiting access to only the state of Washington. The member grant that denies access to USA limits access to USA and all of its children. This means the user can't see USA, CA, OR, WA, and so on. It also means the user can't see Europe or Asia. The next line adds back access to WA. The result is that the user can see USA and WA, but none of the other states or their children.

**Listing 6.15  Limiting access to specific members of the hierarchy**

```
<Role name="Sales Manager - WA">
  <SchemaGrant access="none">                        ←── Deny access to entire schema
    <CubeGrant cube="Product Sales"
               access="all">                          ←┐ Allow access
                                                        │ to Product
                                                        │ Sales cube
      <HierarchyGrant hierarchy="[Location]"
                      access="custom">
        <MemberGrant member="[Location].[Country].[USA]"
          access="none"/>1((mg_no_usa_access))           Custom
                                                          access for
                                                          members
        <MemberGrant member="[Location].[State].[WA]"
          access="all"/>                               ←┐ Add back
                                                        │ access for WA
      </HierarchyGrant>
    </CubeGrant>
  </SchemaGrant>
</Role>
```

Table 6.3 shows how the grants work together. To understand how the restrictions work, assume that you have multiple countries, including [USA] and all of its states. In the table, we only show [CA], [ID], [OR], and [WA]. Note that we're using the {} characters to indicate an MDX set.

**Table 6.3 Comparing member grant combinations**

| [USA] access | [WA] access | State members available |
|---|---|---|
| none | Not specified | { } |
| all | Not specified | { [CA], [ID], [OR], [WA] } |
| none | all | { [WA] } |
| none | none | { } |
| all | none | { } |
| all | all | { [WA] } |

**MEMBER GRANT RULES**

A key concept of member grants is that they are order-dependent, and this can cause confusion when you first start working with them. But if you keep the following in mind when creating member grants, you should be OK.

- *Grants are order-dependent.* If you grant access to a child and then deny access to a parent, then the role can't see the child. For example, if you create a member access that can see [USA].[CA] and then deny access to [USA], the role will no longer be able to see [USA].[CA].
- *Grants inherit from other grants.* For example, if you deny access to [USA], all of the child members are also denied access because access to the children requires access to the parent. But access to children can be granted later. This allows you to block access to a set of members and then only give access back to a limited few.
- *Parents are implicitly granted access if a child is.* This goes with the previous rule about inheritance. In order to reach [USA].[WA], for example, you need to first access [USA].
- *Member grants don't override* topLevel *and* bottomLevel *attributes at the hierarchy grant level.* This means that even if you grant access to an individual store in a state, but you set a bottom level of the city that the store is in, you'll still only see down to the city level.

**ROLLUP POLICIES**

When access is restricted to only certain members, it can cause aggregate values to look incorrect. For example, you may have a list of sales by state for certain states, but the total shown is larger. This is because the aggregate is applied for the given level. To help in managing what users see at the higher aggregation levels, Mondrian provides a concept of rollup policies. Rollup policies tell Mondrian what to return for higher levels of aggregation.

Rollup policies are specified using the rollupPolicy attribute, and there are three possible values: full, partial, and hidden.

A `full` rollup policy lets the user see the aggregate value for all children, including those that they couldn't normally see. This is the default policy used by Mondrian if no rollup policy is specified. Seeing all of the data can be confusing, however, because some higher-level reports show all of the data and others show only the data the user should see.

A `partial` rollup policy means the user will only see the aggregates for the members the user can see. If a user is restricted to the state of Washington, then an aggregate for the US will only reflect values in Washington, not the entire United States. This is usually the policy that makes the most sense to users.

A `hidden` rollup policy will hide all data at the higher levels. This means that aggregates above the restricted level are completely hidden. Note that different UIs reflect `hidden` in different ways. JPivot, for example, will completely hide the aggregate, whereas Analyzer will show no data for the query.

> **AGGREGATE VERSUS TOTAL**  You may have noticed that we're using the term *aggregate* instead of *total* when describing rollup policies. We use this term because the aggregate is not always the total. In Mondrian, you can specify the aggregate to be other values, such as the count or maximum value. The rollup policy will be applied correctly for any of the aggregate types.

An example should make this concept clear. Table 6.4 shows some representative data from a cube: we have four different states with sales for each. Now assume there's a member grant restriction to only see WA. Table 6.5 shows the aggregate (the sum in this case) value for each policy.

**Table 6.4  Sales data by state**

| State | Sales |
|-------|-------|
| CA | 15,000 |
| ID | 3,000 |
| OR | 8,000 |
| WA | 11,000 |
| USA total | 37,000 |

### 6.2.5  *Measure grants*

Measure grants are a special case of member grants. Measures are simply another dimension of the cube; the existing grants can be used to restrict access to measures. There's no way to explicitly specify a measure grant.

You can use `DimensionGrant`, `HierarchyGrant`, and `MemberGrant` to restrict access as you can with any other dimension, but if you completely restrict a role from seeing any measures, Mondrian will throw an exception when you attempt to use the cube. This means that the only way to truly restrict access to measures is to use a combination of `MemberGrant` that allows access to at least one measure.

**Table 6.5  Results of rollup policies with member restricted to WA**

| Rollup policy | USA aggregate sales |
|---------------|---------------------|
| `full` | 37,000 |
| `partial` | 11,000 |
| `hidden` | |

Listing 6.16 shows a partial listing limiting access to measures. In this case the inventory manager is able to see the quantity of items ordered but not the sale price.

As described previously, this restricts the inventory manager to only seeing the quantity of items ordered unless other members have access granted.

**Listing 6.16   Example of restricting access to measures**

```
<Role name="Inventory Manager">
  <SchemaGrant access="all">                        ⟵—— Allow access to entire schema
    <CubeGrant cube="Product Sales"
               access="all">                        ⟵—— Allow access to Product Sales cube

      <HierarchyGrant hierarchy="[Measures]"
                      access="custom">               ⟵—— Specify custom access
        <MemberGrant member="[Measures].[Sales Price]"
          access="none"/>                            ⟵—— Restrict sales info
        <MemberGrant member="[Measures].[Qty Ordered]"
          access="all"/>                             ⟵—— See quantity ordered
      </HierarchyGrant>
    </CubeGrant>
  </SchemaGrant>
</Role>
```

## 6.3   *Summary*

This chapter showed you how roles and security grants can be used to restrict access to data. Roles can be assigned to users, and then those roles are assigned grants. Grants can be any of the following:

- SchemaGrants that can limit access to entire schemas
- CubeGrants that can limit access to specific cubes
- DimensionGrants that can limit access to entire dimensions
- HierarchyGrants that can limit access to dimensional hierarchies
- MemberGrants that can limit access to specific members within a hierarchy level
- Measure grants, a special case of the MemberGrant that limits access to measures

Now that you know how to define schemas and measures and restrict access to the data, it's time to take a look at performance. The next chapter will show you how to make data access faster. This isn't a major problem for smaller datasets, but when data warehouses run into the millions of records, performance becomes a concern.

# Maximizing
# Mondrian performance

**7**

Adventure Works analysts have been generally happy with the Mondrian's abilities. They like the reports and dashboards and particularly being able to do analysis on the fly. Some have even become proficient with MDX queries for performing advanced analysis. But as the amount of data grows, some of the reports and analyses are starting to feel sluggish, and not as quick as users demand.

One of the promises of Mondrian is that it supports *analytics at the speed of thought*. This means that when an analyst makes changes to a report, such as adding or removing dimensions and measures, adding calculations, and applying filters, the report needs to be updated within seconds, rather than minutes or hours. Given that analysis is often done over millions of records, performance is extremely important.

Out of the box, with a well-designed star schema, Mondrian performance is very good for a wide variety of datasets and queries. But some businesses want to do real-time analysis against millions of facts and thousands of dimension members. Eventually, even the fastest database and software will start to bog down with straight database calls. By default, Mondrian will perform some caching to speed things up, but squeezing out the highest levels of performance from your data sometimes takes additional configuration and effort.

There are three main strategies for increasing performance: tuning the database, aggregate tables, and caching. This chapter will discuss how to tune Mondrian using all three approaches. By the end of this chapter, you'll understand the techniques you can use to optimize Mondrian performance and keep the analytics flowing smoothly.

## 7.1 Figuring out where the problems are

Performance is something that you'll want to consider early on. While performance may appear to be fine with small test sets, problems can show up when the amount of data gets large. Some of the possible solutions, such as using aggregation tables, additional servers, and even a different database can be extremely costly and challenging to implement after the system has gone live. This section will present a general process for testing performance and then describe the necessary steps to prepare for performance testing and improvement.

### 7.1.1 Performance improvement process

You can start evaluating performance with any part of the system, but experience has identified a general approach that works best for most Mondrian deployments. Each step in this process has the potential to improve performance, with the early steps usually providing the largest performance gains.

Figure 7.1 shows the high-level process for this performance improvement.

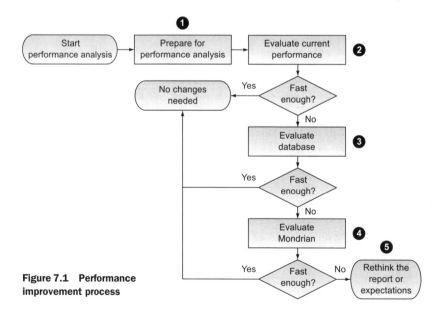

**Figure 7.1   Performance improvement process**

There are five high-level steps to perform when evaluating Mondrian's performance. Figure 7.1 and the following list show the order of analysis, but the order in which you implement solutions may vary. Either way, you can't go wrong following these steps.

1 First, prepare for performance testing. Section 7.1.2 covers the general considerations when preparing for performance testing, such as setting up the test environment and preparing data.

2 Once you're set up, you need to evaluate the current performance. "Executing the queries" in section 7.1.2 covers this topic, but it essentially involves running queries in your test environment.

3 If the performance isn't satisfactory, it's best to start analysis and tuning with the database, as described in section 7.2

4 If tuning the database doesn't solve your performance problems, you'll want to tune your Mondrian schema. Later sections on aggregate tables and caching will show how to speed up your queries.

5 Finally, if you've done all the tuning you can and are still unhappy with the performance, you should look for alternative ways of presenting the information, such as breaking up the data into different cubes or doing analysis with preset filters. These topics aren't covered directly in this book.

**IT MIGHT BE THE SOMETHING ELSE** There are other possible reasons for poor performance, beyond those given here. For example, poor network latency between Mondrian and the database can slow down the system. The system running the Mondrian engine might also be underpowered. To eliminate these variables, it's often ideal to initially do performance testing in a confined environment.

### 7.1.2 *Preparing for performance analysis and establishing current performance*

This section will cover the first two steps of the tuning process shown in figure 7.1. Before you can start your analysis, you need to have an environment, a baseline of test data, and a set of queries to run. It's helpful to have a dedicated environment for testing that's separate from the development environment. Although any improvement helps, some of the tuning that you may want to do involves creating a cluster of servers, which is something not typically found in a development environment.

Figure 7.2 shows what a performance test environment might look like.

#### HARDWARE AND SOFTWARE ENVIRONMENT

First you need the hardware environment and software set up for testing. This architecture should look a lot like what you want your production environment to look like. For instance, suppose you plan on running the data warehouse databases on a separate server from Mondrian. If your test environment has the database and Mondrian running on the same server, you'll miss the impact of bandwidth and latency when you're testing.

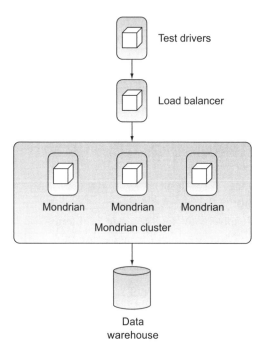

**Figure 7.2   Performance test environment**

The test environment need not be a 100% replica of your production environment, although that can be handy. At a minimum, though, you'll usually want a data warehouse running on the server that you will be using, and at least one server running Mondrian. If you're planning on clustering Mondrian, you'll want to cluster Mondrian in your performance test environment as well, again mainly to capture the cost of clustering. Finally, if you plan on deploying to virtual machines, you should have your performance test environment running in a virtual environment as well.

Memory (RAM) is very important for Mondrian performance, so you'll want the machines running Mondrian to have the same amount of RAM as the production machines. As you'll see later, Mondrian uses a variety of in-memory caches to optimize performance. Physical memory management, however, is up to the operating system. If you have too little memory, the OS will swap page files to the hard drive, and performance can drop dramatically. Increasing memory is one of the easy low-cost approaches to improving performance.

**REPRESENTATIVE TEST DATA**

Test data should represent the production data in both type and volume. Many organizations will simply use a copy of the production database for testing, and if you don't expect the data to grow, this approach can work. But if you're testing to head off future performance problems, it helps to create data that looks like what you expect for the future.

There are several reasons you might want to test with very large datasets. First, small amounts of data are easily held in memory, but when they exceed memory, the data is stored to disk, slowing performance. Certain lookups in the database can also grow non-linearly, such as finding records in a dimension table. If you forgot to index a relationship, that problem wouldn't be obvious on a small dataset, but on large amounts of data it shows up right away. Finally, small datasets don't give you enough data to really see the benefits of aggregate tables on performance. (Aggregate tables will be covered in section 7.3.)

### INITIAL QUERIES

Developing the initial queries is a bit of an art. It's impossible to anticipate every question that an analyst might ask, but you should be able to identify the really important ones. Assuming these cover broad areas of the data, the testing should be adequate, at least initially.

You can start by asking your business users what information they want from the system. A company usually implements OLAP with some idea of what information and reports are desired. These queries are good to start with. Create the underlying queries and run them against Mondrian to see what performance is like.

Next, take a look at the dimensions or cubes you feel will have a lot of data and create additional queries to test analysis performance against those areas. For example, if you have a dimension with a lot of members, be sure you have queries that use that dimension. These queries get added to those identified by business users to anticipate possible problems in the future.

Finally, create queries with any calculations you think might be used but that haven't been covered so far, such as period growth or current period comparisons. There are often tradeoffs to be made on calculated values that can impact performance, so including those in some queries can identify areas for improvement.

You should now have a physical environment for testing that represents the production environment. You should also have a set of test data that is representative of the target environment that needs to run efficiently. Finally, you should have a set of queries that you can run for baseline values, and then run again as changes are made, to determine the impact of the changes on performance. You're now ready to start tweaking the system to make it faster.

### EXECUTING THE QUERIES

Now that the environment is set up, all that remains is to run the queries and monitor performance. You can use a tool, such as Analyzer or Saiku, or you can send MDX to Mondrian via XMLA. The goal is to generate some timing results to see which queries are slow.

Mondrian can log the MDX statements sent to Mondrian and the SQL Mondrian generates. This logging can be turned on by configuring some log4j files. log4j is a common logging framework used by many Java applications, such as Mondrian.

When using Pentaho, the log4j.xml file can be found in the <pentaho-server-folder>. To turn on logging, edit the file, go to the bottom, and uncomment the logger(s) you want to have logged. You can also change the logging location if you like.

You'll need to restart the server after changing the log settings. Note that logging has already been enabled in the virtual machine.

> **PERFORMANCE IS AN ONGOING PROCESS**    For most organizations, performance testing isn't a one-time process and then you're done. It's an ongoing process that you'll continue to perform. Over time, dimensions will likely get added, unanticipated questions will be asked, hardware and software will be upgraded, and so on. All of these changes can affect performance.

With the environment set up and some query performance results logged, you're now ready to begin performance tuning. The rest of the chapter will cover the things you can do to improve performance. You'll also find out how to automate some of the performance steps that would otherwise require manual effort.

## 7.2    *Tuning the database*

Now that you have a baseline and know you want to increase performance, you can move to database tuning (process 3 in figure 7.3). Because Mondrian eventually retrieves data from a relational database, that database can be the performance bottleneck, so it's the first place to start looking for performance enhancements.

Mondrian works against a large number of databases, so our guidance here will be broad and hopefully capture the majority of initial tweaks. The good news is that

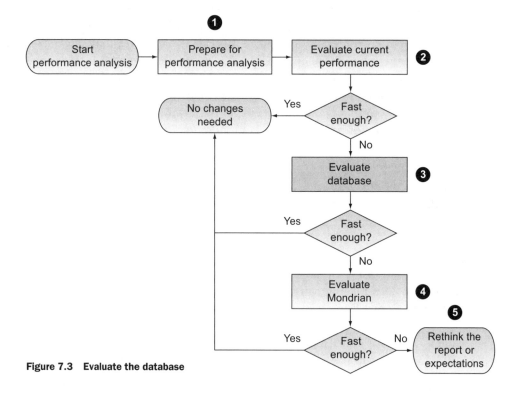

**Figure 7.3    Evaluate the database**

most organizations already have database administrators who understand how to tune the database. They can use their existing tools and experience to get the most out of the database. But there are some common things to look for when dealing with the database.

First, make sure it's really the database that's taking the time to execute the query. The Mondrian MDX and SQL logs can be configured to tell you how long each MDX and SQL query takes. Run the slow queries and view the execution time of both MDX and SQL. Then decide if the time of the SQL query is a significant portion that should be optimized.

Assuming you decide that the SQL queries are a problem, you'll want to figure out how to optimize them. As a first approach, try running the query in the native database tools. This can tell you if there's some database-related problem that's not the database itself. For example, you might be experiencing performance problems with database driver configurations that are separate from the database.

Another recommendation for all databases is to make sure your indexes are properly created. Surrogate keys in dimension tables should always be indexed—these are typically primary keys for the dimension table. If you have other natural keys that will be used for joins in the dimension table, index these as well. A query that takes minutes or even hours without indexing may only take seconds with proper indexes.

Once you have the database tuned for the fastest queries possible, the next step is to look at ways you can tune Mondrian-specific features. Mondrian has two major tuning approaches: aggregation and caching. The rest of this chapter will cover how Mondrian aggregation and caching work.

## 7.3 Aggregate tables

Once you have the database running as fast as possible, the next step is to tune Mondrian's performance as shown in figure 7.4. There are two major ways to improve Mondrian performance. The first is to use aggregate tables, which is covered here. The second is to use in-memory caching, which is covered in the next section.

Analytics databases often contain millions of records, because you want to store data at the lowest grain that might yield useful analysis. But an analyst will likely be interested in higher-level analysis. For example, analysts for Adventure Works might generally want to see how parts are selling at the monthly level, but they still want the ability to drill down to lower levels of detail to see specific days or customer orders. This section will describe aggregate tables and show how they're implemented in Mondrian 4.

Aggregating data across millions of records can be slow for even the fastest hardware and database, so Mondrian allows you to specify aggregate tables that precalculate at a higher level. Then, when analysis is being done, Mondrian can get the higher-level details from the aggregate table and the finer details from the detailed table. All of the data is available at the level needed, but the performance is much better. Figure 7.5 shows the relationship between the aggregate and detailed fact tables.

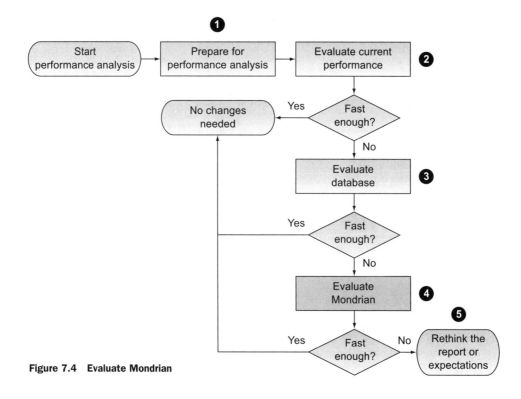

**Figure 7.4    Evaluate Mondrian**

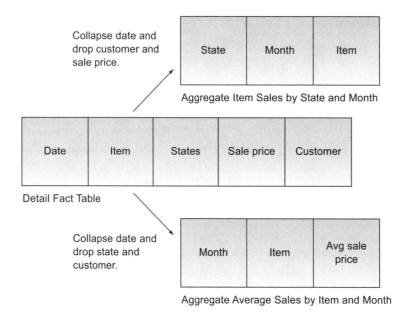

**Figure 7.5    Aggregate versus detail diagram**

Aggregate tables aggregate data by collapsing and dropping dimensions. *Collapsing a dimension* means that the dimension is aggregated at a particular level, eliminating the finer-grained levels. In figure 7.5, the date dimension was collapsed to the month level, leaving off the days. If there were thousands of facts per day, this would reduce the size of the data by tens of thousands of rows.

*Dropping a dimension* means it's left out of the aggregate table completely. You can think of this as the ultimate level of collapsing a dimension. A dropped dimension is essentially the same as the All Members level of the dimension. In figure 7.5, the aggregate average sales by item and month table dropped the customer and sale price columns because the only things we care about are identifying the items sold by state and month. In the average sales by item and month the customer and status were dropped to leave us with only the sales for each item by the given month.

### 7.3.1 Creating aggregate tables

The physical aggregate tables are created in the database and populated as part of the ETL process. There's nothing special about the data in aggregate tables for Mondrian. Mondrian simply uses the data in the aggregate table when it has been configured to do so and the query can be answered by the aggregate table. It's up to the ETL creator and database designer to properly populate the aggregate table.

> **ENABLING AGGREGATE TABLES** Aggregate tables can be enabled or disabled in the mondrian.properties file. For Pentaho they're disabled by default. To enable aggregates, simply set the `mondrian.rolap.aggregates.Use` and `mondrian.rolap.aggregates.Read` properties to `true`.

There are a couple of different approaches that can be used to populate the aggregate table. The first, and most obvious, is to populate the aggregate table as the detailed fact table is being populated. But since the data needed for the aggregate table is in the detailed fact table, it's recommended that you first populate the detailed fact table from the operational or staging data, and then populate the aggregate table from the detailed fact table. This has the secondary advantage that the fact and aggregate tables will be internally consistent. It also removes some of the logic common to populating facts, such as identifying new or modified facts.

> **AGGREGATION DESIGNER** Mondrian includes a tool called Aggregation Designer that can aid in creating summary tables. Aggregation Designer will read a schema and make recommendations for aggregate tables. It'll then generate SQL that can create and populate the aggregate tables for you. You may still need to tweak the results, but this can save time when you're getting started. Due to space limitations, we won't cover Aggregation Designer in this book in detail. The tool and its documentation are available from the Mondrian site.

### 7.3.2  *Declaring an aggregate table*

Aggregate tables are declared as a special usage of the MeasureGroup tag first introduced in chapter 4. Listing 7.1 shows the declaration of an aggregate table for item sales by month. The first thing that makes this an aggregate table is the type='aggregation' attribute in the MeasureGroup element.

**Listing 7.1   Declaring an aggregation table**

```
<MeasureGroup table='agg_sales_by_month'
              type='aggregation'>              ◁─┐ Uses type to declare
                                                 │ an aggregate table
    <Measures>
      <Measure name='Sales' column='SALES'/>   ◁─┐
      <Measure name='Average Sales'              │ Sum of the sales for the item
              column='SALES'
              aggregator='avg'
              formatString='#,###.00'/>        ◁── New measure: average sales

    </Measures>

    <DimensionLinks>
        <ForeignKeyLink dimension='Item'                    ┐ Link to item
                    foreignKeyColumn='item_id'/>  ◁─┘        dimension

        <CopyLink dimension='Time' attribute='Month'>  ◁─┐ Link to month
            <ColumnRef aggColumn='TIME_YEAR'               │ dimension
                    table='time_by_day' column='the_year'/>
            <ColumnRef aggColumn='TIME_QUARTER'
                    table='time_by_day' column='quarter'/>
            <ColumnRef aggColumn='TIME_MONTH'
                    table='time_by_day' column='month_of_year'/>
        </CopyLink>
    </DimensionLinks>

</MeasureGroup>
```

Once the table is declared, a standard measure group is added. In this case, the aggregation includes all of the sales for a given item in a given month. Notice, however, that because this is a measure group, you can also introduce new measures that don't exist in the original fact table. In this case, we're introducing a new measure called [Average Sales], which is the average for all sales for the month for the item.

Now that the measures are defined, it's time to declare the links. The first declaration, for the item, is the same declaration that you'd use in the detailed fact table using the ForeignKeyLink element. The next link, CopyLink, is a special element that specifies using that we're copying a dimension with levels, but only down to the Month level in this case.

**AGGREGATE TABLES IN OLDER VERSIONS OF MONDRIAN** If you're familiar with versions of Mondrian prior to version 4, you'll notice that Mondrian no longer uses the AggName approach to creating aggregates. Mondrian has also made aggregate tables explicit and has dropped the pattern-matching approach to aggregate tables.

### 7.3.3 Which aggregates should you create?

The preceding simple example shows that many different types of aggregate tables can be created. If you have a large fact table with many dimensions and facts, you could create hundreds or thousands of aggregate tables. So how should you decide which aggregate tables to create?

It's tempting to create as many aggregate tables as possible, but this is not recommended for several reasons. For one, the ETL process will grow as more aggregate tables are created and need to be populated. One of the reasons for using a ROLAP tool is to shorten the time needed to move data from OLTP systems to OLAP. Aggregate tables are a step in the direction of "pure" OLAP where intersections are precalculated, sometimes taking hours before data is available for analysis.

Aggregate tables also take up space in the analytics database and possibly in backups of the database. The additional storage in backups can be avoided by just storing the detailed facts and re-creating the fact tables, but this slows down the restoration process as well as makes it more complex.

Because it's undesirable to create all the possible aggregates, careful performance testing can help you determine which ones will be most useful. If you have a good performance test environment and you know the common queries, you can find out which queries could use some performance help. Start with the queries, create an aggregate, and see what impact that has on performance. There are two nice benefits to this approach. First, it's fairly easy to create and populate aggregate tables. Second, aggregates can be added after the fact to speed up slow queries, so it's not essential to create all the aggregates you might eventually want the first time around.

Now let's turn to Mondrian's second significant performance tuning feature: caching. Whereas aggregate tables reduce the amount of data read from the database, caching can eliminate reads entirely by storing data in RAM. Because even the fastest read from the disk or the network is going to be thousands of times slower than in-memory reads, this can lead to another order-of-magnitude gain in performance.

## 7.4 Caching

The process of retrieving schemas, dimension members, and facts and then performing calculations can be costly from an I/O perspective. Even with column-based analytics databases and fast storage, such as solid state drives, disk I/O is still orders of magnitude slower than reading from memory. To speed up analysis, Mondrian can cache the data in memory and use that rather than going to the database for each call.

In this section we'll first take a look at the different types of Mondrian caches, and then we'll study the special case of the external segment cache.

### 7.4.1 Types of caches

Mondrian has three different caches, as shown in figure 7.6.

- The *schema cache* keeps schemas in memory so they don't have to be reread every time a cube is loaded.
- The *member cache* stores member values from dimensions in memory, which reduces the number of reads from the database.
- The *segment cache* stores previously calculated values in memory so they don't need to be retrieved or recalculated. This can significantly speed up analysis by reducing the number of reads for common calculations.

As of Mondrian 3.3, you can use external segment caching. External segment caches store segments in an optional data grid. In section 7.4.2 you'll learn how to configure the external cache using several different technologies and when to use each.

All of the caches work together to maximize Mondrian performance, and the next few sections describe how they work. Understanding the caches is important for understanding when the caches should be primed or cleared.

**SCHEMA CACHE**

The schema cache stores the schema in memory after it has been read the first time, and it will be kept in memory until the cache is cleared. This means that whenever you update the schema, you need to clear the schema cache. If you're using Pentaho as your container, you can clear the schema cache by selecting Tools > Refresh Mondrian Schema Cache. Sometimes clearing all of the caches is required because Mondrian uses a checksum of the schema XML as the key for the cache.

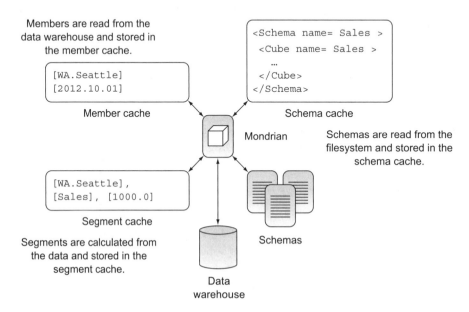

**Figure 7.6  The different Mondrian caches**

This becomes important if you have dynamic schema processors (discussed in chapter 9) because the dynamically generated schemas will be different. Attempting to clear just one schema will not clear all of them.

### MEMBER CACHE

The member cache stores members of dimensions in memory. As with the schema cache, there's not much to worry about as far as configuring the member cache. Just keep in mind that as with the schema cache, the member cache can also get out of synch with the underlying data. Mondrian has a Service Provider Interface (SPI) that allows you to flush the members of the cache, as described in section 7.6.

The member cache is populated when members of a dimension are first read, and the members are retrieved as needed. If the member is in memory, it doesn't need to be reread from the database, increasing performance.

*Members*, in this case, are specific values for levels in a dimension, such as [Time].[2011].[February] or [Customer].[All Customers].[USA].[WA], and they include the root and the children. It's important to remember that a member is more than just a value, such as WA, but rather a value within a dimension level. This is because a member can have the same name for a given level, such as Springfield, for different paths within the hierarchy: [NA].[USA].[Illinois].[Springfield] versus [NA].[USA].[South Dakota].[Springfield].

### SEGMENT CACHING

The segment cache is probably the hardest to understand, but it's also the cache that can have the biggest impact on performance. The segment cache holds data from the fact table, usually the largest table by an order of magnitude or so, and it has aggregated data. Holding data from the largest table can dramatically reduce the amount of I/O that takes place, and caching aggregated data reduces the number of calculations that need to occur.

Listing 7.2 shows the conceptual structure of a segment. First, the segment deals with a particular measure, in this case Internet Sales. Second, the segment contains a set of predicates, or member values, for which the data is relevant. In this case, the data is internet sales for males who graduated high school across all years. Finally, the segment carries the actual data values that make up the segment. If a request includes the predicates already stored, the data values can be quickly aggregated from the in-memory values rather than making a SQL call to the database.

#### Listing 7.2 Conceptual segment structure

```
Measure = [Internet Sales]
Predicates = {
  [Gender = Male],
  [Education Level = High School],
  [Year = All Years]
}
Data = [1224.50, 945.12, ...]
```

### 7.4.2    External segment cache

The external segment cache is a newer feature introduced in Mondrian 3.3. It's an optional physical implementation of the segment cache described previously. Whereas the standard segment cache stores segments in local memory, the external segment cache stores data in a data grid. This allows you to extend the amount of data stored in memory by adding additional servers. In some cases, it also provides in-memory failover of the cache, as you'll see in the next section. Although reading data across the network is substantially slower than reading from local memory, it's typically still an order of magnitude faster than reading from the database and performing calculations.

Figure 7.7 shows the high-level architecture for the external segment cache. Mondrian creates aggregations of measures to return for the query, and each aggregation is made up of segments as described previously. The segment loader is responsible for loading the segments, and it'll first attempt to retrieve the segment from the cache. If the segment isn't stored in the cache, the segment loader will query the database and then put the segment in the cache. The segment is then returned to Mondrian to use as part of the resulting aggregation.

There are currently three external segment caching technologies available for Mondrian. The first two, Infinispan and Memcached, are available as part of the Pentaho Enterprise Edition solution. The third, Community Distributed Cache (CDC), is available as an open source solution. There are tradeoffs to using each of the solutions. If you have an enterprise license for Pentaho, you'll want to stick with Infinispan or Memcached, since those are the only ones supported. If you're using Pentaho CE, then CDC is a good choice.

Note that there is technically another choice, the Pentaho Platform Delegating Cache, but at the time of writing, this cache was still experimental and not recommended for production use. Infinispan and Memcached should be used instead.

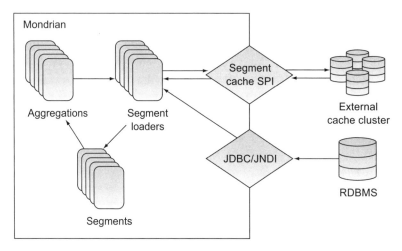

**Figure 7.7    External segment cache architecture**

**YOUR OWN DATA GRID** An additional option that we won't cover is that you can create your own data grid for external segment caching. To do so, you'd need to implement the `mondrian.spi.SegmentCache` interface and then configure Mondrian to use your solution. The three solutions covered in this chapter make the need for such an approach rare.

### INSTALLING THE EXTERNAL CACHE PLUGIN

The external segment cache isn't automatically installed with Pentaho. To use the external cache with Pentaho EE, you need to get the analysis EE plugin, available to users of the Enterprise Edition of Pentaho. You'll need to download the pentaho-analysis-ee plugin package from your software site. Fully up-to-date instructions can be found on Pentaho's Infocenter at http://infocenter.pentaho.com/help/topic/analysis_guide/topic_cache_control.html. Using CDC with Pentaho CE is discussed later in this section.

The plugin consists of two parts. The first is a lib directory that includes all of the JAR files needed to support the plugin. These files get deployed as part of the running application. If you're running inside of Pentaho's BA server, then these are deployed to the lib directory of the app server. For Tomcat, this is the tomcat/webapps/penataho/WEB-INF/lib folder. If you're running Mondrian standalone under Tomcat, this is the tomcat/webapps/mondrian/WEB-INF/lib folder. Other embedded uses of Mondrian need to have all of the files deployed so that they're in the classpath.

**WATCH THE VERSION NUMBERS!** All of the library files for Mondrian contain version numbers, such as jgroups-2.12.0.CR5.jar. This can cause problems if a different version of the same file already exists in the classpath. Be sure to replace such files if they exist.

The second directory, called config, contains all of the configuration files. These files all need to be copied to a location in the classpath as well. For Pentaho and Mondrian running under Tomcat, this is the WEB-INF/classes folder, and other servers will have a similar location. The important thing is that the files must be accessible to the Java classloader when the application is run.

Once everything is deployed, you need to configure Mondrian to use the external segment cache of your choice. The main configuration file is pentaho-analysis-config.xml, and its purpose is to turn external segment caching on or off and to specify the caching technology to use. To enable caching, set the USE_SEGMENT_CACHE entry to `true`. To specify the caching technology to use, set the entry for SEGMENT_CACHE_IMPL to have the name of the class that handles the cache. By default, Pentaho configures the Infinispan version as the recommended implementation, but the other caching technologies are also preconfigured and simply need to be uncommented. If you're using any other approach, add an entry for the custom class.

### INFINISPAN

Infinispan is an in-memory data grid that uses JGroups peer-to-peer communications to communicate between servers. Figure 7.8 shows the architecture when using

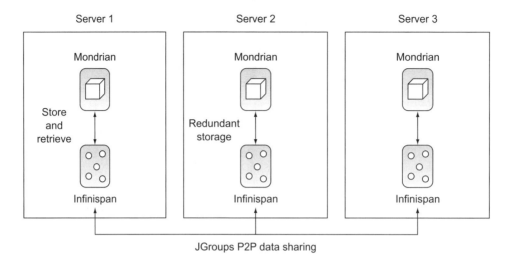

**Figure 7.8   Using Infinispan for the external segment cache**

Infinispan. Each server in the cluster has a copy of Infinispan running locally, and the servers share data across the network using peer-to-peer communications. In the case of Pentaho, the default is to use JGroups.

Infinispan has a few features that make it an ideal default. Infinispan shares segments, which means that any node can store a segment in the cache and any other node can retrieve it. Infinispan also can be configured to have multiple copies of the segment in the cache. This allows a server to fail, and the segment to still be available to the cluster without rereading the data. Finally, Infinispan will attempt to store and retrieve data locally to minimize network traffic and latency. Because most segments will be relevant to the analysis currently being performed within a server, this makes the overall performance better.

Infinispan has one drawback: it has no standalone nodes. To scale Infinispan you have to add additional servers. Because many deployments of Mondrian run in a horizontally scaled environment (one with multiple servers in a cluster), this is not usually a problem. But if you're not running in a cluster, Memcached may be a better choice.

### Configuring Infinispan
You can configure Infinispan by modifying the infinispan-config.xml file. For full configuration instructions, you can refer to the Infinispan site: www.jboss.org/infinispan/. But you may just want to change the numOwners setting. This attribute specifies the number of different nodes that will have a copy of the data. The default is 2, but it can be set higher. The more copies, the safer the data is from loss due to server failure. The tradeoff is that the more copies you have, the slower the cluster becomes. Because the original segment is always persisted in the underlying database, a low number is recommended.

Infinispan comes preconfigured to work with JGroups, a peer-to-peer communication technology. You can change this configuration or replace it altogether. See the Infinispan documentation and JGroups documentation (www.jgroups.org) for details. One change you can easily make, however, is changing the communication protocol used by JGroups. Simply modify the value of the `configurationFile` property in the infinispan-config.xml file to use a different file. By default, UDP is configured, but you can also configure it to use TCP or EC2 if you're deploying to Amazon's EC2 cloud. The filenames are of the form jgroups-*protocol*.xml, where *protocol* is udp, tcp, or ec2.

### MEMCACHED

Memcached is an alternative to Infinispan, and it uses a different architecture, as shown in figure 7.9. Memcached is a master/server data grid that stores key/value pairs. Mondrian interacts with the master to store and retrieve segments from memory. The master node will then store the data in one of the server nodes with a key and a value.

The major benefit that you get from Memcached is that it's easy to add additional memory nodes. Simply create a server with memory, and install and run Memcached. Then configure the master node to use the additional server. This differs from Infinispan, which requires a much heavier-weight server. Memcached is ideal for vertical scaling where a large, fast server is used to support fewer users but lots of data.

The major drawback to Memcached is that there is no sharing or failover. If multiple servers are using the same Memcached servers, the segments won't be shared between nodes. If the master node goes down, the cache is essentially lost from memory, although it can be reread from the database.

### *Configuring Memcached*

Configuration for Memcached is done using the memcached-config.xml file. This file has a number of configuration values, most of which can be left at their default values. But there are two that you'll need to modify: SERVERS and WEIGHTS.

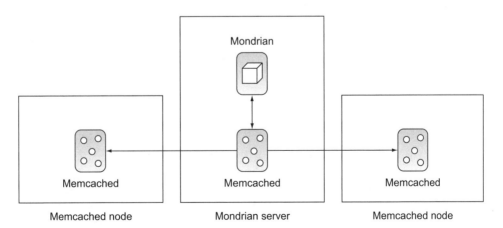

**Figure 7.9  Using Memcached for the external segment cache**

The SERVERS setting contains a comma-separated list of all of the server and port addresses of running Memcached servers. To add another server, simply add the IP address or DNS name plus port number that the Memcached server is listening on.

The WEIGHTS setting is a comma-separated list of integers that describe the relative amount of memory for each server, in the same order as for the SERVERS setting. For example, suppose that you have three servers: the first two have 1 GB of RAM and the third has 4 GB of RAM. The WEIGHTS setting would contain 1, 1, 4, indicating that the fourth server has four times as much RAM available. The weights are relative, so 2, 2, 8 would work just as well. You should try to anticipate the smallest server setting and make that value 1, with all other values being multiples, although you can always change it in the future by reconfiguring. Listing 7.3 shows a snippet of a configuration file with three servers.

> **Listing 7.3  SERVERS and WEIGHTS configuration example**

```
<entry key="SERVERS">                              ⟵—  List of servers
  seg.server1:1642, seg.server2:1642, 10.1.0.12:1642
</entry>
<entry key="WEIGHTS">                              ⟵—  Relative weights for each server
  1, 1, 4
</entry>
```

#### COMMUNITY DISTRIBUTED CACHE (CDC)

CDC is an open source alternative to Infinispan or Memcached from Webdetails (http://cdc.webdetails.org) based on Hazelcast. Its architecture, shown in figure 7.10, is similar to Memcached in that it can support standalone memory nodes. But CDC has additional features that are not standard when using either Infinispan or Memcached.

In addition to caching for Mondrian, CDC provides caching for Community Data Access (CDA), a multisource data abstraction that we'll discuss more in chapter 9. As a

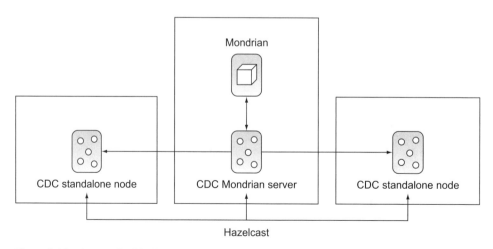

**Figure 7.10  Community Distributed Caching architecture**

Pentaho plugin, CDC provides administration tools that let you see the state of the caching directly in the user console. It also enables you to clear the Mondrian cache, which normally requires writing software.

The easiest way to install CDC is to use the CTools Installer that's available for download from https://github.com/pmalves/ctools-installer. Once you've downloaded the installer, run it as an administrator with the following command: `ctools-installer.sh -s solutionPath -w pentahoWebapPath -y`. The `solutionPath` is the absolute path to your pentaho-solutions directory, and `pentahoWebapPath` is the directory for the Pentaho web application, such as `/.../tomcat/webapps/pentaho`. This latter setting is optional in the script, but it must be specified for CDC to be installed.

> **WGET REQUIRED** The CTools Installer script uses `wget`, a common tool for downloading content from the web. `wget` is not automatically installed on all platforms, particularly Windows and more recent versions of OS X. Download and install `wget` (http://ftp.gnu.org/gnu/wget) before attempting to install CDC.

Once you have CDC installed, you'll want to install one or more standalone servers for caching. The standalone node can be downloaded from http://ci.analytical-labs.com/job/Webdetails-CDC/lastSuccessfulBuild/artifact/dist/cdc-redist-SNAPSHOT.zip. Simply use the launch script appropriate for your operating system to start Hazelcast. The nodes will find one another, so no additional configuration is required. You'll see messages similar to the following in the terminal window showing the known Hazelcast servers.

**Listing 7.4  Hazelcast server showing two servers**

```
Members [2] {
            Member [10.0.1.7]:5701 lite
            Member [10.0.1.7]:5703 this
        }
```

Once CDC and related tools are installed, you need to tell Pentaho to start using CDC for caching. Simply log into the Pentaho User Console and select the CDC icon in the toolbar. Eventually CDC will load and give you an option to start caching (see figure 7.11).

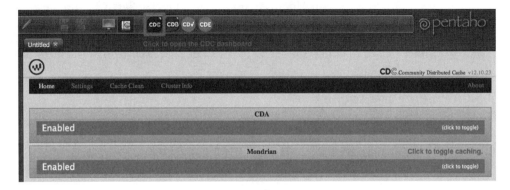

**Figure 7.11  Community Distributed Caching configuration**

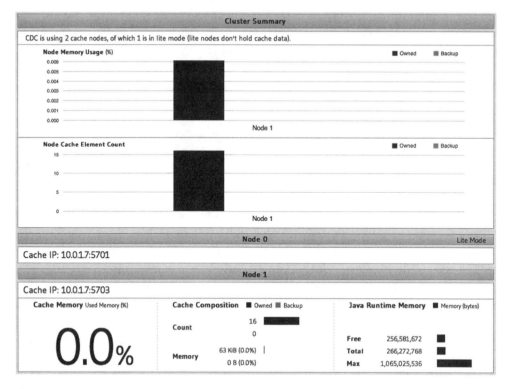

**Figure 7.12  CDC cluster summary**

After toggling or otherwise changing the configuration of CDC, you must restart the Pentaho application server. Once you do, if you use a tool that uses Mondrian you'll see the cache start to fill. CDC provides a simple console that displays information about the cache and memory usage under the Cluster Info tab (see figure 7.12).

> **SETTING SAIKU TO USE THE SAME MONDRIAN AS THE BI SERVER**  By default, Saiku is deployed with its own Mondrian version and files. In this section, we configured CDC to work with Mondrian on the BI Server, so Saiku will not be able to take advantage of CDC clustering. You can change this by running the saiku-shareMondrian.sh script located in the pentaho-solutions/system/saiku folder and providing the path to the Pentaho web app, usually tomcat/webapps/pentaho.

## 7.5  *Priming the cache*

Mondrian will automatically update the caches as schemas and dimensions are read and aggregates are calculated. This means, however, that the first user to access the data is populating the cache rather than getting the benefits of it. What you really want is the ability to prepopulate the cache before business users start performing analysis. Because the cache is populated as part of returning the results of a query, this means any call that makes a query to Mondrian will populate the cache.

The first question you need to ask is which queries need to be run. One approach is to simply wait for users to complain about slow reports, but a much more proactive approach is available. Simply turn on the Mondrian MDX log and monitor it for queries that take a long time. *Long* is relative, but if there are queries that take more than a minute or so, they are good candidates for precaching.

There are a number of approaches available for precaching that can be used. All reports in Pentaho are URL-addressable, so all slow reports can be called from a script, populating the cache. Another approach, when using Pentaho, is to create an action sequence that makes calls to Mondrian, populating the cache. Probably the simplest approach, though, and one that works with most Mondrian installations, is to use XML for Analysis (XMLA) web service calls.

XMLA is a SOAP-based standard for making web service calls. All you need to do for this to work is to expose Mondrian cubes as XMLA data sources. By default, when cubes, called *catalogs* in XMLA, are deployed to Pentaho, they're also made available as XMLA data sources. Other configurations, such as running Mondrian standalone, also support XMLA.

Chapter 10 will give more specifics on XMLA, so we won't cover it in detail here. What we will do here is create a web page that will make calls to XMLA using Ajax. We'll handle the responses, but only to note whether the call was successful or not. This web page could then be called whenever the cache needed to be populated.

**CROSS-DOMAIN CONSIDERATIONS** As a security constraint, JavaScript won't allow calls to other domains. That means a script running on mydomain.com can't call a web service on yourdomain.com. There are ways to get around this constraint, but in this case the cache refresh page can simply be deployed to the same server, because it adds minimal overhead.

Figure 7.13 shows the sequence of messages that our script will handle. The script will send a series of XMLA Execute messages (discussed in chapter 10) to the Mondrian server. The server will then respond with either an error message if there was an error, or a response to the XMLA query. The script will accept responses and log the errors and results to the web page. If MDX logging is enabled, you can also view the logs to see what queries were run.

The details of sending XMLA messages are covered in detail in chapter 10, so we'll just focus on the specifics for enabling caching. To make the script reusable and

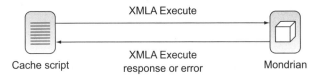

**Figure 7.13 Performance analysis process**

extensible, we've created a separate script that has the catalogs and queries to execute. Listing 7.5 shows the configuration and queries to be made, as well as the connection info.

**Listing 7.5  MDX queries**

```
var xmlaURL = "http://localhost:8080/pentaho/Xmla"          ◁─── Connection info for
var userid = "joe";                                              the XMLA server
var password = "password";

var dataSourceInfo = "Provider=Mondrian;DataSource=Pentaho";   ◁─── Data source info
                                                                    for Mondrian
var queries = [                    ◁─── MDX catalogs
  {                                     and queries
    catalog : "AdventureWorks",
    queries : [
"SELECT [Order Date].[Monthly].[Year].Members ON COLUMNS, " +
      "[Customer].[Gender].[Gender].Members ON ROWS " +
"FROM [Internet Sales] " +
"WHERE [Measures].[Qty Ordered]",

"SELECT [Order Date].[Monthly].[Month].Members ON COLUMNS, " +
      "[Customer].[Education Level].[Education Level].Members " +
        "ON ROWS " +
"FROM [Internet Sales] " +
"WHERE [Measures].[Qty Ordered]",

    ]
  },
  {
    catalog : "UnknownCatalog",
    queries : [
"SELECT [NOTHING] ON COLUMNS, [NOTHING] ON ROWS" +
"FROM [Internet Sales] "
    ]
  }

];
```

The connection information is simply the location of the server and the user information for login. The `DatasourceInfo` is specific to the installation, but it's otherwise static; this example shows the data source info for Pentaho. Other ways of running Mondrian will have a similar data source.

The final part of the file identifies the catalogs (schemas) and queries that will be run by the script. The catalogs are organized in an array with each containing an array of queries. This makes it easy to add additional catalogs and queries to be run. Simply update this one JavaScript file and rerun the script.

**SHARED CACHES**  In this example, we have a single user, joe, that we are using to prime the cache. Only schemas and data that joe has permissions to see will be put into the cache. This may mean that you need to run multiple versions of the queries with different users to prime all the caches.

Listing 7.6 shows the simple page that runs the script. In addition to including the needed scripts and style sheet, it has two <div> sections called results and errors. The script will write the results and errors to these sections when the page is run.

**Listing 7.6 XMLA cache web page**

```
<html>
  <head>
    <title>XMLA Cache</title>
    <link rel="stylesheet" type="text/css" href="XMLACache.css" />
    <script src="jquery-1.7.2.js"></script>
    <script src="MDXQueries.js"></script>
    <script src="XMLACache.js"></script>
  </head>
  <body>
    <h1>Pre-Cache Mondrian via XMLA</h1>
    <div id="results"></div>
    <div id="errors"></div>
  </body>
</html>
```

Listing 7.7 shows the main loop of code that runs the queries. When the main HTML document is ready, the script simply iterates over the catalogs and queries, making an XMLA call for each query.

**Listing 7.7 Execute MDX queries**

```
$(document).ready(function() {

  $("#results").html("<h2>Results</h2>");
  $("#errors").html("<h2>Errors</h2>");

  for (var idx = 0; idx < queries.length; idx++) {
    catalog = queries[idx];

    for (var qidx = 0; qidx < catalog.queries.length; qidx++) {
      postMessage(
        getQueryMessage(catalog.queries[qidx],
                        dataSourceInfo, catalog.catalog),
        'xml', handleQueryCallback);
    }
  }

});
```

Figure 7.14 shows the results of executing the query. In this case, two of the queries were successful and one failed. Examining the error message as well as the Mondrian logs will tell you which queries failed. At this point, the caches have been prepopulated with data from the successful queries and are ready for use.

Now that you know how to prime the caches, the next consideration is how to clear them. You need to do this whenever the underlying data has changed, making

## Pre-Cache Mondrian via XMLA

**Results**

2: success
3: success

**Errors**

1: error (00HSBB01): The Mondrian XML: Mondrian Error:Internal error: Unknown catalog 'UnknownCatalog'

**Figure 7.14   XMLA cache results**

the caches out of date. The next section shows how to programmatically clear each of the caches.

## 7.6    *Flushing the cache*

The drawback to caching is that while the data is stored in memory, the original data source can change, putting the cache out of sync with the true data. This usually occurs when ETL is performed. This section discusses ways to flush the cache, including using the console (for the schema cache) as well as the Cache Control API.

### 7.6.1    *Flushing the schema cache*

The schema cache keeps each of the unique caches in memory. The key for each cache is a checksum for the schema. When the schema is flushed from the cache, its associated member and segment caches are flushed as well, making this a brute-force approach. But if the schema has changed, or if determining the details of what to flush is too complex, this can be the best approach and certainly is the simplest. The caches can be repopulated using the techniques described in the previous section.

Most tools using Mondrian, such as Pentaho, provide a way to manually flush the cache. In Pentaho you can use the Enterprise Console or User Console. If you're logged into the User Console as an administrator, simply select Tools > Refresh > Mondrian Schema Cache.

The manual approach works fine, but administrators usually want to automate cache flushing as part of the overall ETL workflow. Figure 7.15 shows how Mondrian and the cache fit into the overall ETL workflow. After populating the OLAP database, Mondrian is called to flush and then prime the cache. This process makes sure the cache is synchronized with the underlying database so that when analysis is performed, the data is up to date.

To make it easy to integrate flushing the cache into the ETL process, you can create a class that contains methods to flush parts of the cache. You can also create a JSP that uses the new class. It then becomes easy to flush the cache by calling a URL with the appropriate parameters.

Table 7.1 shows the three scenarios that the flushing tool will support. The scenarios run from flushing everything to flushing a specific region of the cache. Mondrian's cache control SPI is very detailed and can allow you to control any parts of the cache, so these are only examples of what's possible.

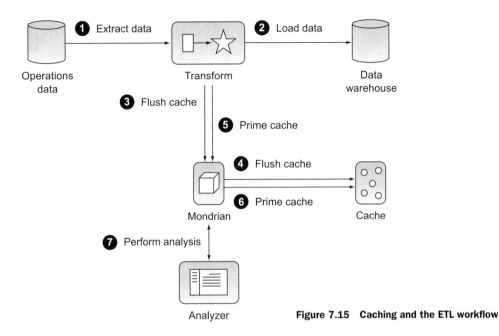

**Figure 7.15    Caching and the ETL workflow**

**Table 7.1    Cache-flushing scenarios**

| What to flush | Parameters required |
|---|---|
| Everything | No parameters |
| Specific cube | Catalog and cube |
| Specific region | Catalog, cube, and members |

Listing 7.8 shows some JSP code that controls caching. It receives parameters and then calls to the CacheFlusher class to flush the appropriate parts of the cache. This makes it easy to separate the work of flushing the cache from the user interface. The same class could be used in an action sequence or be embedded in an application if appropriate.

**Listing 7.8    JSP to flush the cache**

```
<%@ page import="mondrian.in.action.CacheFlusher" %>
<html>
<%
  String title = "Flush Cache";
  StringBuffer msg = new StringBuffer();
  CacheFlusher cacheFlusher = new CacheFlusher();


  String   catalog   = request.getParameter("catalog");          ◁─┐  Get parameters
  String   cube      = request.getParameter("cube");                │  from request
  String[] members   = request.getParameterValues("member");
```

```
  if (catalog == null && cube == null && members == null) {        Flush the
    title = "Flush All";                                           entire cache
    msg.append("<p>Flushing everything.</p>")
      .append (cacheFlusher.flushAll() ?
        "<p>Success!</p>" : "<p>Failure!</p>");
  }

  else if (catalog != null && cube != null) {                 Flush a
    if(members == null) {                                     cube
      title = "Flush Cube";
      msg.append("<p>Flushing ")
        .append(catalog).append(":").append(cube).append("</p>")
        .append (cacheFlusher.flushCube(catalog, cube) ?
          "<p>Success!</p>" : "<p>Failure!</p>");
    }
    else {                                                      Flush a
      title = "Flush Region";                                   region
      msg.append("<p>Flushing region from ")
        .append(catalog).append(":").append(cube).append("</p>")
        .append (cacheFlusher.flushCubeRegion(catalog, cube, members) ?
          "<p>Success!</p>" : "<p>Failure!</p>");
    }
  }
  else {
    msg.append("<p>Invalid argument combination.</p>");
  }
%>
<head>
  <title><%= title %></title>
</head>
<body>
  <%= msg.toString() %>
</body>
</html>
```

To flush the entire cache, you can simply call the JSP with no parameters. For example, if the JSP is deployed to the public folder of the Pentaho web app on the local machine, you'd call http://localhost/pentaho/public/FlushCache.jsp. This would invoke the flushAll() method of the CacheFlusher class, shown in listing 7.9. Note that this will only apply to new connections. Existing connections will continue to use the previous information.

**Listing 7.9   Flush the entire schema cache**

```
public boolean flushAll ()
  throws SQLException, ClassNotFoundException {

  List<RolapSchema> schemas = RolapSchema.getRolapSchemas();      Flush each
  for (RolapSchema schema : schemas) {                           schema
```

```
    CacheControl cacheControl =
      schema.getInternalConnection().getCacheControl(null);      Flush the
    cacheControl.flushSchema(schema);                            schema data

    cacheControl.flushSchemaCache();                             Flush the
  }                                                              cache
    return true;
}
```

Flushing everything when only some data has changed is excessive and will decrease performance unnecessarily for other cubes unless everything is primed again. If only the data for one cube has changed, then only that cube's cache should be flushed. The next section will show how to flush a single cube's cache at a time.

### 7.6.2 *Flushing specific cubes*

In an environment where there are many different schemas and cubes, there may be multiple ETL processes that only apply to a specific cube. After the data has been updated, then only the caches for the cubes that have been impacted need to be changed. This means that other cubes will continue to use the cache. As with clearing everything, this will only affect new connections.

Listing 7.10 shows the code to clear a specific cube's cache. To clear the cache, simply call the JSP and specify the catalog and cube to clear.

#### Listing 7.10   Flush a single cube's cache

```
public boolean flushCube(String schemaName, String cubeName) {
  List<RolapSchema> schemas = RolapSchema.getRolapSchemas();
  for (RolapSchema schema : schemas) {
    if (schema.getName().equals(schemaName)) {              ◁── Flush each schema
      CacheControl cacheControl =
        schema.getInternalConnection().getCacheControl(null);
      for (Cube cube : schema.getCubes()) {
        if (cube.getName().equals(cubeName)) {              ◁── Flush the schema data
          cacheControl.flush(
            cacheControl.createMeasuresRegion(cube));       ◁── Flush the cache
          return true;
        }
      }
    }
  }
  return false;
}
```

This will work fine if you want to clear the cache for the entire cube. But often only parts of the cube will be updated, particularly when time is a dimension, because past facts shouldn't change. The next section describes how to flush specific regions of the cube's cache.

### 7.6.3 *Flushing specific regions of the cache*

Flushing specific regions of the cube's cache gives the finest control over the cache. Suppose that Adventure Works has been tracking sales for several years. They also have a nightly batch process that updates the data warehouse from the operations database. They would only need to clear the cache for any information that has changed, such as the sales for the current month.

Listing 7.11 shows the code needed to flush a region. It looks a bit complex, but it actually only has a few key calls you need to understand. The code for finding the schema and cube should look familiar by now, so we'll only focus on the code for clearing the regions.

**Listing 7.11   Flush the region of a cube**

```
public boolean flushCubeRegion (
    String schemaName,
    String cubeName,
    String [] members
    ) {                                                      Find the schema

    for (RolapSchema schema : RolapSchema.getRolapSchemas()) {
        if (schemaName.equals(schema.getName())) {          Find the
            Cube cube = schema.lookupCube(cubeName, true);   cube
            SchemaReader schemaReader = cube.getSchemaReader(null);
            CacheControl cacheControl =
                schema.getInternalConnection().getCacheControl(null);
            CacheControl.CellRegion [] regions =
                new CacheControl.CellRegion[members.length + 1];
            regions[0] = cacheControl.createMeasuresRegion(cube);    Region for
            int size = 1;                                             measures
            for (String memberName : members) {
                Member member =
                    schemaReader.getMemberByUniqueName(
                        memberNameToSegmentList(memberName),true);
                regions[size++] =
                    cacheControl.createMemberRegion(member, true);   Create member
            }                                                        region
            CacheControl.CellRegion xregion =
                cacheControl.createCrossjoinRegion(regions);    Create cross-
            cacheControl.flush(xregion);                        join of regions
            return true;
        }                                              Flush region
    }
    return false;

}
```

- Create a cache control object
- Cell regions to clear
- Region for each member

The cell regions are a set of cells in the cube that need to be cleared. There's always the measure region, so that gets added as the first region to include. Then each member passed in gets converted to a cell region as well. The `memberNameToSegmentList` method converts from the member name to a special list of members.

Once all of the regions are defined, a cross-join is created and the cache control object flushes the region. The next call to Mondrian that needs the cells in the specific region would read them from the database and populate the cache. If this could be a lot of data, the cache-priming techniques discussed earlier could be used.

## 7.7 *Summary*

This chapter covered a number of topics related to improving the performance of very large Mondrian installations. One or more of these approaches can be used, and each provides a different advantage. These are the key points to remember:

- Performance is something to consider up front and plan for.
- Performance tuning is an iterative process.
- A finely tuned database is the first step to high performance.
- Mondrian uses multiple caches to improve performance, including schema, member, segment, and external segment caches.

Now that you have a grasp on Mondrian performance tuning, it's time to return to data security. The next chapter will show you how to dynamically apply security based on user information.

# Dynamic security

In chapter 6 you saw how Adventure Works was able to use roles and grants to restrict access to data based on a user's role. Most small and medium businesses that use Mondrian for internal only purposes can usually get by with such standard features. But as the numbers of users, roles, cubes, and clients grow, managing a Mondrian installation can become an administrative challenge. In a previous example from chapter 6, you saw how Adventure Works wanted to limit the state sales manager to only see the data from their state. The solution was to create a separate role for each state and assign managers to those roles, a tedious and error-prone solution. Additionally, many companies want to be able to provide Mondrian data to their clients. It's imperative that each client only sees their own data and not data from other clients.

This chapter will discuss the solutions to these challenges. Although there are many approaches to solving these problems, the examples provided in this chapter are specific to Pentaho because most enterprise users of Mondrian use it as part of Pentaho. The examples in this chapter involve Java code and are mainly aimed at

**1** Set session attributes for data restriction.

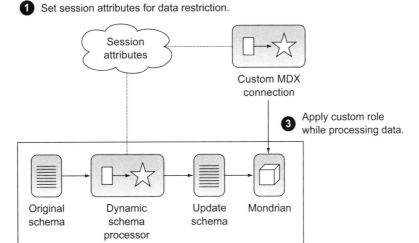

Custom MDX
connection

**3** Apply custom role
while processing data.

Original
schema    Dynamic
schema
processor    Update
schema    Mondrian

**Figure 8.1   Dynamic
security process**

**2** Update the schema when a connection is made.

the software developer, but it's important for the enterprise architect to understand
these concepts as well.

Figure 8.1 shows the high-level process we'll use to restrict data in this chapter.
First, we'll set some values in the user session to restrict data. Then we'll use two
approaches to restrict access to data. The first is to modify the schema to restrict data
based on the database query. The second is to assign users a custom connection and
role that Mondrian uses to evaluate whether a user has access to certain data. The rest
of this chapter will focus on implementing dynamic security.

## 8.1   Preparing for dynamic security

Before data can be restricted, you need a way to determine which data a user is
allowed to see. The approach we'll use in this chapter involves setting session attributes for the users when they log in and then checking the values of these attributes
when queries are made to Mondrian—the values will indicate whether the user is
allowed access to the data.

There are two common approaches to setting session attributes for the user. In scenarios where Pentaho is part of a larger infrastructure with single sign-on, the values
are often set during the sign-on process. In other cases, the values are set using action
sequences when a user logs in.

### 8.1.1   Creating an action sequence

An action sequence is an XML document that the Pentaho runtime engine knows how
to run. It causes various components to execute, it provides access to information
about the user, and it can write to the user session. Finally, there's a special configuration that can cause the action sequences to run when a user logs in.

**ACTION SEQUENCES WILL EVENTUALLY GO AWAY**  Pentaho 5.0 will dramatically reduce the use of action sequences in favor of using Kettle transformations. But startup action sequences will still be supported.

Listing 8.1 shows the main part of a simple action sequence, set_session_vars.xaction, that sets some session attributes in the user session. The first attribute is USER_REGION _CODE, which will be used with a dynamic schema processor (described in section 8.2) to restrict the region for the user. The second is USER_STATE_PROVINCE_NAME, which is used to restrict the state for the user. In this example we're using fixed values. In a real system, this value would come from a database, as a parameter or in some other way. For our purposes, it doesn't matter how the data ends up in the session, so long as it does.

---

**Listing 8.1  Setting user session values**

```
<action-sequence>
  <inputs>
    <USER_REGION_CODE type="string">              ◁─┐ Set country or
      <sources>                                       region for the user
        <request>USER_REGION_CODE</request>
      </sources>
      <default-value><![CDATA[US]]></default-value>
    </USER_REGION_CODE>
    <USER_STATE_PROVINCE_NAME type="string">      ◁─┐ Set state or province
      <sources>                                       for the user
        <request>USER_STATE_PROVINCE_NAME</request>
      </sources>
      <default-value><![CDATA[WA]]></default-value>
    </USER_STATE_PROVINCE_NAME>
  </inputs>
  <outputs>                                       ◁─┐ Write attributes
    <USER_REGION_CODE type="string">                  to the session
      <destinations>
        <session>USER_REGION_CODE</session>
      </destinations>
    </USER_REGION_CODE>
    <USER_STATE_PROVINCE_NAME type="string">
      <destinations>
        <session>USER_STATE_PROVINCE_NAME</session>
      </destinations>
    </USER_STATE_PROVINCE_NAME>
  </outputs>
</action-sequence>
```

## 8.1.2  *Configuring and running the action sequence*

Now that the action sequence is written, it needs to be run. If the action sequence is inside a visible Pentaho folder, it can be run by double-clicking it, the same way you can run saved analyses and reports. This is very convenient for testing because it's easy to see what the results of the action sequence are.

If you run the preceding action sequence, you should see something like figure 8.2.

The final step is to make the action sequence run when a user logs in. Pentaho has a special configuration file called sessionStartupActions.xml in the pentaho-solutions/system folder that allows you to specify action sequences to run when the server starts or a user logs in. To configure a new action sequence, you just need to add the XML in listing 8.2 into the session-StartupActionsList bean's constructor list.

**Figure 8.2   Results showing values from the action sequence**

---

**Listing 8.2   Configuring the action sequence to run on session start**

```
<bean
  class="org.pentaho.platform.engine.core.system.SessionStartupAction"
>                                                            ◁─┐ Declare a startup action
    <property name="sessionType"
      value="org.pentaho.platform.web.http.session.PentahoHttpSession"
    />                                                       ◁─┐ Make this a session action
    <property name="actionPath"
      value="adventure-works/set_session_vars.xaction"/>    ◁─┐ Specify action
    <property name="actionOutputScope"                            sequence to run
      value="session"/>                          ◁─┐ Store results
</bean>                                                in the session
```

Now any time a user logs in, they'll have session attributes of USER_REGION_CODE and USER_STATE_PROVINCE_NAME that can be used by code in the system.

> **TESTING THE ACTION SEQUENCE**   If the action sequence is in a visible solution folder in Pentaho, you can run it like a report from the Pentaho User Console. The displayed content will show the output of the report. This is very useful for initial testing to make sure the action sequence is working as desired.

In the next section, we'll look at how you can use a dynamic schema processor to restrict data based on the region value. Finally, we'll use a different approach and modify the user roles to restrict data based on the state value.

## 8.2   *Restricting data using a dynamic schema processor*

A dynamic schema processor (DSP) is a custom processor that's run whenever Mondrian makes a connection, such as when a user starts a new Analyzer report. Prior to Mondrian using the schema, the DSP can modify the schema. There are no restrictions on what modifications can be made, but the two most common uses of a DSP are to support localization and to restrict access to data in multi-tenanted environments. We'll demonstrate the second use of restricting data in this section.

> **THE DSP IS A MONDRIAN FEATURE**   The DSP is not specific to Pentaho, although the way we'll configure it here is. Any system that includes Mondrian as the analytics engine can use dynamic schema processors.

### 8.2.1   *Modifying the schema to support a DSP*

A multi-tenanted environment is one in which data is stored for multiple different customers (tenants) in the same database. Each of the tables contains a column that specifies which tenant the data is for. For example, Company A might have a 1 in the tenant ID column for records that relate to Company A. Company B would have a 2, and so forth.

The advantage to this approach is that there's only one database to manage for all tenants, rather than a separate database for each tenant. The major concern, however, is that you must ensure that tenants only see their own data. The solution is to make sure all queries use the ID of the tenant.

The Adventure Works database isn't multi-tenanted, so we're going to restrict data based on the region. The technique is the same for tenants; we're just using a different column. This same approach can be used to restrict on any column in the database.

Chapter 4 introduced the PhysicalSchema with the Table and Query elements for declaring tables. In this example, we'll need to use the Query element to restrict the data because it's the only one that allows you to specify the where clause.

Listing 8.3 shows the Query with a SQL element. Notice that the element contains a WHERE clause and %USER_REGION%. At runtime we'll modify the query to replace %USER_REGION% with the value for the specific user.

> **Listing 8.3   Virtual table using a query**

```
<Query alias="dim_customer_geography" keyColumn="CustomerKey">
  <ExpressionView>
    <SQL>
    select c.CustomerKey,
           g.CountryRegionCode, g.StateProvinceName, g.City
    from dim_customer as c
    join dim_geography as g on c.GeographyKey = g.GeographyKey
    where g.CountryRegionCode = %USER_REGION%;
    </SQL>
  </ExpressionView>
</Query>
```

> **SCHEMA CHANGE FROM MONDRIAN 3**   If you're familiar with this technique in Mondrian 3, you'll notice a change. In Mondrian 3, a SQL element could be applied to the Table element to specify a where clause. This functionality was removed in Mondrian 4.

### 8.2.2   *Example dynamic schema processor*

Now that the schema has been modified for use with the dynamic schema processor, you need to create the code to make the runtime modifications. The dynamic schema processor only requires a single class and method, as shown in listing 8.4. This class extends the LocalizingDynamicSchemaProcessor, which is the default schema processor used with Mondrian and which provides support for internationalization of schemas (such as changing column names). Any class that implements the Dynamic-SchemaProcessor interface can work as well.

**Listing 8.4   Dynamic schema processor**

```
public class DynamicSchemaProcessor
  extends LocalizingDynamicSchemaProcessor {                    Override filter
                                                                method
  @Override
  public String filter(String schemaUrl,
    Util.PropertyList connectInfo, InputStream stream)
    throws Exception {

    String schema =                                             Localize the
      super.filter(schemaUrl, connectInfo, stream);             schema

    IPentahoSession session =
      PentahoSessionHolder.getSession();                        Get user region
    String region =                                             from the session
      (String)session.getAttribute("USER_REGION_CODE");

    try {
      schema = schema.replaceAll("%USER_REGION%", region);      Replace
    }                                                           USER_REGION
    catch (PatternSyntaxException pse) {                        in the schema
      pse.printStackTrace();
    }

    return schema;                      Return the
  }                                     modified schema

}
```

The Java code should be compiled to bytecode and deployed in a JAR file to the Pentaho server lib file, usually under tomcat/webapps/pentaho/WEB-INF/lib if you're running in the default configuration with Tomcat. The core requirement is that the class be in a location that can be found by the Java classloader at runtime.

> **WHERE TO PUT THE NEW CODE**   If you're using the DSP with Analyzer, you should put the JAR file in the tomcat/webapps/pentaho/WEB-INF/lib folder. If you're using the DSP with Saiku in its default deployment, put the JAR file in the pentaho-solutions/system/saiku/lib folder.

This example is straightforward. You first localize the schema by calling the parent. Then you get the region for the user and substitute it everywhere it occurs in the schema. Finally, you return the schema as a string to the caller.

### 8.2.3   Configuring the DSP

The last step required to get a DSP to work is to tell Mondrian to use the dynamic schema processor for this schema. This configuration is done in the datasources.xml file located in the pentaho-solutions/system/olap directory.

Listing 8.5 shows the catalog declaration using the dynamic schema processor. DynamicSchemaProcessor is the full class name for our new class, and it must be in the classpath of the Pentaho server as described previously. UseContentChecksum should always be set to `true`—this property tells Mondrian to use the checksum of the schema to determine uniqueness and map to the cache. If this is `false`, it's possible to get incorrect values for a particular user.

**Listing 8.5  Dynamic schema processor configuration**

```
<Catalog name="AdventureWorks">
  <DataSourceInfo>Provider=mondrian;
    DataSource=AdventureWorksDW;
    DynamicSchemaProcessor=
      mondrian.in.action.DynamicSchemaProcessor;
    UseContentChecksum=true
  </DataSourceInfo>
  <Definition>
    solution:adventure-works/adventure_works.mondrian.xml
  </Definition>
</Catalog>
```

**PENTAHO 5.0 CHANGES**  In Pentaho 5.0, you will no longer use the data-sources.xml file to configure Mondrian catalogs.  Instead, you will set the properties when importing a Mondrian schema into the Pentaho repository.

Figure 8.3 shows some of the original data without the filter, and figure 8.4 shows the data with the filter. In the latter case, only the data where the user region is US is shown. The next step is to restrict at the state level using custom roles.

| Product Name | Measures Level | AU | CA | DE | FR | GB | US |
|---|---|---|---|---|---|---|---|
| AWC Logo Cap | Qty Ordered | 424 | 242 | 277 | 237 | 330 | 680 |
| All-Purpose Bike Stand | Qty Ordered | 65 | 32 | 20 | 19 | 28 | 85 |
| Bike Wash - Dissolver | Qty Ordered | 215 | 146 | 64 | 52 | 77 | 354 |
| Classic Vest, L | Qty Ordered | 44 | 28 | 10 | 19 | 14 | 80 |
| Classic Vest, M | Qty Ordered | 39 | 39 | 16 | 17 | 16 | 72 |
| Classic Vest, S | Qty Ordered | 31 | 26 | 16 | 6 | 12 | 77 |
| Fender Set - Mountain | Qty Ordered | 325 | 400 | 161 | 102 | 144 | 989 |
| HL Mountain Tire | Qty Ordered | 240 | 277 | 78 | 65 | 74 | 662 |
| HL Road Tire | Qty Ordered | 167 | 176 | 37 | 73 | 62 | 343 |
| Half-Finger Gloves, L | Qty Ordered | 89 | 82 | 35 | 39 | 34 | 164 |
| Half-Finger Gloves, M | Qty Ordered | 114 | 82 | 23 | 30 | 56 | 194 |
| Half-Finger Gloves, S | Qty Ordered | 114 | 85 | 37 | 32 | 40 | 180 |

**Figure 8.3   Unfiltered data**

| Product Name | Measures Level | US |
|---|---|---|
| AWC Logo Cap | Qty Ordered | 680 |
| All-Purpose Bike Stand | Qty Ordered | 85 |
| Bike Wash - Dissolver | Qty Ordered | 354 |
| Classic Vest, L | Qty Ordered | 80 |
| Classic Vest, M | Qty Ordered | 72 |
| Classic Vest, S | Qty Ordered | 77 |
| Fender Set - Mountain | Qty Ordered | 989 |
| HL Mountain Tire | Qty Ordered | 662 |
| HL Road Tire | Qty Ordered | 343 |
| Half-Finger Gloves, L | Qty Ordered | 164 |
| Half-Finger Gloves, M | Qty Ordered | 194 |
| Half-Finger Gloves, S | Qty Ordered | 180 |

Figure 8.4  Data filtered by region

## 8.3   *Restricting data using dynamic role modification*

Adventure Works wants to restrict sales managers so they can only see information about customers in their state. For example, the sales manager for the state of Washington should only see the sales for Washington. As you saw in chapter 6, Adventure Works could create a separate role for each sales manager and assign each manager to that role, but this adds fifty roles in just the United States. That alone would be very complex to manage. Now imagine an organization that wants to filter thousands of stores and limit managers to see only data for their store. The management of roles would become quite complex.

Most organizations already have information about users that defines what roles they have, where they work, who their clients are, and so on. This information can be used at runtime to dynamically create roles for users and restrict data access. This is possible because Mondrian supports the concept of a delegate role that determines access.

In section 8.1 you saw how to set session variables for a user. In a production environment, these action sequences would retrieve data about the user from a database or other location and put it into the session. In our example, we manually set the state via the action sequence for testing. Now we'll use the session variable to restrict the data.

**CUSTOM ROLES ARE NOT COMBINED**  Normally if a user belongs to multiple roles, the roles are combined. But when you use a custom role as described here, it's the only role that's applied for the user. It's not combined with other roles.

With the dynamic schema processor, we only needed to create one class. For this approach, three classes are needed; they're all simple, but each provides a different customization. These are the three classes:

- `CustomMDXConnection` replaces the defined role with a custom role.
- `CustomRoleDelegate` controls access to member data.
- `CustomHierarchyAccess` is an inner class of `CustomRoleDelegate` and helps with access control.

In the rest of this section, we'll look at preparing the schema for the custom delegate role and at each of these three classes.

**CACHE CONSIDERATIONS**  One consideration when deciding to use a dynamic schema processor instead of a custom role is the cache. Mondrian uses the checksum of the schema to distinguish caches, and because the DSP modifies the schema, there's a separate cache for each resulting schema. The custom role is applied at a higher level than the schema, so cache data can be shared even if the results are different for each user. The downside is that the custom role can be slower than the dynamic schema processor.

### 8.3.1 *Preparing the schema*

Before you can apply a custom role, you need an existing role to modify. This can be any role that the user will have, but you should consider the access for users who don't have that specific role. As shown in listing 8.6, we're limiting the sales manager role. When the connection is made, the existing role will be replaced with the custom role. Keep in mind that you may need to limit other users who aren't in the sales manager role by restricting access to the cube, because those users won't be affected by the custom role and won't have their data restricted.

**Listing 8.6  Predefined role**

```
<Role name="Sales Manager">
  <SchemaGrant access="all">
    <CubeGrant cube="Internet Sales" access="all">
      <HierarchyGrant hierarchy="[Customer Geography].[Geography]"
                      access="custom" rollupPolicy="partial">
        <MemberGrant member="[Customer Geography].[Country].[US]"
                     access="none"/>
        <MemberGrant member="[Customer Geography].[State].[California]"
                     access="all"/>
      </HierarchyGrant>
    </CubeGrant>
  </SchemaGrant>
</Role>
```

One additional aspect of this role is that it must include a valid MemberGrant that has a legitimate member that exists in the database. If the MemberGrant isn't included or the member doesn't exist, the call to check for access is optimized away and the code will never be invoked.

Note that as this is written, the user will never see any members in the given hierarchy because access specified for the MemberGrant is none. This effectively disables access by default so the custom role can give it back.

> **RESTRICTING ALL DIMENSIONS**  A role only restricts access to the dimensions that it's told to restrict. In Analyzer you can drag a dimension to the canvas and see all of the members. If there's an unrestricted role, all members are shown unless the restricted dimension or a measure is included. For example, if a user is restricted only by state and they drag only the customer names to the canvas, they would see all customer names, even those for other states, until a measure or the state level is added. If this is a problem, customers also need to be restricted.

### 8.3.2 Custom MDX connection

The custom MDX connection is what allows the custom role to be used by Mondrian when determining access. Listing 8.7 shows the custom MDX connection class.

**Listing 8.7  Custom MDX connect**

```
public class CustomMDXConnection extends MDXConnection {      ◁─┐ Extend
                                                                │ MDXConnection class
  @Override
  protected void init (Util.PropertyList properties) {
    super.init(properties);
    Connection thisConn = this.getConnection();               ◁── Call parent init
    Role authRole =                                           ◁── Use Sales Manager role
      thisConn.getSchema().lookupRole("Sales Manager");

    CustomRoleDelegate customRole =                           ◁── Create new custom role
      new CustomRoleDelegate(authRole);

    thisConn.setRole(customRole);                             ◁─┐ Set custom role
    setRole(customRole);                                       │ for this user
  }
}
```

The class extends the MDXConnection that's normally used and overrides the init method. This method is called whenever a connection is made to Mondrian. All this class does is create a new custom role and assign it to the connection.

One important thing to note about the example is that you must have an Authenticated role already defined. You could use any role, but the role should already exist as a starting point, and it must be a role that the user will have.

### 8.3.3   *Custom delegate role and custom hierarchy access*

Now that you have a custom delegate role assigned to the connection, you need to create the role and its helper class. Listing 8.8 may appear complex, but most of it is boilerplate code that routes the decision to the getAccess method.

**Listing 8.8   Custom role delegate**

```
public class CustomRoleDelegate extends DelegatingRole {

  private String state;                                         ┌─ Specify hierarchy
  private static String HIERARCHY_NAME = "Geography";    ◁──────┘  to restrict

  public CustomRoleDelegate(Role role) {          ◁─── Create new delegate role
    super(((RoleImpl) role).makeMutableClone());
    this.state =                                  ◁─── Get state from the session
      (String) PentahoSessionHolder.getSession().
        getAttribute("USER_STATE_PROVINCE_NAME");
  }
                                                                 ┌─ Return access
                                                                 │  details for the
  @Override                                                      │  hierarchy
  public HierarchyAccess getAccessDetails(Hierarchy hierarchy) {  ◁─┘
    HierarchyAccess ha = super.getAccessDetails(hierarchy);
    return (ha == null ? null : new CustomHierarchyAccess(ha));
  }

  protected class CustomHierarchyAccess                          ┌─ Create inner delegate
    extends RoleImpl.DelegatingHierarchyAccess {         ◁───────┘  for controlling access

    public CustomHierarchyAccess(HierarchyAccess ha) {
      super(ha);
    }
                                                              ┌─ Handle access for
    public Access getAccess(Member member) {          ◁───────┘  member access
      return CustomRoleDelegate.this.
        getAccess(member, hierarchyAccess.getAccess(member));
    }
  }

  @Override                                                   ┌─ Return access for
  public Access getAccess(Hierarchy hierarchy) {       ◁──────┘  the hierarchy
    return role.getAccess(hierarchy);
  }

  @Override                                                   ┌─ Return access
  public Access getAccess(Member member) {             ◁──────┘  for members
    return getAccess(member, role.getAccess(member));
  }                                                          ┌─ Determine
                                                             │  member
  protected Access getAccess(Member member, Access access) {  ◁─┘ access
    String memberHierarchyName = member.getHierarchy().getName();
    if (memberHierarchyName.contains(HIERARCHY_NAME)) {       ◁─── Check if
      if (member.getName().equalsIgnoreCase(this.state)) {        controlled
        return Access.ALL;                                        hierarchy
      }
```

```
    for (Member mem : member.getAncestorMembers()) {          Check for access
      if (mem.getName().equalsIgnoreCase(this.state)) {       to higher levels
        return Access.ALL;
      }
    }

    Access acc = (access == Access.CUSTOM) ? access : Access.NONE;
    return acc;                                               Return access
  }                                                           for member

  return access;                          Return standard access
}                                         if not controlled

@Override
public Access getAccess(Level level) {      Return level
  return role.getAccess(level);             access
}

}
```

The getAccess method is where the decision is made as to whether or not the user has access to the data member. The first check determines whether this is the member the user is allowed to see. If not, a check is made to see if the member is in the hierarchy of the restricted member. Finally, the original access is returned if the access is custom, or NONE if not.

### 8.3.4 Configuring the custom MDX connection

The final step in getting the custom delegate role to work is to configure it in pentaho-Objects.spring.xml. Simply replace the existing MDX connection declaration with one like that in listing 8.9. This configuration tells Pentaho to use the custom class whenever a connection to Mondrian is made.

**Listing 8.9   Configure custom MDX connection**

```
<bean id="connection-MDX"
      class="mondrian.in.action.CustomMDXConnection"
      scope="prototype">
  <property name="useExtendedColumnNames" value="true" />
</bean>
```

Figure 8.5 shows the data without the restriction by state. As you can see, the user sees all states and not just those they should be restricted to. Figure 8.6 shows the results when the dynamic roles are applied. In this case, the user can only see the state they're granted access to.

The custom delegate role approach is very powerful because it allows you to dynamically modify a role at runtime. You can implement virtually any customization, but you have to understand how the role will be invoked. There are currently plans to simplify and improve dynamic roles in a future version of Mondrian, but this approach works with the existing version.

| Country | State | Quantity Ordered |
|---------|-------|-----------------:|
| US | AL | 2 |
| | AZ | 2 |
| | CA | 12,248 |
| | FL | 11 |
| | GA | 7 |
| | IL | 14 |
| | KY | 5 |
| | MA | 1 |
| | MN | 3 |
| | MO | 3 |
| | MS | 2 |
| | MT | 3 |
| | NC | 2 |
| | NY | 11 |
| | OH | 15 |
| | OR | 2,876 |
| | SC | 8 |
| | TX | 15 |
| | UT | 6 |
| | VA | 2 |
| | WA | 6,101 |
| | WY | 7 |

**Figure 8.5   No restriction on state**

| Country | State | Quantity Ordered |
|---------|-------|-----------------:|
| US | WA | 6,101 |

**Figure 8.6   Restricting by state**

## 8.4   Deciding which security approach to use

The dynamic schema processor and custom roles are two different ways you can achieve the same goal of restricting data, but which approach you should use is not always obvious. This section describes some factors to consider when making your decision.

To use a DSP for data security, you must have something in your data to restrict on. This is usually an ID for the user or the group the user belongs to. The nice thing about using a DSP is that it can significantly reduce the amount of data returned to Mondrian for processing. The drawback is that each DSP causes a separate in-memory cache that can impact performance and lead to complexity in clearing the caches.

The custom-role approach requires that you know what you want to restrict for the user. Usually the restriction is at the member level, so you must have all of the members available for restriction. If you want to restrict members within more than one dimension, you'll have to restrict all of them, which can lead to some fairly significant data being stored in the user session.

Although custom roles share a common cache, possibly improving performance, they also require that all data be brought back from the database for a given user. If there is a large number of users who all have custom views of the data, this may not be faster than reducing the data returned by using a DSP. You'll have to think about how the data will be returned and possibly experiment to see which approach provides security while maintaining performance.

## 8.5   *Summary*

This chapter showed you how to apply custom security when running Mondrian in Pentaho. We first looked at one approach to setting values in the user session that can be used to restrict data access. Then we looked at two approaches to restricting data:

- A dynamic schema processor that rewrites the schema to restrict access to data
- A custom role that restricted data at runtime to a single state

Both of these scenarios are common for enterprise users of Mondrian as well as for multi-tenanted environments.

In the next chapter, we'll examine various ways that Mondrian data can be presented to users with Pentaho. The security techniques in this chapter apply in all of those cases as well. No matter what the presentation is—table, report, chart, or dashboard—the same security restrictions will be applied in all cases.

# Working with Mondrian and Pentaho

As we pointed out in chapter 1, Mondrian is an OLAP engine. It provides a lot of power, but you need to couple it with an end-user tool to make it effective. As we've explored Mondrian's various capabilities, we've used examples of end-user tools use to explain particular points, but we haven't looked very deeply into any of the specific tools.

In this chapter, we'll broaden our scope and cover topics that should be of interest to all users of Mondrian. We're going to take a look at several tools that are commonly used with Mondrian and show how they're used. These tools are written and maintained by Pentaho, as well as several tools from other companies that work closely with Pentaho. As you'll see, there is a rich variety of tools tailored to specific needs:

- Pentaho Analyzer—An Enterprise Edition plugin that provides drag-and-drop analysis as well as advanced charting.
- Saiku—An open source, thin-client interface that provides drag-and-drop analysis and charting.
- Community Dashboard Framework (CDF)—An open source tool that allows users to create dashboards based on Mondrian data.
- Pentaho Report Designer (PRD)—An open source desktop application that allows users to create pixel-perfect reports.
- Pentaho Data Integration (PDI)—An ETL tool that's usually used to populate the data used by Mondrian as described in chapter 3, but it can also use Mondrian as a source of data.

We won't be providing a complete user guide to each tool—that would take another complete book. But you should get an understanding of what each tool can do for you and how to use it with Mondrian. We'll also point out any peculiarities associated with each tool as it relates to Mondrian.

## 9.1 Pentaho Analyzer

Pentaho Analyzer is an enterprise analysis and charting tool. It uses Mondrian as a source of information and provides a graphical interface that allows analysts to easily perform analysis. Analyzer is an Enterprise Edition feature that requires a license from Pentaho to use. It has similar functionality to Saiku with some advanced features such as geomapping and plugin visualizations.

The rest of this section will provide an overview of some of Analyzer's features as well as some special additions to schemas to support mapping and time dimensions in Analyzer.

### 9.1.1 Overview of Pentaho Analyzer

Figure 9.1 shows Analyzer with data in a tabular format. On the left is the list of dimensions and measures that you can add to the analysis. These values all come from the cube that you choose when creating an Analyzer report.

Next to the fields is the current layout. This panel is context sensitive and will change based on the report view. For example, a stacked bar chart allows you to specify a dimension to use for multiple charts, as shown in figure 9.2. In this case, we're creating a separate chart for each country.

The toolbar contains some basic tools such as undo and redo, showing and hiding panels, and other settings. The toolbar also allows you to switch from tabular mode to charts, selecting the specific chart you want to use. Hovering over an icon on the toolbar gives a tip to show what the icon does.

The analysis results area will show either a table of the results or the chosen chart. Through the use of context menus, you can also add things like subtotals and coloring to tables. We'll describe how to use some of these features in the next section.

Toolbar

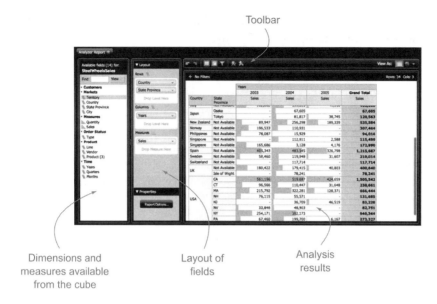

Dimensions and measures available from the cube

Layout of fields

Analysis results

**Figure 9.1   Pentaho Analyzer**

Layout for chart

Multiple charts

**Figure 9.2   Multiple bar charts for each country**

### 9.1.2   *Using Analyzer for analysis*

Let's use Analyzer to create a report on Adventure Works' internet sales. We'll find customers who purchased more than 10 items, and target them with a new promotion.

Select File > New > Analyzer Report to create a new Analyzer report, and you'll get the dialog box shown in figure 9.3. (You could also click one of the icons on the main User Console toolbar.) Choose the Internet Sales cube, and then click OK to enter a new Analyzer report.

Selected schema
and cube

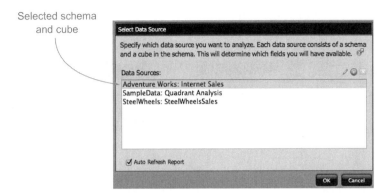

**Figure 9.3   Select cube for analysis**

Click the Report Options button to open the Report Options dialog box, as shown in figure 9.4. You're not interested in seeing customers who haven't made a purchase, so make sure the Also show Rows/Columns where the Measure cell is blank check box is unchecked. You can also specify what value is shown in blank cells, and whether totals are shown. Cell drillthrough causes each measure to have a link that can be clicked to see the source data that went into that cell. Freezing headers is useful for large reports so that you can see them when scrolling.

To restrict the report to customers with 10 purchases, you need a filter. To do this, drag the Sales field to the filter pane. (You can also right-click on a header and select Filter.) The dialog box is shown in figure 9.5.

There are different kinds of filters based on the type of thing being filtered. The sales filter is based on numeric value, and there are also filters for standard dimensions or time dimensions, shown in figures 9.6 and 9.7.

Numeric filters can filter based on values or can be set to show the top or bottom values. For example, you could identify the lowest performing stores to see how they can be improved. Numeric filters make it possible to limit the report to only the important values.

Rules for empty cells

Show totals

Turn on drillthrough

Always show headers

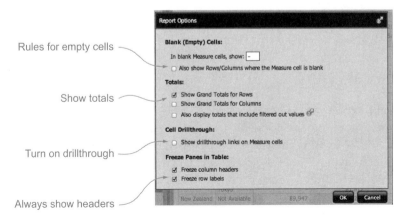

**Figure 9.4   Set report options**

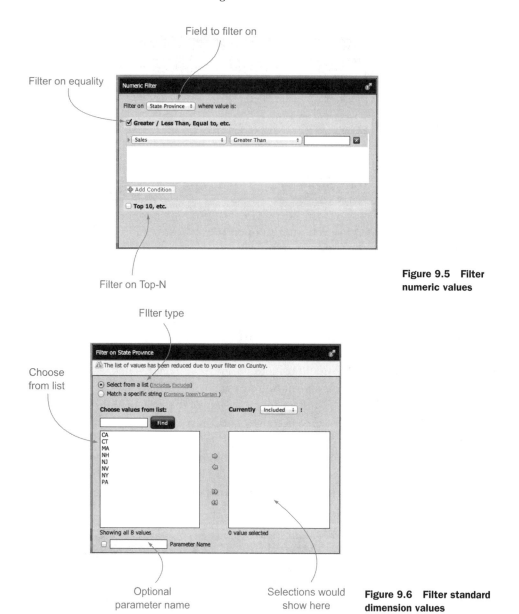

Field to filter on

Filter on equality

Filter on Top-N

**Figure 9.5   Filter numeric values**

Filter type

Choose from list

Optional parameter name

Selections would show here

**Figure 9.6   Filter standard dimension values**

Dimensional filters let you filter on specific levels in a dimension. This can be very helpful if you just want to see a specific territory or state, for example. You can select a value from a list of existing members or even specify a substring to match on. The filters let you include or exclude the matching data.

The final type of filter is based on dates. When a dimension is properly defined as a time dimension, Analyzer will allow you to specify dates related to the type of time, such as year or month. As with standard dimensions, you can include and exclude

Choose time filter

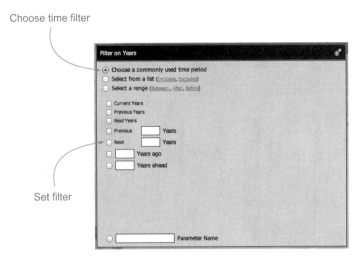

Set filter

**Figure 9.7   Filter time dimension values**

specific values, but you can also use more interesting filters, such as searching between dates, choosing dates from the last time period, and so on.

### 9.1.3   *Charting with Analyzer*

Tables are very powerful for analysis, but graphical representations of data can be even more powerful. Charts give a view of the data that can quickly highlight differences. For example, you may have a bar chart of sales by store where one bar is significantly higher or lower than others. Such a result would suggest further analysis to see why a store is performing above or below average.

Creating charts is as simple as creating tabular reports. But because of the context-based layout panel described previously, it's much easier to start in the chart mode and create the report rather than start with a table and convert it to a chart. To create a new chart, simply create a new Analyzer report, click the chart icon in the toolbar, and then drag the fields to the appropriate location.

Figure 9.8 shows an example of a stacked bar chart. Unfortunately, this example also demonstrates one of the dangers of charts. If they aren't all at the same scale, they can misrepresent the data. In this case, New Zealand appears to have dramatically more canceled orders than the United States. But if you look closely, you'll see that the difference isn't quite that large.

A particularly compelling chart that has been recently added to Analyzer is the Geo Map. This map presents data on a global map and allows you to drill down locally. Figure 9.9 shows the sales of shipped items by country. The size of the bubble indicates the quantity shipped, and the color specifies the quantity of sales. This allows the viewer to easily see where the most sales are in an easy-to-understand visual form.

One final point on charts is that Analyzer uses Pentaho's plugin architecture and allows you to create and use new visualizations. Some users need more than what's available from the standard charts, so assuming you have the technical skills, you can

**Figure 9.8    Example of a stacked bar chart**

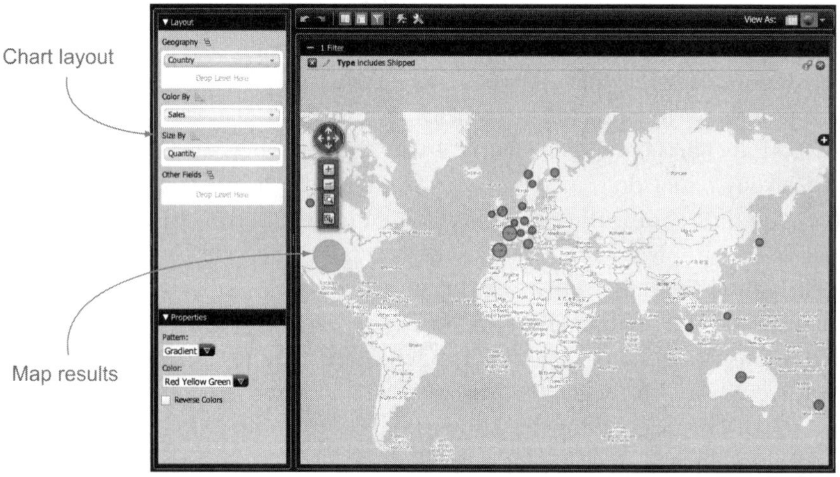

**Figure 9.9    Plotting data on a Geo Map chart**

create your own visualizations. Figure 9.10 shows a *chord chart*, which links two metrics and uses the width of the connection as a relative size.

Not only can you create your own charts, but because these are plugins, you can reuse charts that are created by others. In the future, it's likely that the Pentaho community will provide a number of charts to represent data in a variety of ways. At this

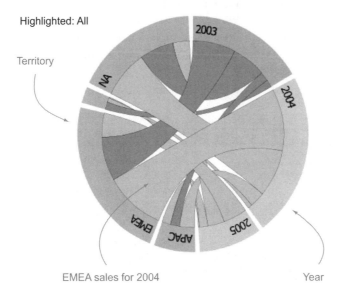

Highlighted: All

Territory

EMEA sales for 2004

Year

**Figure 9.10 Plotting data as a chord chart**

time, the process isn't well documented, but you should be able to find examples on the Pentaho site.

### 9.1.4 Special schema annotations for using Analyzer

When dealing with time and geomapped data, Analyzer requires special annotations in the Mondrian schema to make these data types work well. Time annotations allow Analyzer to create special time-based calculations, and geomapped data allows Analyzer to show the data on maps. In this section, we'll show you what to add to your schema to get the full benefits of time and geomapped data.

#### ANNOTATING FOR TIME DIMENSIONS

Analyzer requires that levels in a time dimension have an `AnalyzerDateFormat` annotation for each level. This tells Analyzer how to format the date for queries, and it uses Java date format notation. For example, a four-digit year is specified as `[yyyy]`. Listing 9.1 shows an example of annotating the month level.

**Listing 9.1 Annotating the month level for Analyzer**

```
<Level name="Months" column="MONTH_NAME"
       ordinalColumn="MONTH_ID"
       type="String" uniqueMembers="false"
       levelType="TimeMonths" hideMemberIf="Never">
  <Annotations>
    <Annotation name="AnalyzerDateFormat">
      [yyyy].['QTR'q].[MMM]
    </Annotation>
  </Annotations>
</Level>
```

## ANNOTATING FOR GEO MAPS

For Analyzer to display items on a map, you need to tell it how to find the geographical location of dimension members. There are two different approaches for annotating locations. The first is to specify a level, such as country, state, or city. The second is to specify latitude and longitude. This means, of course, that the location information must exist in the data warehouse.

Listing 9.2 shows the declaration of a state level. Table 9.1 shows the possible annotations.

**Listing 9.2  Annotating the state level for Analyzer**

```
<Level name="State Province"
       column="STATE"
       type="String"
       levelType="Regular"
       hideMemberIf="Never">
  <Annotations>
    <Annotation name="Data.Role">Geography</Annotation>
    <Annotation name="Geo.Role">state</Annotation>
    <Annotation name="Geo.RequiredParents">country</Annotation>
  </Annotations>
</Level>
```

**Table 9.1  Geo annotations**

| Annotation | Required? | Value(s) |
| --- | --- | --- |
| Data.Role | Required | Geography— indicates that members of the level have a geographical location. |
| Geo.Role | Required | Name of a geographical classification; country, state, city, and zip are typical values, but you can use any value supported by the location service. If Geo.Role has the special value location, Analyzer will look for properties of the level called latitude and longitude. |
| Geo.RequiredParents | Optional | Comma-separated list of parent classifications. |

If you don't have a geography dimension, you can still geotag data using latitude and longitude, and it will be shown on the map. Latitude and longitude are added as properties and tagged with the Geo roles to indicate that they are latitude and longitude, as shown in listing 9.3. As long as you have the data, you can geotag any level where it makes sense.

**Listing 9.3  Annotating the latitude and longitude for Analyzer**

```
<Level name="Customer Location"
       column="CUSTOMERNUMBER"
       type="Numeric"
       uniqueMembers="false">
```

```
<Annotations>
  <Annotation name="Data.Role">Geography</Annotation>
  <Annotation name="Geo.Role">location</Annotation>
</Annotations>
<Property name="Latitude" column="CUSTLAT" type="Numeric" />
<Property name="Longitude" column="CUSTLON" type="Numeric"/>
</Level>
```

Now that you understand how to use Analyzer, let's look at how to use Saiku, an open source alternative to Analyzer.

## 9.2   *Saiku*

We covered Saiku in chapter 2, so we won't go into detail about how to use it again here. Because Analyzer requires an enterprise license, Saiku is a good choice for a drag-and-drop tool that has no licensing costs. Even if you do have Analyzer, many people use Saiku for its ability to generate MDX queries because it generates much easier-to-read MDX than Analyzer.

Another reason to use Saiku is that it has a standalone version that doesn't require Pentaho at all. Simply download the server and start it running. This is a very handy approach if you simply want to do analysis without the other overhead that comes with the entire Pentaho suite. And because Saiku is open source, you can even contribute to the project.

When running Saiku as a plugin, there are some things to be aware of. First, Saiku has its own library of files in the saiku/lib folder. This means that if you should need a different library for only Saiku, you can place it in this folder.

A second consideration is that by default Saiku will not use Mondrian's cache, so if you install something like the Community Data Cache, you might wonder why nothing is being cached. Reconfiguring Saiku to use Mondrian's cache is easy. Simply run the script saiku-shareMondrian.sh to have Saiku use the same Mondrian version as Pentaho, including sharing the cache. Note that this means Saiku will also use the same libraries as Pentaho.

Hopefully you now have a feel for Analyzer and Saiku and understand some of the trade-offs between the two. In the next section, we'll show you how to create dashboards based on Mondrian data.

## 9.3   *Community Dashboard Framework*

The Community Dashboard Framework (CDF) is another project from Webdetails for creating interactive dashboards. The dashboards are written in a combination of HTML, JavaScript, and CSS, which means that you will need technically skilled people to develop CDF dashboards. It also means that the dashboards can be highly interactive and do anything that a dynamic web page can do.

This section will give you a brief introduction to CDF and describe how to use Mondrian as a source of data for CDF components. We'll also discuss a complementary project, Community Data Access (CDA), that abstracts the Mondrian connection from the dashboard while adding additional features.

### 9.3.1  *Creating a CDF dashboard*

A typical dashboard consists of at least three files:

- An .xcdf file that defines the dashboard
- An HTML file that serves as a template for dashboard
- A JavaScript file that contains the actions of the dashboard, including the MDX queries

Additional files commonly seen in more complex dashboards include cascading style sheets, static images, and possibly additional JavaScript files. Because CDF dashboards are essentially dynamic HTML pages, they can include anything that a regular dynamic HTML page can, including jQuery or other framework files. The additional files don't even have to reside in the same directory, allowing you to create common files for reuse by other dashboards.

Listing 9.4 shows the contents of an .xcdf file. The two most important values are the title and template. The title is what will be displayed in the Pentaho User Console and can be localized. The template is the HTML file that will be used to create the dashboard.

#### Listing 9.4   Declaring a CDF dashboard

```
<?xml version="1.0" encoding="UTF-8"?>
<cdf>                                              Title and
    <title>MDX Chart</title>           ◁─┘        description
    <author>Bill Back</author>
    <description>Sample chart based on MDX Query</description>
    <icon></icon>                                          Location
    <template>charts.html</template>       ◁─┘             of chart
    <style>mia</style>               ◁─┐  Name of style
</cdf>                                 │  template
```

The .xcdf file tells Pentaho that this is a dashboard, and it calls the CDF plugin to render the dashboard. CDF will use the template file to load all of the resources needed for the dashboard. The template file actually gets loaded into a separate template that can be used globally by all CDF dashboards, allowing you to customize the look and feel of all dashboards. The `style` tag specifies which outermost template to use. See the CDF documentation for information on how to change the global template files, because this involves creating and deploying a new HTML file.

The template file contains three logical sections, as shown in listing 9.5. The first is basic HTML that will define locations for CDF to render the objects. In this example, we're only adding a pie chart, so we just have a single `div` to hold the resulting chart. For a complex dashboard, you might have multiple `div` tags and use tables or CSS to lay out the dashboard.

The second section is the declaration of the objects. In this example, we first define the pie chart and then create a pie chart based on the definition. Because we're using Mondrian, we specify an MDX type, the catalog to use, the data source for the data, and the actual query. This example uses Steel Wheels, the sample dataset that comes with Pentaho. There are a few additional settings, such as height and width, that should also be specified but that are not shown here.

> **Listing 9.5   Defining a CDF dashboard with a pie chart**

```
<div id="pieChart_object"></div>
<script language="javascript" type="text/javascript">

var pieChartDefinition = {                          Define chart
  chartType: "PieChart",                            content
  datasetType: "CategoryDataset",
  title: "Territory Sales",                         Use MDX
  queryType: 'mdx',                                 with catalog
  catalog:
    "solution:steel-wheels/analysis/steelwheels.mondrian.xml",   JNDI data
  jndi: "SampleData",                                            source
  query: function(){            <---  MDX query

    var query = "select " +
                "NON EMPTY {[Measures].[Quantity]} ON COLUMNS, " +
                "NON EMPTY [Markets].[Territory].Members ON ROWS " +
                "FROM [SteelWheelsSales]";

    return query;
  }
};

pieChart = {                   <---  Create pie chart
  name: "pieChart",
  type: "jFreeChartComponent",
  listeners:[],
  chartDefinition: pieChartDefinition,
  htmlObject: "pieChart_object",
  executeAtStart: true
};

var components = [pieChart];        Create and init
Dashboards.init(components);        components
</script>
```

Once the dashboard has been loaded into the repository, you can run it and see the results, as shown in figure 9.11. In this case, we have the sales by territory as a pie chart.

### 9.3.2   *Using Community Data Access*

In the previous example, we embedded the query directly into the dashboard, but there

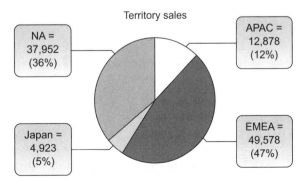

**Figure 9.11   CDF pie chart**

are a few problems with this approach. First, it potentially exposes the details of your data to anyone who has access to the dashboard. Second, it makes the data access difficult to change should you decide to change the type of data source.

To solve these problems and add extra functionality, there's another project called Community Data Access (CDA) that allows you to separate the source of data from the dashboard. Users will only see that you're using CDA, but not the original source of the data. CDA supports a wide variety of data source types in addition to Mondrian, such as SQL and Pentaho Data Integration (PDI). You can also combine data from multiple sources into a single query using CDA and make that available to the dashboard as well.

CDA data access is defined in a separate file with a .cda extension. Listing 9.6 shows a CDA file that returns the same results as the previous query. There are two sections: the first defines the data sources to use and the second defines the specific query and the results returned.

**Listing 9.6    Declaring a CDA descriptor**

```xml
<?xml version="1.0" encoding="utf-8"?>
<CDADescriptor>                                          ⟵  Define a connection
  <DataSources>                                              to the schema
    <Connection id="1" type="mondrian.jndi">
      <Jndi>SampleData</Jndi>
      <Catalog>
        ../steel-wheels/analysis/steelwheels.mondrian.xml
      </Catalog>
      <Cube>SteelWheelsSales</Cube>
    </Connection>
  </DataSources>
  <DataAccess id="1" connection="1" type="mdx" access="public">
    <Name>Mdx Query on SampleData - Jndi</Name>
    <Query>                                        ⟵  MDX query
      SELECT
        NON EMPTY {[Measures].[Quantity]} ON COLUMNS,
        NON EMPTY [Markets].[Territory].Members ON ROWS
        FROM [SteelWheelsSales]
    </Query>
    <Columns>                                      ⟵  Column descriptions
      <Column idx="1">
        <Name>Territory</Name>
      </Column>
      <Column idx="2">
        <Name>Quantity</Name>
      </Column>
    </Columns>
    <Output indexes="1,2"/>                         ⟵  Columns to return
  </DataAccess>
</CDADescriptor>
```

Once you have a CDA file defined, you can edit the original CDF file to change the data access from MDX to CDA. Listing 9.7 shows the new definition for the pie chart.

It's all the same except that the MDX has been replaced with CDA settings. Once you run the chart, it looks identical to the previous one.

---

**Listing 9.7   Defining a CDF dashboard with a pie chart**

```
var pieChartDefinition = {
  chartType: "PieChart",
  datasetType: "CategoryDataset",
  title: "Territory Sales",              Use CDA
  queryType: "cda",
  cdaFile: "/mia/mia.cda",          CDA file
  dataAccessId: "1"
};                          Data access ID in file
```

CDF and CDA provide a nice way to create a dashboard, but many users also want data in reports. The next section will show you how to create tabular reports with Mondrian data.

## 9.4   *Pentaho Report Designer*

Pentaho Report Designer (PRD) is a pixel-perfect report-designing tool. It's a stand-alone tool that runs independently of the Pentaho BA server, and it can be downloaded from http://reporting.pentaho.com. If you install using the Pentaho graphical installer, it will be placed in the design-tools directory. Start it as you would any other Java application.

PRD allows you to use a variety of data sources to create nicely formatted reports for users. Reports typically contain header and footer information, tabular data, and charts. Furthermore, a Pentaho report can include parameters that allow a user to filter the data. In this section, we'll give you a brief overview of what reports can do, show you how to use Mondrian as a source of data, and discuss how to use a dynamic schema processor with reports. We won't show you all the details of creating reports, but we'll focus on the Mondrian-specific aspects.

Reports are most commonly based on data from relational databases using SQL to get the data. But PRD supports a wide variety of input sources, such as Mondrian, Pentaho Data Integration, big data sources such as Hadoop, and NoSQL databases such as MongoDB. With the use of scripted data sources for languages such as Groovy and Beanshell, the number of data sources is almost limitless.

### 9.4.1   *Creating an OLAP data source*

Let's look at how you can use PRD to create a report based on Mondrian. First, open up PRD and select New Report. You'll see something very similar to the blank canvas shown in figure 9.12.

The first thing to do is set a source of data. There are a number of ways to specify the data type, but we'll use the Data tab. Click the Data tab, and then click the database icon at the top. You'll see a pop-up menu like that shown in figure 9.13. Click OLAP and choose Pentaho Analysis to create a Mondrian-based connection. You'll notice that

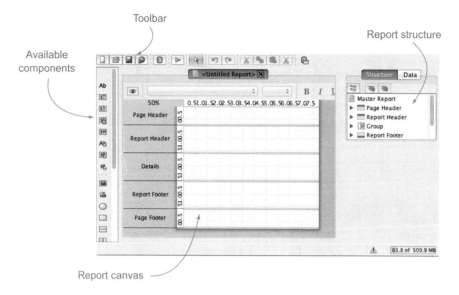

**Figure 9.12   Blank report**

there are multiple OLAP options. We'll just cover the basic one here, since that's the most common one.

After the data source editor opens (as shown in figure 9.14), you can set the values for the data source. You can use the Browse button and browse to the Mondrian schema. Note that the path to the schema will become part of the report definition—when the report is deployed, it'll look for the schema at the same path. This means

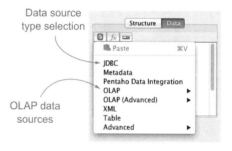

**Figure 9.13   Choose OLAP data source**

that you need some approach to make sure the report will find the schema in the environment it's deployed to, or else the report will need to be updated to point to the correct path.

The next thing to select is the data source you want to use. This is a configured connection. Pentaho has a standard way of configuring connections to the database that we won't cover here, but you can choose to use standard JDBC settings or JNDI. Whenever possible, you should use JNDI because it allows you to have a development report that points to development data, and then as the report goes through QA and into production, only the JNDI settings need to change, not the report.

After setting the database, click the green button with a "+" sign on it, to the right of Available Queries. This creates a new query. Give the query a descriptive name that makes it easy to tell what the query does. Finally, enter a valid MDX query. This query will return the values to use in the report.

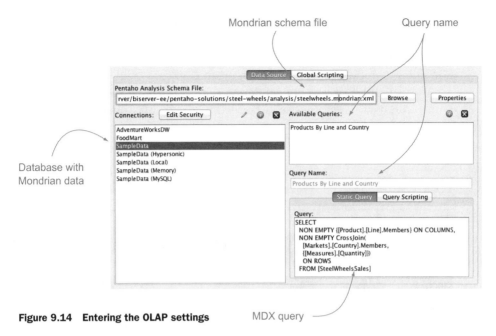

**Figure 9.14   Entering the OLAP settings**

**EXPERIMENT WITH THE ORDER OF ROWS AND COLUMNS**   One word of caution: the order of the columns and rows can cause your report to get different values, including member names rather than the measures you might expect. You may need to experiment with the query to get the values you want in your report.

Now that you have the query, close the data source editor and you'll see the available fields you can use in the report. Figure 9.15 shows the completed report. Several data fields have been put onto the details section, and this section will repeat for each line

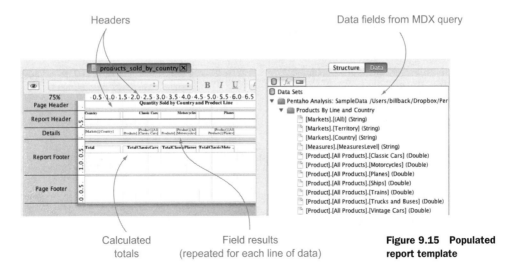

**Figure 9.15   Populated report template**

in the results. There's also a page header that gets added to each page, containing the report name. The report header will be displayed before the details, so you can put the column headers there. You can also put a total in the report footer that will show how many items were ordered by each product line.

At this point, you have a complete report that can be run. Figure 9.16 shows the report with data. The values are all pulled from the MDX query executing against the database. You could now publish this report to the Pentaho server for other users to run.

## Quantity Sold by Country and Product Line

| Country | Classic Cars | Motorcycles | Planes |
|---|---|---|---|
| Australia | 1,818 | 876 | 813 |
| New Zealand | 1,526 | 976 | 517 |
| Singapore | 508 | | |
| Austria | 937 | 197 | 200 |
| Belgium | 147 | | 41 |
| Denmark | 1,244 | | 70 |
| Finland | 1,284 | 447 | 421 |
| France | 3,540 | 2,404 | 1,136 |
| Germany | 1,281 | 121 | 245 |
| Ireland | 202 | 58 | 115 |
| Italy | 982 | 111 | 1,276 |
| Norway | 1,158 | 484 | 325 |
| Spain | 4,380 | 780 | 1,101 |
| Sweden | 552 | 133 | 104 |
| Switzerland | 1,078 | | |
| UK | 1,507 | 371 | 479 |
| Hong Kong | | 35 | 462 |
| Japan | 314 | 309 | 547 |
| Philippines | 478 | 241 | 215 |
| Singapore | 535 | 44 | |
| Canada | 456 | 41 | 317 |
| USA | 11,625 | 5,080 | 3,476 |
| **Total** | **35,552** | **11,860** | **12,708** |

**Figure 9.16   Report with data**

### 9.4.2 Using parameters

One problem with reports is that they can get pretty long. Users often want to see only some of the data at any given time. In Analyzer you can create filters to restrict the data, and Pentaho Report Designer offers a similar capability through the use of parameters.

The first step is to create a query to populate the parameters. You could also just hard code the value (for example, if you want to specify a dimension), but in this case we're going to parameterize the country to allow users to restrict by country. Because of the way the query is returned, the territory needs to be in the rows, and since you can't specify a ROWS value in MDX without a column, you need to also specify something on the COLUMNS. In this case, we'll just ignore the column values. Listing 9.8 shows the MDX query for the territories.

---

**Listing 9.8 Getting the territories for parameters**

```
SELECT
  NON EMPTY {[Product].[Line].Members} ON COLUMNS,
  NON EMPTY {[Markets].[Territory].Members} ON ROWS
  FROM [SteelWheelsSales]
```

Once you have a query, you can create a parameter to use. Figure 9.17 shows the configuration for the parameter. Select the query, and then select the fields to use. In this case, we'll use a drop-down list.

Now that the parameter has been defined, it needs to be added to the original query to filter the data. There are really two ways to filter in MDX. The first is to use a

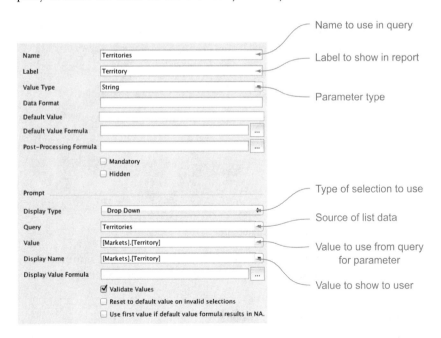

**Figure 9.17  Defining the territory parameter**

WHERE clause, which is essentially the same as adding a hidden axis that selects only some data. Because we're restricting on a dimension that's already in the query, we can't use a WHERE, because that would cause Markets to be on two axes. In this case, we can filter by specifying the territory in the SELECT.

The last step is to update the original query to use the parameter. Listing 9.9 shows the new query. Note that the market will now be populated with the children values of the territory selected from the parameter, as indicated by ${Territories}. Figure 9.18 shows the results of running the report with a parameter.

**Listing 9.9   Restricting the territory with a parameter**

```
SELECT
  NON EMPTY {[Product].[Line].Members} ON COLUMNS,
  NON EMPTY CrossJoin(
    [Markets].[${Territories}].Children,
    {[Measures].[Quantity]})
    ON ROWS
  FROM [SteelWheelsSales]
```

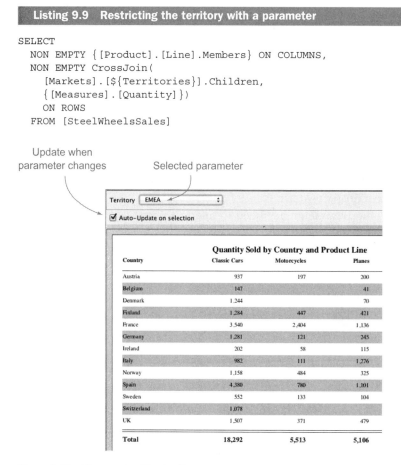

**Figure 9.18   The report with a territory parameter**

**SLICING**   We've been using the term *filter* because that's a common term for reporting. It's also common to see the term *slicing* used in OLAP when talking about restricting data.

### 9.4.3   *PRD and the dynamic schema processor*

The last thing to mention about Mondrian and PRD is the use of dynamic schema processors. PRD uses a different connection approach than Analyzer, Saiku, and other

**Figure 9.19   Adding a global script**

tools. PRD contains the definition as part of the report. Because of this, you need to set a dynamic schema processor in the report definition.

To specify the DSP you want to use, edit the data source and add a new global script, as shown in figure 9.19. This script will be called when the report is generated and will set the DSP to use; the value specified is the class name of the DSP. Note that you need to deploy the class into the classpath of the reporting engine so it can be found at runtime.

The previous sections showed you how to create visualizations based on Mondrian data. But sometimes users just want to get data from Mondrian and do something with it. The next section covers extracting Mondrian data using PDI.

## 9.5   *Pentaho Data Integration*

Pentaho Data Integration (PDI) is a desktop tool that allows you to extract data from a variety of sources, modify the data, and then send it to a variety of outputs. The most common use of PDI is to perform ETL, as described in some detail in chapter 3, but PDI can be used in any situation where you need to get and manipulate data. This section will describe how to use PDI to extract data from Mondrian. From there, you can use the data as you would from any other data source.

The first step is to create a new transformation. This is done by selecting File > New > Transformation. Once you have a transformation, you can connect to the database.

Figure 9.20 shows the View tab. Right-click Database Connections and select New. You'll get the standard database connection form shown in figure 9.21. Enter the connection information for the data mart being used by Mondrian.

So far you've created a connection to the database with the data for Mondrian. Now you just need to hook it up to a schema and get some data. From the Design tab, open the Input folder and drag a Mondrian Input step onto the canvas. You should now have a transformation that looks similar to figure 9.22.

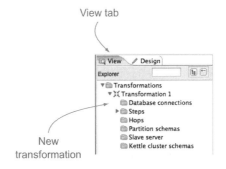

**Figure 9.20   PDI view**

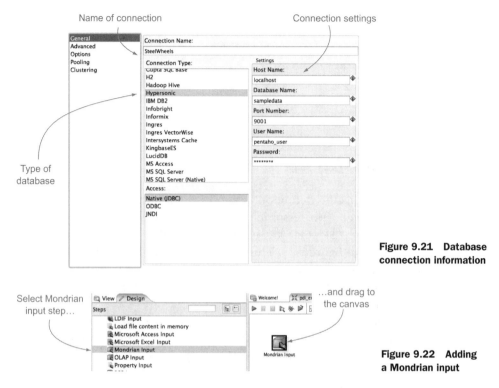

**Figure 9.21   Database connection information**

**Figure 9.22   Adding a Mondrian input**

Next, enter the catalog, database connection, and query into the step dialog box, as shown in figure 9.23. After the settings are entered, click the Preview button to see the results. Figure 9.24 shows the sales by category.

**Figure 9.23   Setting Mondrian values**

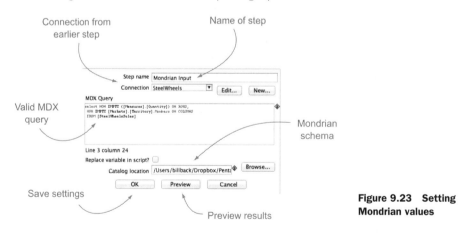

Rows of step: Mondrian Input (1 rows)

| # ▲ | [Measures] | [Markets].[APAC] | [Markets].[EMEA] | [Markets].[Japan] | [Markets].[NA] |
|---|---|---|---|---|---|
| 1 | [Measures].[Quantity] | 12878.0 | 49578.0 | 4923.0 | 37952.0 |

**Figure 9.24   Results of query**

At this point, you can use the data as you would any other input from PDI.

## 9.6   *Summary*

In this chapter, we took a look at some of the most widely used tools for working with Mondrian data sources. For each tool, we provided a brief overview and some high-level instructions on how to use it with Mondrian. We also provided some tips and considerations to be aware of when using each tool. You should now have a good idea of what each tool provides in the way of functionality and generally understand when it might be useful.

In particular, we covered the following tools:

- Pentaho Analyzer
- Saiku
- Community Dashboard Framework
- Pentaho Report Designer
- Pentaho Data Integration

Despite all the power these tools provide, they may not meet all your needs. Perhaps you want to link Mondrian directly to your system, or perhaps you want to create a simplified user interface. In the next chapter, we'll take a look at how developers can create new tools to work directly with Mondrian to meet these needs.

# *Developing with Mondrian* 10

**This chapter is recommended for**

Business analysts

✓ Data architects

Enterprise architects

✓ Application developers

All of the previous chapters dealt with creating Mondrian content and using Mondrian from existing tools. You learned the steps necessary to create a data warehouse and populate it for Mondrian. You learned how to create a schema and optimize performance. You also learned how to apply security to Mondrian, including dynamic security. Finally, you learned about a variety of tools that can use Mondrian.

In this chapter you take the next step and learn how to use Mondrian from your own applications. This chapter is mainly written for software developers. It's expected that you have the ability to read HTML, JavaScript, and Java code to fully understand the examples.

Adventure Works management has decided that they want to add analytical information to their existing web and desktop applications. This functionality would allow them to let analysts and managers see reports and trends against their data while using their existing applications rather than needing multiple tools.

They want to use Mondrian to do so because of its rich feature set, built-in security, and existing user base.

They discover that there are two main ways to use Mondrian from within their applications (figure 10.1). If they have a thin-client application, they can use XML for Analysis (XMLA) and JavaScript to make calls to Mondrian. In this case Mondrian would run on a web server configured as an XMLA source. In section 10.1 we'll show how to use Mondrian using jQuery with Ajax as well as the xmla4js JavaScript libraries.

If they're writing an application using Java or some other JVM language, they can use olap4j to talk to Mondrian. olap4j works both with Mondrian configured as a web service or directly embedded within your application. Using olap4j you can also access additional functionality, such as access to the cache control service provider interface (SPI), that isn't available when making XMLA calls from a thin client. In section 10.2 we'll show how to use olap4j to make both types of connections.

> **CODE SNIPPETS IN THIS CHAPTER**   Note that we only show the parts of the code that are relevant to Mondrian and XMLA. We've also generally kept error detection to a minimum to make the code clearer as well. Please see the book's web-site (http://www.manning.com/back) to download the complete code examples.

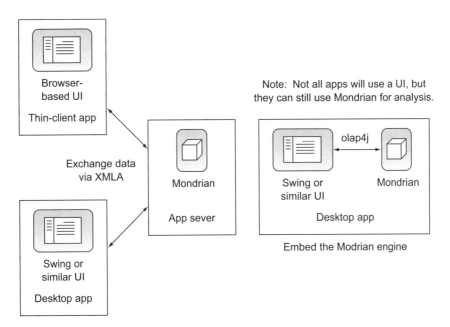

**Figure 10.1   Mondrian can be used from web and desktop clients via XMLA, and it can be embedded in Java applications.**

## 10.1   *Calling Mondrian from a thin client*

As we described, Mondrian can be invoked from both a thin client and desktop application. The techniques are similar but take different approaches. We'll first introduce XMLA to provide some background. Next, we'll describe how to invoke Mondrian as an XMLA service using JavaScript and Ajax. Finally we'll describe how to use an open source library, xmla4js, that makes working with XMLA easier. Though the xmla4js approach is simpler, it's worth understanding the more complex approach with straight XMLA since xmla4js assumes you understand the messages being passed.

### 10.1.1   *XML for Analysis (XMLA)*

*XML for Analysis (XMLA)* is a standard that allows systems to interact with OLAP servers via SOAP messages. XMLA was first proposed by Microsoft in 2000, and the XMLA council was formed in 2001. Since that time, most OLAP providers, including Mondrian, have added support for XMLA.

*SOAP,* which originally stood for Simple Object Access Protocol, is a message passing protocol designed for system-to-system communications. SOAP exchanges can be thought of as two friends sending letters back and forth. SOAP messages have an *envelope* that contains a header and a body. The content of the message is put into the *body* and is an XML document (listing 10.1). In our case, the message body will be our XMLA messages. The receiver of the message typically responds back with another SOAP message. SOAP message exchange is often implemented as an asynchronous communication using a JavaScript library such as jQuery. The sender won't wait for a response, but rather listens for one to show up. When the SOAP message is received, a function is called to handle the message and do something with it.

#### Listing 10.1   Basic SOAP message

```
<SOAP-ENV:Envelope
    xmlns:SOAP-ENV="http://schemas.xmlsoap.org/soap/envelope/"
    SOAP-ENV:encodingStyle="http://schemas.xmlsoap.org/soap/encoding/">
  <SOAP-ENV:Header />
  <SOAP-ENV:Body>
    XML message here
  </SOAP-ENV:Body>
</SOAP-ENV:Envelope>
```

XMLA consists of two types of messages: *discover messages* that allow the calling system to retrieve information about the data sources and cubes and *execute messages* that let the calling system execute remote MDX queries (figure 10.2). By using a series of messages, you can create applications that can interact with an XMLA server for analysis without writing your own analysis code. This allows you to support a variety of applications using the same back end. And since XMLA is a standard, you could potentially switch between vendors.

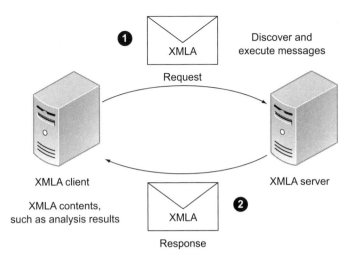

Figure 10.2  Exchanging
XMLA messages via SOAP

### 10.1.2  Configuring Mondrian as an XMLA web service

Before Mondrian can be used as an XMLA service, it has to be properly configured.
When Mondrian is deployed with Pentaho, it's already configured to be used as an XMLA
service. If you examine the pentaho-solutions/system/olap/datasources.xml file, you'll
see the configuration information for the data source. Listing 10.2 shows some of the
key values. The URL is the one you'll want to use when making connections to the XMLA
server. Note that you should pass the username and password for a valid user.

---

**Listing 10.2  Mondrian configuration in datasources.xml**

```
<DataSourceName>                                          ⟵── Name of data source
  Provider=Mondrian;DataSource=Pentaho
</DataSourceName>                              ⟵─┐ URL to call
<URL>
  http://localhost:8080/pentaho/Xmla?userid=joe&amp;password=password
</URL>
<DataSourceInfo>                                      ⟵── Information about data source
  Provider=mondrian
</DataSourceInfo>
<ProviderName>                              ⟵── Sets provider name
  PentahoXMLA
</ProviderName>
```

If you're deploying Mondrian as part of your own web application, the steps are similar to what the BI server does. You create a datasources.xml file in your web application WEB-INF directory. The format of the file is the same as the Pentaho one shown in
the preceding listing. You also configure the XMLA servlet in your web.xml configuration file, as shown in listing 10.3. Full details with an example can be found on the
Mondrian configuration page at http://mondrian.pentaho.com/documentation/
installation.php#5_How_to_configure_Mondrian_as_an_XMLA_provider.

**Listing 10.3   Mondrian configuration in web.xml**

```
<servlet>
  <servlet-name>MondrianXmlaServlet</servlet-name>
  <servlet-class>mondrian.xmla.impl.DefaultXmlaServlet</servlet-class>
</servlet>
```

Now that Mondrian is configured to provide XMLA services, the next step is to use the service. Using the service can be done using either JavaScript or olap4j. The next section will describe how to access the service using direct Ajax SOAP calls. After that we'll look at a library that makes it a lot simpler.

### 10.1.3   Calling XMLA services with Ajax

To learn how to use XMLA services in the thin clients, we'll first build a simple web page that will allow us to discover the available data sources from the Mondrian XMLA server and make analytical queries. We can use this knowledge to interface from a variety of clients. We'll base the interface on jQuery and Ajax, since that will allow us to create the type of dynamic interfaces that users have come to expect.

> **THIS IS THE HARD WAY**   This section provides you with the low-level details of how to use the XMLA service. If you prefer to use libraries and simplify your work, you can skip ahead to section 10.1.4.

#### CREATING THE THIN-CLIENT APPLICATION

The first thing to do is create an HTML page to define the layout of this application. Figure 10.3 shows the client proof of concept to be built. With this client, we'll be able to enter the URL for the Mondrian server along with a user-name and password and discover the available data sources and cubes. Once a data source is selected, we can enter an MDX query and get the results as a table of data. Although simple, this example shows how you can easily embed access to Mondrian in any thin client.

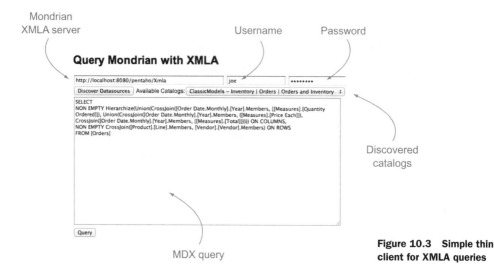

**Figure 10.3   Simple thin client for XMLA queries**

The solution consists of four files:

- *QueryXMLA.html*—An HTML document that defines the layout of the page
- *QueryXMLA.js*—A JavaScript file that uses jQuery and does the bulk of the work
- *XMLAResponse.js*—A JavaScript class that will aid in parsing responses from XMLA
- *QueryXMLA.css*—A cascading stylesheet to make the page look nice

Listing 10.4 shows the simplified HTML we use to lay out the page. JavaScript will populate the page as the user enters data and makes selections. The user first enters and selects values, then enters an MDX query, and then views the results of the query.

**Listing 10.4   HTML layout**

```html
<html>
  <head>
    <title>XMLA Query</title>
    <script src="jquery-1.7.2.js"></script>
    <script src="XMLAResponse.js"></script>
    <script src="QueryXMLA.js"></script>
  </head>
  <body>
    <h1>Query Mondrian with XMLA</h1>
    <form id="queryForm">                              ⟵┐ Form for XMLA
      <input type="text" name="serverURL" />              │ parameters
      <input type="text" name="userId" />
      <input type="password"name="password" />
      <input type="button" name="discoverButton" >
            value="Discover Datasources"/>
      Available Catalogs:<select id="catalogSelect"></select>   ⟵┐ User MDX
      <textarea type="textarea" name="mdxQuery"></textarea><br/>  ⟵┘ query
      <input type="button" name="queryButton" value="Query" />
    </form>
    <div>
      <table id="results">                   ⟵── Table for results
        <tbody></tbody>
      </table>
    </div>
    <div id="errors"></div>                   ⟵── Error messages
  </body>
</html>
```

**XMLA DISCOVERY**

Once the layout has been defined, the JavaScript that performs the work in the thin-client application needs to be written. Retrieving information about the data sources and cubes is done by sending a series of XMLA Discover messages. The end goal is to have enough information to be able to make MDX queries. To make MDX queries, we need the data source and the schema, also called a *catalog* in XMLA. To get this information, we send a series of three discover messages: DISCOVER_DATASOURCES, DBSCHEMA_CATALOGS, and MDSCHEMA_CUBES. Figure 10.4 shows the exchange of messages used to discover the data sources, catalogs, and cubes.

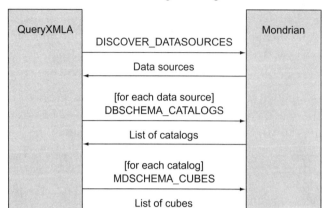

**Figure 10.4   SOAP message exchange for discovery**

Each of the discover messages is sent as a SOAP message. The message is embedded into the SOAP body, as shown earlier in listing 10.1. Listing 10.5 shows the messages sent to discover all of the cube information needed to make queries.

**Listing 10.5   Discover data sources query**

```
<Discover xmlns="urn:schemas-microsoft-com:xml-analysis">
  <RequestType>DISCOVER_DATASOURCES</RequestType>          ◁─┐ Discovers available
  <Restrictions>                                              │ data sources
    <RestrictionList/>
  </Restrictions>
  <Properties>
    <PropertyList>
      <Format>Tabular</Format>
    </PropertyList>
  </Properties>
</Discover>

<Discover xmlns="urn:schemas-microsoft-com:xml-analysis">   ┐ Discovers
  <RequestType>DBSCHEMA_CATALOGS</RequestType>          ◁──┘ available schemas
  <Restrictions />
  <Properties />
</Discover>

<Discover xmlns="urn:schemas-microsoft-com:xml-analysis">   ┐ Discovers
  <RequestType>MDSCHEMA_CUBES</RequestType>            ◁──┘ available cubes
  <Restrictions>
    <RestrictionList>
      <CATALOG_NAME>xxxCATALOGxxx</CATALOG_NAME>    ◁──── Catalog name
    </RestrictionList>
  </Restrictions>
  <Properties>
```

```
Data source    ⌐▷ <PropertyList>
 info from              <DataSourceInfo>xxxDATA_SOURCE_INFOxxx</DataSourceInfo>
    above              <Catalog>xxxCATALOGxxx</Catalog>                    ◁─────┐
                       <Format>Tabular</Format>                          | Catalog name
                  </PropertyList>
              </Properties>
          </Discover>
```

To make the call, the user will enter a URL and username and password and then click the Discover Datasources button. When the button is clicked, the application will retrieve the discover message defined here and will post the message to the XMLA server using a jQuery Ajax function.

To handle posting messages to the XMLA server, you can define a general purpose JavaScript function to be used each time you need to send a message. Listing 10.8 shows the function that will post messages using the jQuery Ajax call. This function takes three parameters. The first is the message to send to the XMLA server. The message must be a valid XMLA SOAP message. The second parameter is the type of content to send to the callback handler. The valid options are text or xml. Text is convenient for debugging or getting back generic content. Since the XMLA server returns SOAP messages, we'll generally specify XML. The third parameter is the function to call when the response is received from the XMLA server. We'll describe the format of this function in a bit.

Since XMLA is based on message passing, a few types of errors can occur. The first is general Ajax errors that can be handled with standard Ajax calls. The second is XMLA errors. If the message passed to the XMLA server isn't correct, then an error message will be returned. Listing 10.6 shows the general form of an error message. The main element to look for is the <error> element. If it exists, then this is an error message and the code and description elements will tell you what the error is.

---

**Listing 10.6   Example XMLA error**

```
<faultcode>SOAP-ENV:Server.00HSBE02</faultcode>
<faultstring>XMLA Discover unparse results error</faultstring>       ┌─ <error> element
<faultactor>Mondrian</faultactor>                                  ◁─┘  indicates an error
<detail>
  <XA:error xmlns:XA="http://mondrian.sourceforge.net">
    <code>00HSBE02</code>                                       ◁─── Error code
    <desc>Mondrian XMLA error message.</desc>                   ◁──┐
  </XA:error>                                                      | Error description
</detail>
```

To support error handling, we'll create a function to check for XMLA errors and let us know if one occurred. Listing 10.7 shows the code to check for an error (without the SOAP header information). If an error is found, an alert will be shown with the error, and the function will return true. The return value can then be used by callback functions to know if there was an error or if it has valid content to process.

**Listing 10.7  Function to check for XMLA errors**

```
function checkForXMLAError (response) {
  var hasError = false;
  $(response).find('error').each (function() {          Check for <error>
    hasError = true;                                    element
    var code = $(this).find('code').text();            Get error code
    var desc = $(this).find('desc').text();
    alert ('found an error (' + code + '): ' + desc);   Get description
  });
  return hasError;
}
```

In order to post a message to the server, it's necessary that the URL be set. The post-Message function will verify that a URL has been entered, as shown in the following listing. It's up to the user to make sure that the URL is correct. Mondrian also allows you to pass a user ID and password when making XMLA calls, so the postMessage function will add those if they're provided.

**Listing 10.8  Function to post XMLA SOAP messages via Ajax**

```
function postMessage (message, returnDataType, successCallback) {
  var baseURL  = queryFormElement("serverURL").val();   Get URL and
  var userid   = queryFormElement("userId").val();      parameters
  var password = queryFormElement("password").val();

  if (baseURL == '') {
    alert ('Error: you must set the server URL prior to any calls');
    return;
  }                                                      Verify URL exists

  var url = baseURL + "?";                               Add user ID and
  if (userid != '') { url += "userid=" + userid + "&";}  password
  if (password != '') {url += "password=" + password;}

  $.ajax({                            POST using Ajax
    type: 'POST',
    url: url,
    contentType: "text/xml",
    data: message,
    success: successCallback,
    dataType: returnDataType
  });
}
```

Once the message has been successfully sent, the results need to be handled in the callback function. jQuery Ajax callback functions take three parameters: the data returned from the call (either text or an XML DOM object), a text status indicating whether the Ajax call succeeded, and a jQuery object that contains information about the query. For our program we're only going to use the data. Note that the success text will indicate success if the Ajax query was successful even if the XMLA query wasn't.

The data source information callback will provide the data source information. Theoretically, multiple data sources can be returned, but in the case of Mondrian embedded inside of Pentaho, only a single data source is returned so a single object is sufficient to hold the data.

Listing 10.9 shows a partial example of the content of the SOAP message returned. The data source information is listed inside of a row element. The data source info is the primary data that we'll need, but we'll go ahead and save all of the information returned in case we want to display or use it later.

**Listing 10.9    Content of a discover response message**

```
<row>
  <DataSourceName>
    Provider=Mondrian;DataSource=Pentaho          Name of
  </DataSourceName>                               data source
  <DataSourceDescription>
    Pentaho BI Platform Datasources
  </DataSourceDescription>                         Same URL
  <URL>                                            we called,
    http://localhost:8080/pentaho/Xmla?userid=joe&password=password   but doesn't
  </URL>                                           have to be
  <DataSourceInfo>
    Provider=Mondrian;DataSource=Pentaho          Usually same
  </DataSourceInfo>                               as the name
  <ProviderName>
    PentahoXMLA
  </ProviderName>
  <ProviderType>
    MDP
  </ProviderType>
  <AuthenticationMode>
    Unauthenticated
  </AuthenticationMode>
</row>
```

Listing 10.10 shows the callback function that's called when the response to DISCOVER_DATASOURCES is received. It parses the response and saves the information to the data source object. It also clears the catalogs object in case there were earlier queries. Finally it calls to get the catalog information.

**Listing 10.10    Callback function for handling discover data source messages**

```
function handleDiscoverCallback (data, textStatus, jqXHR) {
  if (checkForXMLAError(data) == true) {return;}          Stop on
                                                          errors
  $("#datasourcesSelect").html("");
  datasource = {};
  catalogs = {};

  $(data).find('row').each(function() {          Each row is a data source

    datasource.dataSourceName        =          Get data source properties
      $(this).find('DataSourceName').text();
    datasource.dataSourceDescription
```

```
      = $(this).find('DataSourceDescription').text();
    datasource.url
      = $(this).find('URL').text();
    datasource.dataSourceInfo
      = $(this).find('DataSourceInfo').text();
    datasource.providerName
      = $(this).find('ProviderName').text();
    datasource.providerType
      = $(this).find('ProviderType').text();
    datasource.authenticationMode
      = $(this).find('AuthenticationMode').text();

    postMessage(getDiscoverCatalogsMessage(), 'xml',            ◁──┐ Get catalogs
      function(catalogData, catalogTextStatus, jqXHR) {            └─ for data source
        $(catalogData).find('row').each(function() {            ◁── Handles return message
          var catalogName = $(this).find('CATALOG_NAME').text();
          postMessage(                                          ◁── Get cubes for catalog
            getDiscoverCubesMessage(
              datasource.dataSourceInfo, catalogName),
            'xml', handleDiscoverCube);
        });
      });
    });
}
```

The calls to discover the catalogs (Mondrian schemas) and cubes for each catalog provide the data needed to select the schema for the query. Listing 10.11 shows the message used to retrieve the catalogs. The response to this query is a set of catalogs available for requests. Each of the catalogs can then be used to find the cubes for the query.

**Listing 10.11   XMLA query to discover catalogs**

```
var discoverCatalogsQuery =
'<Discover xmlns="urn:schemas-microsoft-com:xml-analysis">
   <RequestType>DBSCHEMA_CATALOGS</RequestType>         ◁── Discovery type
   <Restrictions />                                  ◁──┐ No restrictions
   <Properties />                                       └─ or properties
</Discover>';

function getDiscoverCatalogsMessage() {
  return getSOAPMessage(discoverCatalogsQuery);        ◁── Send message
}
```

Listing 10.12 shows the body of the response back from the XMLA server. Several additional properties are returned, but these are the main ones we're interested in for now. They allow us to provide the name and description for the interface and make MDX query calls. Each row contains information about a different catalog that can contain cubes.

**Listing 10.12   XMLA response for discover DBSCHEMA_CATALOGS query**

```
<row>
  <CATALOG_NAME>ClassicModels</CATALOG_NAME>          ◁── Schema name
```

```
<DESCRIPTION>No description available</DESCRIPTION>   ◁—— Description
  <ROLES/>                                            ◁—┐
</row>                                                   │ Defined roles,
<row>                                                    │ if any
  <CATALOG_NAME>SampleData</CATALOG_NAME>
  <DESCRIPTION>No description available</DESCRIPTION>
  <ROLES/>
</row>
<row>
  <CATALOG_NAME>SteelWheels</CATALOG_NAME>
  <DESCRIPTION>No description available</DESCRIPTION>
  <ROLES/>
</row>
```

Listing 10.13 shows the calls to get the cubes for a given catalog. Note that the data source information and the catalog must be included in the message. This message is sent for each catalog.

**Listing 10.13   XMLA query to discover cubes for a given catalog**

```
var discoverCubesQuery =
'<Discover xmlns="urn:schemas-microsoft-com:xml-analysis">
   <RequestType>MDSCHEMA_CUBES</RequestType>          ◁—— Discover cubes
   <Restrictions>
      <RestrictionList>
         <CATALOG_NAME>xxxCATALOGxxx</CATALOG_NAME>   ◁—— Restrict catalog returned
      </RestrictionList>
   </Restrictions>
   <Properties>
      <PropertyList>
         <DataSourceInfo>xxxDATA_SOURCE_INFOxxx</DataSourceInfo>  ◁—— Data source info
         <Catalog>xxxCATALOGxxx</Catalog>             ◁—┐
         <Format>Tabular</Format>                        │ Catalog to get cubes for
      </PropertyList>
   </Properties>
</Discover>';

function getDiscoverCubesMessage (dataSourceInfo, catalog) {
  return getSOAPMessage(discoverCubesQuery
    .replace(/xxxDATA_SOURCE_INFOxxx/g, dataSourceInfo)
    .replace(/xxxCATALOGxxx/g, catalog));
}
```

A response like that shown in listing 10.14 is returned for the discover message. Each row is a cube for the given catalog (schema). Each cube can be used for analysis queries.

**Listing 10.14   XMLA response for discover MDSCHEMA_CUBES query**

```
<row>                                                 │ Catalog name
  <CATALOG_NAME>ClassicModels</CATALOG_NAME>          ◁—┘
  <CUBE_NAME>Inventory</CUBE_NAME>                    ◁—— Cube name for query
  <CUBE_CAPTION>Inventory</CUBE_CAPTION>
  <DESCRIPTION>ClassicModels Schema - Inventory Cube</DESCRIPTION>
</row>
```

```
<row>
  <CATALOG_NAME>ClassicModels</CATALOG_NAME>
  <CUBE_NAME>Orders</CUBE_NAME>
  <CUBE_CAPTION>Orders</CUBE_CAPTION>                    Caption for display
  <DESCRIPTION>ClassicModels Schema - Orders Cube</DESCRIPTION>
</row>
```

As each response to the MDSCHEMA_CUBES message is received, the handle-
DiscoverCube function (listing 10.15) is called with the results. This will check each
row and store the properties of the catalog and cube. This information will be needed
for the user to execute queries later.

**Listing 10.15   Function to handle MDSCHEMA_CUBES response**

```
function handleDiscoverCube(cubeData, textStatus, jqXHR) {

  if (checkForXMLAError(cubeData) == true) {return;}    ◁——— Stop on errors

  $(cubeData).find('row').each (function () {           ◁——— Each row is a cube
    var catalogName = $(this).find('CATALOG_NAME').text();  ◁—
    var cubeName = $(this).find('CUBE_NAME').text();          │  Get cube properties
    var description = $(this).find('DESCRIPTION').text();

    var catalog = catalogs[catalogName];
    if (catalog == null) {
      catalog = new Object();                           ◁——— New catalog, create new
      catalog.catalogName = catalogName;
      catalog.cubes = new Array();
      catalogs[catalogName] = catalog;
    }
    catalog.cubes.push(cubeName);                       ◁——— Add cube to catalog

    setCatalogSelect();                                 ◁——— Update select element
  });
}
```

Once the cubes have been processed and added to the list of catalogs, the select input
is updated with the list of catalogs and cubes as shown in listing 10.16. A complete
update needs to be made each time, because the user could've pointed to a different
XMLA server. At this point the user has a populated list of cubes to use for querying. In
the next section we'll see how to create and send the queries.

**Listing 10.16   Function to set the catalogs and cubes to select**

```
function setCatalogSelect() {
  var html = "";
  for (var catalogName in catalogs) {                  ◁——— Each catalog
    var catalog = catalogs[catalogName];                   │  Get catalog
    var cubes      = catalog.cubes;                     ◁——— Get cubes

    html += "<option value='" + catalogName + "'>" +   ◁——— Add select option
              catalogName + " - " + cubes.join(" | ") +
            "</option>";
```

```
    }
    $("#catalogSelect").html(html);                    ⟵── Add to page

}
```

**EXECUTING XMLA QUERIES**

Now that we have all the information needed to execute a query, the application user can enter straight MDX queries and run them. Listing 10.17 shows the message that's sent to the XMLA server and the JavaScript function used to get the message. The *xxxMDX_STATEMENTxxx* will be replaced with the actual MDX query entered by the user. The data source info and catalog information are set from values retrieved and chosen earlier.

**Listing 10.17   Execute MDX query message**

```
var executeQuery =
'<Execute xmlns="urn:schemas-microsoft-com:xml-analysis">   ⟵── Execute message

    <Command>
        <Statement>xxxMDX_STATEMENTxxx</Statement>        ⟵── MDX query
    </Command>
    <Properties>
        <PropertyList>
            <DataSourceInfo>xxxDATASOURCE_INFOxxx</DataSourceInfo>  ⟵┘ Data source info
            <Catalog>xxxCATALOGxxx</Catalog>              ⟵── Catalog name
            <Format>Multidimensional</Format>             ⟵┐
            <AxisFormat>TupleFormat</AxisFormat>          │ Result and axis format
        </PropertyList>
    </Properties>
</Execute>';
/
```

When the user clicks the Query button, the code checks that a query of some sort has been entered. If not, the user gets an error message and no query is made. Assuming a query has been entered, an Ajax call is made to the XMLA server as shown in listing 10.18.

**Listing 10.18   Execute MDX query**

```
function getQueryMessage (mdxQuery, dataSourceInfo, catalog) {
    return getSOAPMessage(                                    ⟵── Send query
        executeQuery.replace(/xxxMDX_STATEMENTxxx/g, mdxQuery)
                  .replace(/xxxDATASOURCE_INFOxxx/g, dataSourceInfo)
                  .replace(/xxxCATALOGxxx/g, catalog)
    );
}
```

**DISPLAYING THE RESULTS**

After studying the return results from the query, it should be apparent that parsing the results is going to be complex. So we'll put the code for parsing the query results into its own class to make it easier to understand, and we can potentially reuse it in future projects. Two major steps are involved: parse the column and row headers, and parse the data. We'll create a new JavaScript class called XMLAResponse to parse the response and provide access to the headers and the data. Listing 10.19 shows the new class with a constructor.

**Listing 10.19   Class to parse XMLA response**

```
function XMLAResponse(XMLAContent) {
    this.rowHeaders = new Array();
    this.colHeaders = new Array();
    this.cellData = new Array();

    this.parseHeaders(XMLAContent);
    this.parseData(XMLAContent);
}
```

**Array of arrays, one per row of data**

When the class is created, the XML content is passed to the class. The class has three arrays to hold the row and column headers and the data returned. The class then calls to parse the headers and the data so they're available to the user of the class. The headers and data arrays hold an array of values for each row so that they can be easily processed as shown in figure 10.5.

Two rows of column headers.

Two rows of column headers.

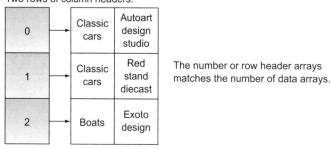

The number or row header arrays matches the number of data arrays.

Six columns of data matching number of column headers.

| 0 | 337 | $166.55 | $56,128 | 416 | $174.63 | $72,644 |
| 1 | 312 | $117.08 | $36,530 | 369 | $120.12 | $44,324 |
| 2 | 284 | $87.57 | $24,869 | 473 | $89.82 | $42,486 |

**Figure 10.5   Table of query results**

Listing 10.20 shows the format of the axes returned. Of interest to us are the level and the caption. In this example, the levels are lined neatly, but that isn't always the case. Sometimes the levels have a single value followed by multiple values for lower levels. The solution is to check the level and make sure captions are at the proper level for all of the columns and rows.

**Listing 10.20   XMLA response axis headers**

```
<Axes>
  <Axis name="Axis0">                          ⟵── Rows axis
    <Tuples>
      <Tuple>
        <Member Hierarchy="Product.Product">    ⟵── Hierarchy name
          <Caption>Classic Cars</Caption>        ⟵
          <LName>[Product].[Line]</LName>        ⟵      Caption
        </Member>                                    Level
        <Member Hierarchy="Scale.Scale">
          <Caption>1:10</Caption>
          <LName>[Scale].[Scale]</LName>
        </Member>
      </Tuple>
      <Tuple>
        <Member Hierarchy="Product.Product">
          <Caption>Classic Cars</Caption>
          <LName>[Product].[Line]</LName>
        </Member>
        <Member Hierarchy="Scale.Scale">
          <Caption>1:12</Caption>
          <LName>[Scale].[Scale]</LName>
        </Member>
      </Tuple>
    </Tuples>
  </Axis>
  <Axis name="Axis1">                          ⟵── Columns axis
    <Tuples>
      <Tuple>
        <Member Hierarchy="Vendor.Vendor">
          <Caption>Autoart Studio Design</Caption>
          <LName>[Vendor].[Vendor]</LName>
        </Member>
        <Member Hierarchy="Order Month.Month">
          <Caption>January</Caption>
          <LName>[Month].[Month]</LName>
        </Member>
        <Member Hierarchy="Measures">
          <Caption>Quantity Ordered</Caption>
          <LName>[Measures].[MeasuresLevel]</LName>
        </Member>
      </Tuple>
      <Tuple>
        <Member Hierarchy="Vendor.Vendor">
          <Caption>Autoart Studio Design</Caption>
          <LName>[Vendor].[Vendor]</LName>
        </Member>
```

```
        <Member Hierarchy="Order Month.Month">
          <Caption>January</Caption>
          <LName>[Month].[Month]</LName>
        </Member>
        <Member Hierarchy="Measures">
          <Caption>Price Each</Caption>
          <LName>[Measures].[MeasuresLevel]</LName>
        </Member>
      </Tuple>
    </Tuples>
  </Axis>
</Axes>
```

Listing 10.21 shows the parsing of the headers. The code reads the tuples from each axis to get the level and caption. It then finds the correct level in the header and gets the caption for that level. By definition in MDX, columns are axis 0 and rows are axis 1. You can theoretically have more than two axes, but that's difficult to display in two dimensions, so the typical approach when presenting the data is to only handle two axes and put them into a table. For this reason any axis above two will be ignored. Since the values for the headers are returned the same way for all axes, we can rotates the headers for the row to convert from column form to row form as shown in listing 10.22.

#### Listing 10.21  Parse the row and column headers

```
XMLAResponse.prototype.parseHeaders = function(XMLAContent) {
  var axisCount = 0;

  var xr = this;                                      ◁─┐ "this" is contextual so
                                                         │ keep reference to object
  $(XMLAContent).find("Axis").each(function() {
    var lname = "";
    axisCount++;

    var levelNames = new Array();                      ─┐ First axis is columns,
    var headers;                                     ◁──┘ second is rows
    if      (axisCount == 1) headers = xr.colHeaders;
    else if (axisCount == 2) headers = xr.rowHeaders;
    else {                                            ◁─┐ Only allow two
      return;                                           │ axes for tables
    }

    var currentLevel;
    var level;

    $(this).find("Tuple").each(function() {           ─┐ Each member
      $(this).find("Member").each(function() {      ◁──┘ is a value
        var caption = $(this).find("Caption").text();
        var newlname = $(this).find("LName").text();
        if (newlname != currentLevel) {              ◁── Different level
          level = xr.findHeaderLevel(levelNames, headers, newlname);
        }
        level.push(caption);                        ◁── Add caption value to level
      });
```

```
    });
    if (axisCount == 2) xr.rotateRowHeaders();        ◁─── Rotate row headers
  });
}
```

**Listing 10.22  Rotate the row headers**

```
XMLAResponse.prototype.rotateRowHeaders = function () {        ┐ Create new array
  var nbrOldHeaders = this.rowHeaders.length;                 │ of correct size
  if (nbrOldHeaders > 0) {                              ◁─────┘
    var newRowHeaders = new Array();
    var newLength = this.rowHeaders[0].length;
    for (var cnt = 0; cnt < newLength; cnt++) {
      newRowHeaders.push(new Array());
    }
    for (var rcnt = 0; rcnt < nbrOldHeaders; rcnt++) {        ◁─── Copy header values
      for (var ccnt = 0; ccnt < newLength; ccnt++) {
        newRowHeaders[ccnt].push(this.rowHeaders[rcnt][ccnt]);
      }
    }
    this.rowHeaders = newRowHeaders;                          ◁─── Set row header
  }
}
```

Finding the correct level in the data has to account for both new levels and jagged headers, as shown in listing 10.23. First the code checks through the levels to see if this is one of the existing levels. Once the level is found, all of the levels are made to be the same length. This is done by populating any shorter rows with the same value. Finally, if this is a new level, it's created and added to the levels to be used for future values. The current level is returned to let the value be added.

**Listing 10.23  Find the right level**

```
XMLAResponse.prototype.findHeaderLevel =
  function (levelNames, headers, newlname) {

  var level = null;                                     ◁─── Find level by name
  for (var cnt = 0; cnt < levelNames.length; cnt++) {
    if (newlname == levelNames[cnt]) {
      level = headers[cnt];
      break;
    }
  }

  if (headers.length > 0) {                             ◁─── Make higher rows same size
    var max = headers[headers.length - 1].length;
    for (cnt = headers.length - 2; cnt >= 0; cnt -= 1) {
      var row = headers[cnt];
      var lval = row[row.length - 1];
      while (row.length < max) {
        row.push(lval);                                 ◁─── Copy current value
      }
    }
  }
```

```
    if (!level) {                              ◁——  Create and add new level
      level = new Array();
      headers.push(level);
      levelNames.push(newlname);
    }

    return level;

}
```

Now that the headers have been properly handled, the cell values need to be read and put into the right location. The data's complexity comes from the fact that it's all in one, flat list. It's up to the receiver to figure out how to handle the data. Also, only the cells that have values are returned—empty cells aren't. Rather, a CellOrdinal value is returned that tells where the data belongs.

There are two ways that the data can be populated. One alternative is to parse through the data and fill the arrays as data is read. This approach would mean that each cell is populated once. But it makes the code fairly complex and difficult to maintain. An easier if less computationally efficient approach as shown in listing 10.24. First create the arrays for the data and prepopulate them with blanks. Then use the Cell-Ordinal value to put the cell into the correct row and column, since a value now exists for each cell.

**Listing 10.24   Parse the data**

```
XMLAResponse.prototype.parseData = function(XMLAContent) {
  var cnt = 0;
  var rowLength = this.colHeaders[0].length;
  var data = this.cellData;

  for (var rcnt = 0; rcnt < this.rowHeaders.length; rcnt++) {
    var row = new Array();                              ◁┐  Create data
    data.push(row);                                     │   with blanks
    for (var ccnt = 0; ccnt < rowLength; ccnt++) {
      row.push("");
    }
  }

  $(XMLAContent).find("Cell").each(function() {         ◁——  Process all data cells
    var value = $(this).find("FmtValue").text();
    var cellOrdinalValue = $(this).attr("CellOrdinal");
    var cloc = cellOrdinalValue % rowLength;            ◁——  Calculate column
    var rloc = Math.floor(cellOrdinalValue / rowLength); ◁┐
    data[rloc][cloc] = value;                           │   Calculate row
  });
}
```

The final step is to display the results to the user, as shown in listing 10.25. First the columns headers are added, leaving spaces for each of the row headers. Then the row headers followed by data are added. The final result is a table of all the data returned from the query. Figure 10.6 shows the final results for the user.

**Listing 10.25   Show query results**

```
function handleQueryCallback (data, textStatus, jqXHR) {
  if (checkForXMLAError(data) == true) {
    return;                                  ⟵─── Stop on MDX error
  }

  var response = new XMLAResponse(data);
                                        ┐  Clear previous results
  $("#results tr").remove();            ⟵─┘
  for (var ccnt = 0; ccnt < response.colHeaders.length; ccnt++) {   ┐ Row for each
    var row = "<tr>";                                            ⟵─┘ column header
    var ch = response.colHeaders[ccnt];
    for (var rcnt = 0; rcnt < response.rowHeaders[0].length; rcnt++) {
      row += "<th></th>";                       ⟵─┐ Blanks for
    }                                              ┘ row headers
    for (var ccnt2 = 0; ccnt2 < ch.length; ccnt2++) {   ⟵─┐
      row += "<th>" + ch[ccnt2] + "</th>";                │
    }                                              Add column
    row += "</tr>";                                header value
    $("#results > tbody:last").append(row);
  }

  for (var rcnt = 0; rcnt < response.rowHeaders.length; rcnt++) {
    var rh = response.rowHeaders[rcnt];
    var data = response.cellData[rcnt];
    row = "<tr>";                          ⟵─── Each row of data

    for (rcnt2 = 0; rcnt2 < rh.length; rcnt2++) {   ⟵─── Add row header
      row += "<th>" + rh[rcnt2] + "</th>";
    }
    for (dcnt = 0; dcnt < data.length; dcnt++) {    ⟵─── Add data value
      row += "<td>" + data[dcnt] + "</td>";
    }
    row += "</tr>";
    $("#results > tbody:last").append(row);
  }

}
```

| | | 2003 | 2003 | 2003 | 2004 | 2004 | 2004 |
| --- | --- | --- | --- | --- | --- | --- | --- |
| | | Quantity Ordered | Price Each | Total | Quantity Ordered | Price Each | Total |
| Classic Cars | Autoart Studio Design | 337 | $166.55 | $56,128.02 | 416 | $174.63 | $72,644.00 |
| Classic Cars | Carousel DieCast Legends | 1,043 | $55.02 | $57,390.73 | 1,320 | $56.42 | $74,472.97 |
| Classic Cars | Classic Metal Creations | 2,056 | $122.40 | $251,644.12 | 2,601 | $121.25 | $315,372.32 |
| Classic Cars | Exoto Designs | 983 | $96.47 | $94,828.37 | 1,183 | $98.73 | $116,802.81 |
| Classic Cars | Gearbox Collectibles | 1,746 | $113.83 | $198,747.18 | 2,147 | $115.14 | $247,203.40 |
| Classic Cars | Highway 66 Mini Classics | 639 | $87.28 | $55,771.60 | 930 | $84.14 | $78,247.97 |
| Classic Cars | Min Lin Diecast | 1,009 | $108.44 | $109,420.67 | 1,255 | $111.62 | $140,079.37 |
| Classic Cars | Motor City Art Classics | 349 | $123.31 | $43,034.03 | 463 | $124.83 | $57,795.63 |
| Classic Cars | Red Start Diecast | 312 | $117.08 | $36,530.21 | 369 | $120.12 | $44,324.28 |
| Classic Cars | Second Gear Diecast | 1,288 | $124.10 | $159,835.72 | 1,932 | $132.32 | $255,648.07 |
| Classic Cars | Studio M Art Models | 610 | $67.66 | $41,271.99 | 682 | $69.02 | $47,073.81 |
| Classic Cars | Unimax Art Galleries | 1,000 | $123.89 | $123,894.33 | 1,123 | $125.36 | $140,779.92 |
| Classic Cars | Welly Diecast Productions | 1,390 | $99.84 | $138,774.75 | 1,664 | $101.58 | $169,023.46 |
| Motorcycles | Autoart Studio Design | 684 | $87.35 | $59,750.06 | 884 | $88.22 | $77,989.20 |
| Motorcycles | Exoto Designs | 284 | $87.57 | $24,869.88 | 473 | $89.82 | $42,486.68 |
| Motorcycles | Gearbox Collectibles | 290 | $36.65 | $10,629.79 | 414 | $36.36 | $15,053.68 |
| Motorcycles | Highway 66 Mini Classics | 921 | $79.37 | $73,102.84 | 1,391 | $79.31 | $110,319.86 |

**Figure 10.6   Table of query results**

Now we're satisfied with our prototype and understand what needs to be done for thin clients. A large part of the work was creating and sending standard SOAP messages. This seems to be a common requirement for many developers. When there's a common technical problem, there's often a common technical solution. The next section will describe just such a solution for XMLA.

### 10.1.4 XMLA for JavaScript (xmla4js)

If you do research into XMLA for reusable libraries, you'll find xmla4js. Xmla4js is a JavaScript library that wraps the effort of interacting with XMLA. Although you need to understand the messages to call and the properties to set, you no longer need to create and parse SOAP messages. Since this approach sounds good, we can head to http://code.google.com/p/xmla4js/ and download the library and documentation. Now we can rework the original prototype, but using xmla4js. Though you could write your own library, having one that has been tested and is community supported makes a lot of sense and can save you a lot of development and testing efforts.

Since we're replacing the original prototype, we can reuse the same HTML and CSS. We'll also use jQuery as we did in the previous example. But we can replace the XMLAResponse class by using xmla4js.

The first step is to replace the code that gets the cubes to populate the selection for the user. After a user enters the URL, username, and password as before, they can click the Discover Datasources button. Before using xmla4js, this process involved formatting SOAP messages, sending the messages, handling the callbacks, and parsing XML documents. As you can see from listing 10.26, the code is now much simpler.

---

**Listing 10.26  Get catalogs and cubes**

```
queryFormElement("discoverButton").click(function() {
  xmla = new Xmla({url: getServiceURL()});

  datasource =                                                    Get available
    xmla.discoverDataSources().fetchAsObject();                   data sources
  var catalogs =
    xmla.discoverDBCatalogs().fetchAllAsObject();      ⟵── Get catalogs

  catalogsAndCubes = {}; // clear any previous.

  for (var cnt = 0; cnt < catalogs.length; cnt++) {   ⟵── For each catalog...
    var catalogName = catalogs[cnt].CATALOG_NAME;
    var cubesRS = xmla.discoverMDCubes({                  ⟵── ...get all cubes
      properties : {DataSourceInfo : datasource.DataSourceInfo,
                    Catalog : catalogName},
      restrictions : {CATALOG_NAME : catalogName}
    });

    var cubes = cubesRS.fetchAllAsObject();                       For each
    for (var cubeCnt = 0; cubeCnt < cubes.length; cubeCnt++) {  ⟵── cube...
      var cubeName = cubes[cubeCnt].CUBE_NAME;
      var catalog = catalogsAndCubes[catalogName];
```

```
      if (catalog == null) {
        catalog = new Object();                      ⟵— ...add catalog...
        catalog.catalogName = catalogName;
        catalog.cubes = new Array();
        catalogsAndCubes[catalogName] = catalog;
      }
      catalog.cubes.push(cubeName);                 ⟵— ...add cube to catalog
    }
  }
  setCatalogSelect();                      ⟵— Update select with cubes and catalogs

});
```

Xmla4js makes the discover process straightforward. Each discovery is basically one line of code. Though Xmla4js supports both synchronous and asynchronous calls, it makes the code cleaner to use synchronous calls. This is especially nice since we need the data for future calls. We can reuse the same selection code as the previous prototype to set the select options.

Now the user can select the cube to use and enter a query. Listing 10.27 shows the code that gets executed when the user clicks the Query button. First the values set by the user are retrieved. Then a single call is made to execute the query and return the value as tabular results. Tabular results are easy to put into a table, which is our goal.

**Listing 10.27 Execute the MDX query**

```
var mdxQuery = $("#queryForm").find('textarea[name=mdxQuery]').val();    ⟵┐
var dataSourceInfo = datasource.DataSourceInfo;
var catalog = catalogsAndCubes[$("#catalogSelect").val()].catalogName;   │

var resultsRS = xmla.executeTabular({   ⟵ Execute            Get user-
  statement : mdxQuery,                   query              provided
  properties : {                                            parameters
    DataSourceInfo : dataSourceInfo,
    Catalog : catalog
  }
});
```

Among the various data returned as part of the results are the field names that specify the columns and rows. Handling the field names is probably the most difficult part of the effort, whereas handling the data is straightforward. Listing 10.28 shows the code that retrieves the field names and adds them to the results. First it calls to get the fields from the results and calls a function that parses the header data. Finally, the headers are dynamically added to the HTML document.

**Listing 10.28 Execute the MDX query**

```
var fieldNames = resultsRS.getFieldNames();          ⟵— Get headers

var headers = parseFieldNames(fieldNames);           ⟵— Parse headers
```

```
$("#results tr").remove();
for (var hcnt = 0; hcnt < headers.length; hcnt++) {          ⟵— Add header rows
  var row = "<tr>";
  var h = headers[hcnt];
  for (var ccnt = 0; ccnt < h.length; ccnt++) {
    row += "<th>" + h[ccnt] + "</th>";
  }
  row += "</tr>";
  $("#results > tbody:last").append(row);
}
```

Parsing the headers is the most difficult part of this effort. This is because the headers
are returned as a single array with the full path to indicate which column they
apply to. For example, a member caption has the form `[dimension].[level]`
`.[MEMBER_CAPTION]` and a column header has the form `[level].[member]`
`.[level].[member]....` Headers in OLAP are generally more complex than dealing
with headers in a JDBC result set because OLAP is multidimensional, whereas JDBC is tabular (two dimensional). Listing 10.29 shows the code to parse the field names and put
them into a set of arrays where each array is a row of headers that can be displayed.

**Listing 10.29   Parse field names**

```
function parseFieldNames (fieldNames) {
  var rowHeaders = [];
  var colHeaders = [];                                  Parse all headers

  for (var fcnt = 0; fcnt < fieldNames.length; fcnt++) {  ⟵                 Parse row
    if (fieldNames[fcnt].indexOf("MEMBER_CAPTION") != -1) {  ⟵              header
      rowHeaders[rowHeaders.length] = splitField (fieldNames[fcnt]);
    }                                                     Parse column header
    else {                                              ⟵
      colHeaders[colHeaders.length] = splitField (fieldNames[fcnt]);
    }
  }
                                                          Number of
  var nbrColHeaderLevels = colHeaders[0].length;        ⟵ rows to return
  var headers = [];                                     ⟵

                                                        Header rows to return
  for (hcnt = 0; hcnt < nbrColHeaderLevels; hcnt++) {
    headers[headers.length] = [];                         ⟵— New header row

    var lastRow = (hcnt == nbrColHeaderLevels - 1);
    for (rhcnt = 0; rhcnt < rowHeaders.length; rhcnt++) {  ⟵— Add row header...
      if (lastRow) {
        headers[hcnt].push(rowHeaders[rhcnt][0]);       ⟵— ... but only to last row
      }
      else {
        headers[hcnt].push("");
      }
    }

    for (ccnt = 0; ccnt < colHeaders.length; ccnt++) {    ⟵— Add column headers
```

```
        headers[hcnt].push(colHeaders[ccnt][hcnt]);
    }
  }

  return headers;
}
```

In the previous example there was a call to split the fields. This is because the format needs to be broken up to create multiple header cells based on the number of levels. Listing 10.30 shows the JavaScript to parse the field. First the outside brackets are removed, then the fields are split on the ].[ separator. This results in a set of fields. Only the odd-numbered fields are needed for display, so they're added to the output and returned.

**Listing 10.30   Parse individual field**

```
function splitField (field) {
  var fieldNames = [];

  var f = field.substr(1, field.length-2);          ◁─── Strip outer
                                                          brackets
  var fieldTokens = f.split("].[");                 ◁─── Split fields

  for (var fcnt = 1;                                ◁─── Get odd tokens

      fcnt < fieldTokens.length;
      fcnt += 2) {
    fieldNames[fieldNames.length] = fieldTokens[fcnt];
  }
  return fieldNames;
}
```

The last step is to add the results to the form. The results can be returned as an array of rows, making it simple to add them. The following listing shows how to add the results after fetching them as an array.

**Listing 10.31   Add results data**

```
var resArray = resultsRS.fetchAllAsArray();       ◁─── Get results data
for (var rcnt = 0; rcnt < resArray.length; rcnt++) {   ◁─┐
  row = "<tr>";                                          │ Add data to form
  var r = resArray[rcnt];
  for (var ccnt = 0; ccnt < r.length; ccnt++) {
    row += "<td>" + r[ccnt] + "</td>";
  }
  row += "</tr>";
  $("#results > tbody:last").append(row);
}
```

And that's it! Using xmla4js dramatically simplified the effort of retrieving data from XMLA. Figure 10.7 shows the results. As you can see, they look basically the same as the longer effort that we previously performed.

| Line | MeasuresLevel | APAC 2003 | APAC 2004 | APAC 2005 | EMEA 2003 | EMEA 2004 | EMEA 2005 | Japan 2003 | Japan 2004 | Japan 2005 | NA 2003 | NA 2004 | NA 2005 |
|---|---|---|---|---|---|---|---|---|---|---|---|---|---|
| Classic Cars | Quantity | 1052 | 1785 | 1015 | 5853 | 8976 | 3463 | 898 | 307 | 122 | 4959 | 5017 | 2105 |
| Motorcycles | Quantity | 654 | 540 | 658 | 1428 | 2177 | 1501 | 205 | 380 | 44 | 1744 | 2809 | 568 |
| Planes | Quantity | 456 | 723 | 151 | 1723 | 2326 | 1464 | 677 | 547 | null | 977 | 2224 | 592 |
| Ships | Quantity | null | 396 | 32 | 1968 | 2144 | 696 | 174 | 127 | 81 | 702 | 1642 | 537 |
| Trains | Quantity | 33 | 106 | null | 384 | 977 | 183 | 174 | null | 49 | 409 | 326 | 177 |
| Trucks and Buses | Quantity | 91 | 801 | 488 | 2261 | 1558 | 836 | 415 | 102 | null | 1289 | 2563 | 597 |
| Vintage Cars | Quantity | 1243 | 1587 | 1067 | 3094 | 5472 | 1094 | 308 | 229 | 84 | 3268 | 3576 | 1871 |

**Figure 10.7  xmla4js query results**

Although many other things can be done with XMLA and xmla4js, we've seen the basics of how to integrate with XMLA via a thin client. Though xmla4js was much simpler, the lessons learned from writing SOAP messages were useful for understanding the process better. Now we're ready to tackle integrating with Mondrian from a desktop application, which we'll cover in the next section. Though you'd probably want to start with xmla4js, hopefully you have a better understanding of what xmla4js is doing when you make calls.

## 10.2   *Calling Mondrian from a Java application*

Now that we've seen how to connect to Mondrian via XMLA using thin-client applications, we'll look at how to connect to Mondrian from Java applications. Though you could create an application that exchanges XMLA SOAP messages with Mondrian, there's a much easier way: use olap4j.

Olap4j is a standard API and driver for connecting to OLAP systems. It allows users to generically connect to XMLA servers as well as embed Mondrian directly into an application. The API is written in Java, so it can easily be embedded into any Java or JVM application, including desktop applications or web service applications. The libraries and documentation can be found at the project site: http://olap4j.org.

> **JDBC AND olap4j**   If you're familiar with JDBC, much of olap4j will look similar. olap4j was inspired by JDBC and uses a number of JDBC classes and techniques.

> **JAVA OLAP INTERFACE (JOLAP)**   In addition to olap4j, there was a Java Specification Request (JSR-69) called JOLAP that would've created a pure Java interface for OLAP systems. JSR-69 has since been withdrawn by the specification lead.

### 10.2.1  *Creating connections via olap4j*

Currently two drivers are available for olap4j. The first is the `XmlaOlap4jDriver` that provides connections to XMLA systems. You create an instance of the driver and then a connection to the XMLA server. The server can be based on Mondrian, but it also works with Microsoft Analysis Services (MSAS) and other OLAP servers that support XMLA. Listing 10.32 shows creating the class and connecting to a remote server.

**Listing 10.32  Create XMLA connection**

```
Class.forName("org.olap4j.driver.xmla.XmlaOlap4jDriver");          Instantiate
                                                                    XMLA driver
Connection cnx =
  DriverManager.getConnection(
    "jdbc:xmla:" +
    "Server=http://yourserver.com/applicationContext/xmla",        URL to server
    "username",                                                     Server username
    "password")                                                     Server password
```

To embed Mondrian directly, you create a different driver and create a connection. Listing 10.33 shows the code needed to create the Mondrian driver and connect to the database. Note that we need to unwrap the connection to an `OlapConnection` before it's ready for use. No matter which driver you choose to use, the rest of the API is now the same.

**Listing 10.33  Create Mondrian connection**

```
Class.forName("mondrian.olap4j.MondrianOlap4jDriver");             Create Mondrian
                                                                    driver
String cnxURL =
  "jdbc:mondrian:Jdbc=jdbc:" +                      DB URL
    "mysql://localhost:3306/adventure_works_dw;" +
  "JdbcDrivers=com.mysql.jdbc.Driver;" +                           DB driver
  "JdbcUser=username;" +                            DB username
  "JdbcPassword=password;" +                                       DB password
  "Catalog=file:/path/to/adventure_works.mondrian.xml;"           Path to schema

Connection connection = DriverManager.getConnection(cnxURL);       Create connection
OlapConnection olapConnection = connection.unwrap(OlapConnection.class);

                                                   Unwrap connection
```

> **UNSUPPORTED METHODS**  Many of the methods in the driver specification aren't required to be implemented. So even though you may see a method in the JavaDoc, you should verify that it's supported.

Now that you have a connection, you can start making queries to the server from your application. If you're using the XMLA driver, SOAP messages will be sent between the application and the server. If you're using Mondrian, then direct API calls are made. After you're finished working with the data, make sure you call the `close()` method to close the connection.

### 10.2.2  Querying data

The first thing we might want to do is find out which cubes are available to query. Getting the list of cubes is one simple line of code: `NamedList<Cube> cubes =connection` `.getOlapSchema().getCubes();`. The cubes can now be used to allow the user to specify which one to use.

Querying data can be done one of two ways. The first is to create a query model (org.olap4j.query.Query) that represents the equivalent MDX query. The benefit is that it's all code and you don't really have to understand MDX. The drawback is that the query model isn't as rich as MDX, so you may need to create MDX query strings. Since MDX query strings will always work, that's the approach we'll use here.

The following listing shows the code needed to create the MDX query. All you need is a string value and then call to execute the query. You will get the results back as a CellSet.

#### Listing 10.34   Execute MDX query

```
String mdx =
  "select {Measures.[Qty Ordered], " +
      "Measures.[Unit Price]} on columns, " +
      "Customer.Gender.Members on rows " +
  "from [Internet Sales]";

CellSet cellSet =
  this.connection.createStatement().executeOlapQuery(mdx);
```

The last step in the example code will loop through the results and print them out. Listing 10.35 shows how this is done. First you get a list of all of the positions for the columns and rows. Then you get a list of the member values for the particular position. Finally you get the cell and show its value.

#### Listing 10.35   Show the results of the query

```
for (Position row : cellset.getAxes().get(1)) {          ◁── Loop through rows

  for (Position column : cellset.getAxes().get(0)) {     ◁── Loop through columns

    for (Member member : row.getMembers()) {             ◁── Get members for the row
      System.out.println(member.getUniqueName());
    }

    for (Member member : column.getMembers()) {          ◁── Get members for the column
      System.out.println(member.getUniqueName());
    }
                                                         Get result cell
    final Cell cell = cellset.getCell(column, row);      ◁─┘
    System.out.println(cell.getFormattedValue());        ◁── Get cell's value
    System.out.println();
  }
}
```

The results will look like listing 10.36. Each set of data shows the value for one aggregate of the given members. Note that you got the aggregate for [All Gender] as well as the values for each gender.

#### Listing 10.36   Output of query results

```
[Customer].[Gender].[All Gender]
[Measures].[Qty Ordered]
```

```
60,398

[Customer].[Gender].[All Gender]
[Measures].[Unit Price]
$29,358,677.22

[Customer].[Gender].[Female]
[Measures].[Qty Ordered]
30,017

[Customer].[Gender].[Female]
[Measures].[Unit Price]
$14,813,618.68

[Customer].[Gender].[Male]
[Measures].[Qty Ordered]
30,381

[Customer].[Gender].[Male]
[Measures].[Unit Price]
$14,545,058.55
```

The last feature we'll explore is performing *drillthrough*. Drillthrough returns the underlying data that was used to create the contents of a cell. There are two approaches to use. One is to make an MDX DRILLTHROUGH query. This approach differs from the previous query in that you'd call `this.connection.createStatement()` `.executeOlapQuery(mdx);` rather than `executeOlapQuery`. This is because you're making a relational and not a multidimensional query. An advantage of the MDX approach is that you can specify the maximum number of rows to return. The disadvantage is that you have to determine the right query to create.

The second option is to call the `drillThrough()` method on a `Cell` as shown in the following listing. You can then iterate through the `ResultSet` and display the source data.

##### Listing 10.37  Drilling through a cell

```
Cell cell = cellset.getCell(                              ◁─── Get a cell
  cellset.getAxes().get(1).getPositions().get(0),
  cellset.getAxes().get(0).getPositions().get(1));

ResultSet rs = cell.drillThrough();                      ◁─── Drill through cell

ResultSetMetaData rsmd = rs.getMetaData();               ◁─── Get results metadata

int nbrColumns = rsmd.getColumnCount();
for (int ccnt = 1; ccnt < nbrColumns + 1; ccnt++) {      ◁─── Show column labels
  System.out.print(rsmd.getColumnLabel(ccnt) + "\t");
}
System.out.println();

for (rs.first(); !rs.isAfterLast(); rs.next()) {         ◁─── All rows
  for (int ccnt = 1; ccnt < nbrColumns + 1; ccnt++) {    ◁─── All columns
```

```
    System.out.print(rs.getObject(ccnt).toString() + "\t");      <—— Show value
  }
}
System.out.println();

rs.close();                              <—— Close resultset
```

Listing 10.38 shows the source of data from a slightly more complex query. In this case it's a single row, but in some cases there can be very many rows of data.

**Listing 10.38   Cell drillthrough results**

```
Promotion Name      Product Name      Qty Ordered
No Discount     AWC Logo Cap         2190
```

This section showed how to connect to Mondrian or an XMLA server, execute an MDX query, and get the results. Adventure Works can now integrate Mondrian into their company's applications to provide rich analytics capabilities without a lot of work. And since both Mondrian and olap4j are open source projects, they'll get the benefits of any improvements that are made to either.

## 10.3   *Summary*

This chapter introduced integrating with Mondrian in four ways:

1. Integrating from a thin client by exchanging SOAP messages
2. Integrating from a thin client using xmla4js
3. Integrating from a desktop client using olap4j and the XMLA driver
4. Integrating from a desktop client using olap4j and embedded Mondrian

If you want to create a completely thin client, then you should consider either XMLA and SOAP or xmla4js, the latter being much easier. If you're creating a Java application, then you should consider using olap4j and either integrating Mondrian directly or calling Mondrian via XMLA. In both cases, the driver is the main difference.

   All of the APIs discussed in this chapter have many more classes and methods available for exploration. Each also has dedicated sites with documentation and examples that you can draw on as you explore them and integrate with Mondrian. Finally, the code is available for you to experiment with and use to truly understand the APIs. Now we'll turn to some advanced topics related to Mondrian and analytics in the next chapter.

# Advanced analytics

In this chapter we'll cover how to do more advanced analytics both inside Mondrian and with external tools. The advanced analytics inside Mondrian, through MDX, meet many use cases. Adventure Works will find many of their common analytics, metrics, and scorecards can be built using these. You can run the MDX examples we present in this chapter; we cover the MDX in more detail than external tools. We'll also explore some limited "What If" support to allow Mondrian to help you model and think about various scenarios. We'll then delve into the external tools and briefly cover where Mondrian fits within the Big Data landscape and what tools are often used with Mondrian for data mining. These topics are primarily aimed at the business analyst and enterprise architect.

## 11.1 Advanced analytics in Mondrian with MDX

Mondrian's query language, MDX, provides a variety of advanced time-based analytics that you can leverage immediately on top of your existing cubes. MDX supports (and makes rather easy) things like "year to date" accumulations, this quarter versus the same quarter last year, percent increase of this quarter over last quarter, and on and on. We'll explore and build some of these calculations in this section.

MDX stands for *Multidimensional Expressions*; it was made popular by Microsoft as part of their SQL Server Analysis Services. Until 2000, no consistent vendor-agnostic way to query OLAP cubes existed. Unlike relational databases that had a similar SQL dialect between vendors, OLAP systems all had individual and disparate APIs. At about the same time, Microsoft's dominance and market leadership in the OLAP server space made MDX a de facto standard, since the majority of the market (already SQL Server) already knew MDX. Made official, as part of a multi vendor standard (XML for Analysis), MDX has become the only well-implemented query language for OLAP systems. Mondrian, like many other OLAP systems, chose it for its compatibility and eloquence.

Calculations in MDX are powerful, not necessarily because of their raw function. For instance, knowing that you can do arithmetic such as (A - B) in a language isn't that impressive. What's impressive about MDX is that every calculation is aggregation- and level-aware. What does that mean? Our simple calculation (A - B) need not explicitly say at which level of aggregation it applies. For Adventure Works, this means they can define (A - B) in MDX and it works if A and B are calculated at the [Year] level, [Month] level, [All Products] level, [Product Category] level, and so on. Calculations are inherently and magically useful all over the cube at different levels of aggregation. In fact, unless you deliberately make your MDX use a specific level ([Country]), it'll apply to all levels. Contrast that to SQL, which requires the level of aggregation (aka the GROUP BY clause) to be defined in the query with the calculation. In MDX, the calculation is defined and MDX makes sure the calculation is done on the proper level of aggregation.

MDX is a big topic; there are entire books on writing MDX, and we've linked to resources devoted to the query structure and basics in appendix B. Here we hope to give you the basics to be able to run, see the results from, and have a quick list of common MDX calculations you can use on your Mondrian project.

> **ONE TIME VERSUS SAVED IN CUBE**    Often, fancy MDX fragments are developed using a free-form MDX query tool (such as the query box in Saiku). Once developed, and useful, it's best to take the new calculation (This Quarter versus Same Quarter Last Year) and make it a calculated member. This allows anyone using the cube in Saiku or Analyzer to use the powerful calculation, without needing to know anything about MDX (refer back to section 5.4.2 for details).

This saving of MDX fragments into the cube is the Mondrian equivalent of a database view. It's a prebuilt set of logic ready to execute, but for the user it appears as a simple "thing" to get data from.

### 11.1.1 *Running MDX queries*

In this section, we'll make sure you know how to run MDX queries and see the results using the sample platform. We'll also show you the `WITH MEMBER` syntax.

First, in order to run the MDX fragments in this section, you'll need to use Saiku. Using the sample virtual machine provided for the book, you'll need to make sure that Pentaho is running. Once it is, to launch Saiku you'll want to log in to the User Console, and then click the File menu, then New, then Saiku Analysis. Once you see Saiku, you'll want to select the FoodMart Schema/Sales Cube from the drop-down list. Once you've done that, you should see Saiku ready to help you drag and drop to create a query. But we're going to use the MDX editor to manually write our MDX instead.

There's a button on the toolbar titled Switch to MDX Mode. You'll want to click this button, and then you should see a free-form text box that will allow you to enter the MDX examples in this chapter. You can copy and paste (if you have the eBook) directly into the text box, then click the Green arrow to run the query.

We'll make extensive use of the `WITH MEMBER` MDX syntax. This MDX construct allows us to create calculations that exist only in the single query. Earlier in this chapter we covered how to make those changes more permanent.

Now that you know how to run MDX queries and see the results, let's get on to specific formulas that you'll hopefully find useful.

### 11.1.2 *Ratios and growth*

We'll start with a straightforward post aggregation calculation using arithmetic. Say Adventure Works would like to calculate `[Gross Profit]`. Its calculation is straightforward: `[Store Sales] - [Store Cost]`. We can make this calculation simply in MDX (listing 11.1 and displayed in figure 11.1).

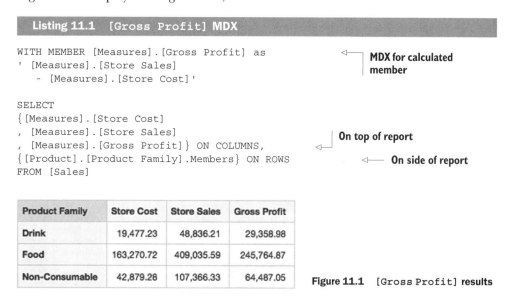

Listing 11.1 `[Gross Profit]` MDX

```
WITH MEMBER [Measures].[Gross Profit] as          ◁─┐ MDX for calculated
' [Measures].[Store Sales]                            member
   - [Measures].[Store Cost]'

SELECT
{[Measures].[Store Cost]
, [Measures].[Store Sales]                         ◁── On top of report
, [Measures].[Gross Profit]} ON COLUMNS,
{[Product].[Product Family].Members} ON ROWS       ◁── On side of report
FROM [Sales]
```

| Product Family | Store Cost | Store Sales | Gross Profit |
|---|---|---|---|
| Drink | 19,477.23 | 48,836.21 | 29,358.98 |
| Food | 163,270.72 | 409,035.59 | 245,764.87 |
| Non-Consumable | 42,879.28 | 107,366.33 | 64,487.05 |

Figure 11.1 `[Gross Profit]` results

The results in figure 11.1 demonstrate simple subtraction; it's worth noting that this calculation is happening in memory in Mondrian after the main aggregation and [Store Sales] and [Store Cost] is calculated in the database. Remember, as we mentioned previously in this section, this calculation is aggregation-safe so it'll work the same if it's at the [Product Family] level, or one level below at the [Product Department] level. For instance, here is the exact same calculation working at the [Product Department] level; note that the WITH MEMBER fragment is identical (listing 11.2 and figure 11.2)!

**Listing 11.2  [Gross Profit] at [Product Department] level**

```
WITH MEMBER [Measures].[Gross Profit] as
' [Measures].[Store Sales]
   - [Measures].[Store Cost]'

SELECT
{[Measures].[Store Cost]
, [Measures].[Store Sales]
, [Measures].[Gross Profit]} ON COLUMNS,
{[Product].[Product Department].Members} ON ROWS
FROM [Sales]
```

| Product Department | Store Cost | Store Sales | Gross Profit |
|---|---|---|---|
| Alcoholic Beverages | 5,576.79 | 14,029.08 | 8,452.29 |
| Beverages | 11,069.53 | 27,748.53 | 16,679.00 |
| Dairy | 2,830.92 | 7,058.60 | 4,227.68 |
| Baked Goods | 6,564.09 | 16,455.43 | 9,891.34 |
| Baking Goods | 15,370.61 | 38,670.41 | 23,299.80 |
| Breakfast Foods | 2,756.80 | 6,941.46 | 4,184.66 |
| Canned Foods | 15,894.53 | 39,774.34 | 23,879.81 |
| Canned Products | 1,317.13 | 3,314.52 | 1,997.39 |
| Dairy | 12,228.85 | 30,508.85 | 18,280.00 |
| Deli | 10,108.87 | 25,318.93 | 15,210.06 |
| Eggs | 3,684.90 | 9,200.76 | 5,515.86 |
| Frozen Foods | 22,030.66 | 55,207.50 | 33,176.84 |
| Meat | 1,465.42 | 3,669.89 | 2,204.47 |
| Produce | 32,831.33 | 82,248.42 | 49,417.09 |
| Seafood | 1,520.70 | 3,809.14 | 2,288.44 |
| Snack Foods | 26,963.34 | 67,609.82 | 40,646.48 |
| Snacks | 5,827.58 | 14,550.05 | 8,722.47 |
| Starchy Foods | 4,705.91 | 11,756.07 | 7,050.16 |
| Carousel | 595.97 | 1,500.11 | 904.14 |
| Checkout | 1,525.04 | 3,767.71 | 2,242.67 |
| Health and Hygiene | 12,972.99 | 32,571.86 | 19,598.87 |
| Household | 24,170.73 | 60,469.89 | 36,299.16 |
| Periodicals | 3,614.55 | 9,056.76 | 5,442.21 |

Figure 11.2  [Gross Profit] at [Product Department] level

The simple arithmetic in MDX also allows us to create important ratios and proportions. For Adventure Works, the overall gross profit percentage (the [Gross Profit] as a proportion of the [Store Sales]) is also salient. Without these types of proportions and percentages, it would be hard to gauge relative effectiveness when comparing scalar values of different magnitudes. For instance, looking at the raw [Gross Profit] for individual [Product Family]s might not help you figure out which [Product Family]s are contributing to Profit effectively (as a percentage) if you're looking at raw numbers. As we see in figure 11.3 the [Product Family]s have orders of magnitude difference [Gross Profit]; you have to look at the ratio to determine the relative profitability of each [Product Family].

**Listing 11.3  [Gross Profit Margin] MDX**

```
WITH MEMBER [Measures].[Gross Profit] as
' [Measures].[Store Sales]
   - [Measures].[Store Cost]'
MEMBER [Measures].[Gross Profit Margin] as
'[Measures].[Gross Profit] / [Measures].[Store Sales]'

SELECT
{[Measures].[Gross Profit]
 ,[Measures].[Gross Profit Margin]} ON COLUMNS,
{[Product].[Product Family].Members} ON ROWS
FROM [Sales]
```

Note in figure 11.3 that the [Gross Profit] is wildly different for different [Product Family]s but the [Gross Profit Margin] is identical. Drinks, Food, and Non-Consumables all have a gross margin of 60%.

| Product Family | Gross Profit | Gross Profit Margin |
|---|---|---|
| Drink | 29,358.98 | .60 |
| Food | 245,764.87 | .60 |
| Non-Consumable | 64,487.05 | .60 |

**Figure 11.3**  [Gross Profit Margin]

The last piece we'll cover, in terms of cool arithmetic in MDX, is the ability to also create ratios and proportions at different levels. For instance, say we want to see what a particular [Customer].[State]'s contribution is toward the [Store Sales] for the [Country]. We can use the simple MDX arithmetic along with MDX's ability to navigate levels in a hierarchy to display this data. We'll use two MDX constructs. First, we'll find our current member (Seattle, WA, or CA) in the hierarchy that's currently being evaluated for calculation. The syntax for this is [Customer Geography].CurrentMember. Next, we'll use the ability of *any* member to navigate to other places in the hierarchy. We'll do this using the [Member].Parent function that gets the parent of any member ([USA] is the parent of [WA]). We'll explore both CurrentMember and Parent in listing 11.4; we'll divide each member's sales by its parent's sales—[State]'s total divided by the [Country] total.

**Listing 11.4   [Sales % of Geography] MDX**

```
WITH
MEMBER [Measures].[Sales % of Geography] as
'([Customers].CurrentMember, [Measures].[Store Sales])
/([Customers].CurrentMember.Parent, [Measures].[Store Sales])'

SELECT
{[Measures].[Store Sales]
 , [Measures].[Sales % of Geography]} ON COLUMNS,
NON EMPTY Hierarchize(
{[Customers].[State Province].Members,[Customers].[Country].Members
}) ON ROWS
FROM [Sales]
```

In figures 11.4 and 11.5 we can see the results of expressing the [Member].Parent as a percentage. OR represents approximately 25% of USA's profit.

| Country | State Province | Store Sales | Sales % of Geography |
|---------|----------------|-------------|----------------------|
| USA     |                | 565,238.13  | 1.00                 |
|         | CA             | 159,167.84  | .28                  |
|         | OR             | 142,277.07  | .25                  |
|         | WA             | 263,793.22  | .47                  |

**Figure 11.4   Sales percentage of total table**

**LEVEL-AGNOSTIC CALCULATIONS**  Remember, as long as you don't pick a specific level, such as [Customer Geography].[State] in your MDX statements, and you use CurrentMember and the general CurrentMember.Parent for these types of calculations, they'll work "up and down" the hierarchy. The same calculation, [Measures].[Sales % of Geography], can be used for City to State, State to Country, and Country to All Geographies.

■ CA [1]      ▨ OR [2]      ▨ WA [3]

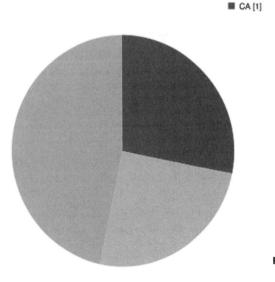

**Figure 11.5   Sales percentage of total chart**

### 11.1.3 Time-specific MDX

Prior Period is useful when you're trying to calculate the classic month-over-month growth. Adventure Works has built this month-to-month growth report many times in SQL and knows their users will need to see it regularly! Using the MDX Member function .PrevMember you can positionally go back one day, month, quarter, or year. The .PrevMember is level-agnostic, so the same calculation can be used for any level in the hierarchy. We've also built on these raw growth figures and added some simple ratios using the arithmetic MDX we covered in section 11.1.2 to give an idea of the total velocity of the data. Adventure Works knows that although the raw growth values are interesting, their users want to see it as a percentage, ideally.

**Listing 11.5  [Prior Sales] MDX**

```
WITH
MEMBER [Measures].[Prior Sales] as
'([Time].CurrentMember.PrevMember, [Measures].[Unit Sales])'
MEMBER [Measures].[Prior Sales Growth] as
'[Measures].[Unit Sales] - [Measures].[Prior Sales]'
MEMBER [Measures].[Growth %] as
'[Measures].[Prior Sales Growth] / [Measures].[Prior Sales]'
,FORMAT_STRING='0%'

SELECT
{[Measures].[Unit Sales]
 ,[Measures].[Prior Sales]
 ,[Measures].[Prior Sales Growth]
 ,[Measures].[Growth %]
} ON COLUMNS,
NON EMPTY {[Time].[Month].Members} ON ROWS
from [Sales]
```

In figures 11.6 and 11.7, we can see, on a month-by-month basis, the growth (as a percentage) of sales over the previous month's sales. Once again, we've used the scalar figure (such as -671 for Month 2) and arithmetic to arrive at the percentage which is preferred.

Adventure Works also knows that it's common for their users to need to calculate the aggregated year-to-date totals for a variety of measures. They know this cumulative type aggregation is useful and often requested from their users. The

| Month | Unit Sales | Prior Sales | Prior Sales Growth | Growth % |
|---|---|---|---|---|
| 1 | 21,628 | | 21,628 | |
| 2 | 20,957 | 21,628 | -671 | -3% |
| 3 | 23,706 | 20,957 | 2,749 | 13% |
| 4 | 20,179 | 23,706 | -3,527 | -15% |
| 5 | 21,081 | 20,179 | 902 | 4% |
| 6 | 21,350 | 21,081 | 269 | 1% |
| 7 | 23,763 | 21,350 | 2,413 | 11% |
| 8 | 21,697 | 23,763 | -2,066 | -9% |
| 9 | 20,388 | 21,697 | -1,309 | -6% |
| 10 | 19,958 | 20,388 | -430 | -2% |
| 11 | 25,270 | 19,958 | 5,312 | 27% |
| 12 | 26,796 | 25,270 | 1,526 | 6% |
| 1 | | 26,796 | -26,796 | -100% |

**Figure 11.6  [Prior Sales] results**

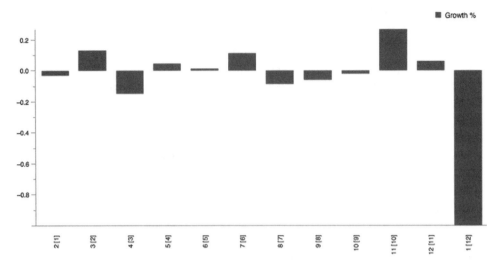

**Figure 11.7   Prior Period chart**

MDX YTD() shortcut function (see listing 11.6) returns all periods from the beginning of the year right up to the current period and aggregates the totals to give the total year-to-date value. Figures 11.8 and 11.9 show the results.

---

**Listing 11.6   [YTD Sales] MDX**

```
WITH
MEMBER [Measures].[YTD Sales] as
'Aggregate(YTD([Time].CurrentMember), [Measures].[Unit Sales])'
```

```
SELECT
{[Measures].[Unit Sales]
 ,[Measures].[YTD Sales]
} ON COLUMNS,
NON EMPTY {[Time].[Month].Members} ON ROWS
from [Sales]
```

We've seen how Adventure Works can use YTD(), which returns the periods up to this point in the year and then use the generic Aggregate() MDX function to total those periods. The Aggregate MDX function will use the basic aggregator for the measure (Count, Sum, and so forth).

| Month | Unit Sales | YTD Sales |
|---|---|---|
| 1 | 21,628 | 21,628 |
| 2 | 20,957 | 42,585 |
| 3 | 23,706 | 66,291 |
| 4 | 20,179 | 86,470 |
| 5 | 21,081 | 107,551 |
| 6 | 21,350 | 128,901 |
| 7 | 23,763 | 152,664 |
| 8 | 21,697 | 174,361 |
| 9 | 20,388 | 194,749 |
| 10 | 19,958 | 214,707 |
| 11 | 25,270 | 239,977 |
| 12 | 26,796 | 266,773 |

**Figure 11.8   [YTD Sales] results**

### 11.1.4   *Advanced MDX*

It's common to develop some sort of target to base your current results against. Adventure Works sometimes has fixed targets (145,000 in sales per quarter), and other times they're calculated from

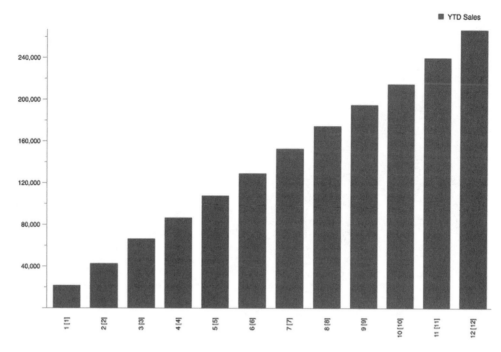

**Figure 11.9   Year-to-date chart**

past performance. Though listing 11.7 shows a fixed target, it'd be just as easy to find the previous quarter's figures, add 5%, and make that the "target." Just like many of the other raw figures, we also adorn it with some percentages to make the real metric and velocity of the figures easily apparent to Adventure Works users.

**Listing 11.7   Fixed-goal MDX**

```
WITH
MEMBER [Measures].[Sales Goal] as
'145000'
MEMBER [Measures].[% from Goal] as
'([Measures].[Sales Goal] - [Measures].[Store Sales])
  / [Measures].[Sales Goal]',FORMAT_STRING='0%'

SELECT
{[Measures].[Store Sales]
,[Measures].[Sales Goal]
,[Measures].[% from Goal]
} ON COLUMNS,
NON EMPTY {[Time].[1997].Children} ON ROWS
from [Sales]
```

Note in figures 11.10 and 11.11 that the deviation from the goal, as a percentage, is readily apparent in the line chart.

| Quarter | Store Sales | Sales Goal | % from Goal |
|---------|-------------|------------|-------------|
| Q1 | 139,628.35 | 145,000 | 4% |
| Q2 | 132,666.27 | 145,000 | 9% |
| Q3 | 140,271.89 | 145,000 | 3% |
| Q4 | 152,671.62 | 145,000 | -5% |

Figure 11.10   Fixed-goal table

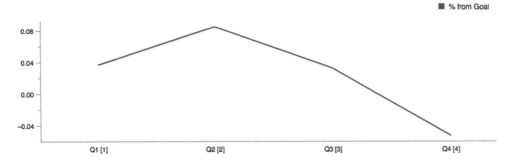

Figure 11.11   Fixed-goal chart

Adventure Works knows their users will want to see "What's the overall trend?" If we continue on this general sales pattern, ignoring the natural noise of the month-to-month data, what will our sales be like in three months? Performing a *linear regression* (with the LinRegPoint() MDX function) allows Adventure Works to show the overall trend over a period of time. This avoids anxious calls from analysts who are worried about a single-month drop-off; linear regressions help to smooth out data and make general, unsophisticated forecasts for the future. We'll discuss the ability to employ more sophisticated forecasting options later in section 11.3.

Listing 11.8   Trend-line MDX

```
WITH
MEMBER [Measures].[Sales Trend] as
'LinRegPoint(
  Rank(
     [Time].CurrentMember,
     [Time].CurrentMember.Level.Members),
  {[Time].CurrentMember.Level.Members},
   [Measures].[Unit Sales],
   Rank(
       [Time].CurrentMember,
       [Time].CurrentMember.Level.Members)
)'
```

```
SELECT
{
[Measures].[Unit Sales]
,[Measures].[Sales Trend]
} ON COLUMNS,
NON EMPTY {
[Time].[Month].Members} ON ROWS
from [Sales]
```

| Month | Unit Sales | Sales Trend |
|-------|-----------|-------------|
| 1 | 21,628 | 20,794 |
| 2 | 20,957 | 21,055 |
| 3 | 23,706 | 21,316 |
| 4 | 20,179 | 21,578 |
| 5 | 21,081 | 21,839 |
| 6 | 21,350 | 22,100 |
| 7 | 23,763 | 22,362 |
| 8 | 21,697 | 22,623 |
| 9 | 20,388 | 22,884 |
| 10 | 19,958 | 23,146 |
| 11 | 25,270 | 23,407 |
| 12 | 26,796 | 23,668 |
| 1 | | 23,930 |
| 2 | | 24,191 |
| 3 | | 24,452 |

**Figure 11.12  Trend-line table**

Note in figures 11.12 and 11.13 that a general trend for sales over the past 12 months is now projecting out into the future where we don't have sales figures. Lin-RegPoint() gives Adventure Works the ability to do simple forecasting on any measure.

Adventure Works also needs to explore "What are the best months for sales in the past 12 months?" In listing 11.9 we explore how to discover the 10 best months across the entire company. Ranking (via the MDX Rank() function) allows you to order and rank results and determine sets of performers. Figure 11.14 shows the output for Adventure Works.

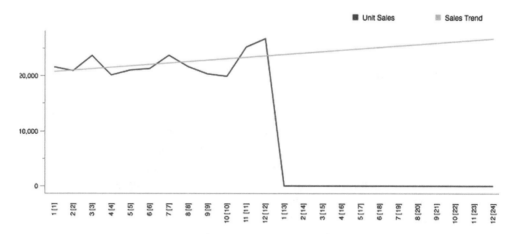

**Figure 11.13  Trend-line chart**

**Listing 11.9  Ranking in MDX**

```
WITH
MEMBER [Measures].[Sales Rank] as
' Rank(
    [Time].CurrentMember
```

```
,[Time].CurrentMember.Level.Members
,[Measures].[Store Sales])'

SELECT
{
[Measures].[Store Sales]
,[Measures].[Sales Rank]
} ON COLUMNS,
NON EMPTY {
Head(
 Order([Time].[Month].Members, [Measures].[Sales Rank], BASC)
 , 10)
} ON ROWS
from [Sales]
```

In listing 11.9 we saw how to get the relative, ordinal rank of a figure among its peers. We also tacked on the use of two additional MDX functions that are commonly used with this type of analysis. Order() changes the order of members based on a value. In listing 11.9 we ordered by the Rank() we just created. Next we used Head() to only grab the first 10 items in the list of all ranked months.

Now that we've covered some of the advanced analytics we can accomplish using Mondrian by itself, with MDX we move on to more advanced analytics. Next we discuss what happens when we want to play around and make changes to data values for what-if analysis.

| Month | Store Sales | Sales Rank |
|-------|-------------|------------|
| 12 | 56,965.64 | 1 |
| 11 | 53,363.71 | 2 |
| 7 | 50,246.88 | 3 |
| 3 | 50,029.87 | 4 |
| 8 | 46,199.04 | 5 |
| 1 | 45,539.69 | 6 |
| 6 | 45,331.73 | 7 |
| 5 | 44,456.29 | 8 |
| 2 | 44,058.79 | 9 |
| 9 | 43,825.97 | 10 |

**Figure 11.14   Ranking table**

## 11.2  *What-if analysis*

Mondrian has some support for helping you explore some "What If" analysis. Most reporting systems present the user with data as it is; static data provides little if any help for the data analyst's desire to explore scenarios that haven't actually happened. In fact, Mondrian's term for such what-if analysis is *scenarios.*

Scenarios allow users to make nonpermanent changes to values in the cube for the purpose of seeing how those changes affect totals, other ratios, and other metrics. Take for instance a hypothetical Adventure Works knows their analysts investigate on a regular basis: If we increased our gross sales for a particular product line, what does that do to our overall bottom line? Let's explore a scenario where we want to understand whether increasing our store sales in [Drinks] by $5,000 USD, keeping costs fixed, will dramatically increase our company's profitability in a year.

This example should work with the Saiku Sales Scenario cube. Make sure you create a new Saiku report using the Sales Scenario cube to see the scenario button, not start with an existing report. In all scenario cases, you'll start with your base cube with actual data in Mondrian and the underlying database. In this case (shown

| (All) | Product Family | Store Sales | Profit |
|-------|---------------|-------------|--------|
| All Products | | 565,238.13 | $339,610.90 |
| | Drink | 48836.21 | $29,358.98 |
| | Food | 409,035.59 | $245,764.87 |
| | Non-Consumable | 107,366.33 | $64,487.05 |

**Figure 11.15   Saiku scenario start. This is the baseline data from Mondrian without any modification.**

in figure 11.15), we'll start with a report that has [All Products] and [Product Family] (on rows), with the measures [Store Sales] and [Profit] (on columns), and filter to one year ([1997]).

This is our data as it is now and represents what our cube tells us with no scenarios in play. This initial Saiku report represents our baseline.

Next, we'll enable our ability to make changes to the data and create our Scenario for evaluation. In our example, we want to increase our sales by 5,000 from $48,836.21 to $53,836.21. To do so, we first start by clicking the Query Scenario button on the toolbar, typing in the new value (58836.21), and pressing Return (see figure 11.16). At this point, Saiku has enabled the scenario, given the changed value to Mondrian, and Mondrian is ready to rerun the MDX query with the modified values. We'd expect to see the value we just changed retain its +5000 value, but we'd also expect to see our totals and other calculated members changed in other spots as well.

Figure 11.17 shows that, as expected, the figures for the [Store Sales] totals and [Profit] have adjusted by the 5,000 change we made to [Drink] for [1997]. What's also worth noting is that [Profit], which is a calculated member, has also adjusted.

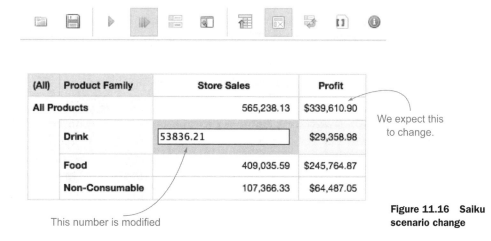

| (All) | Product Family | Store Sales | Profit | |
|-------|---------------|-------------|--------|--|
| All Products | | 565,238.13 | $339,610.90 | We expect this to change. |
| | Drink | 53836.21 | $29,358.98 | |
| | Food | 409,035.59 | $245,764.87 | |
| | Non-Consumable | 107,366.33 | $64,487.05 | |

This number is modified

**Figure 11.16   Saiku scenario change**

| (All) | Product Family | Store Sales | Profit |
|---|---|---|---|
| **All Products** | | 570,238.13 | $344,610.90 |
| | **Drink** | 53,836.21 | $34,358.98 |
| | **Food** | 409,035.59 | $245,764.87 |
| | **Non-Consumable** | 107,366.33 | $64,487.05 |

This calculation shows an increased amount.

**Figure 11.17  Saiku scenario result**

This means that Mondrian is not just updating the base figures, but when connected with this scenario, it's ensuring the results of all calculations also reflect that scenario change.

Though calculated members do reflect the changes made to it in a scenario, they themselves can't be changed. In our example, we can't change [Profit] because it's a calculated member; we can only change a value that's a core measure aggregated from the database.

In our example, we saw the results of reflecting the change of a lower level in a hierarchy ([Drink]) on the total ([All Products]). But it's also common to explore scenarios where you'd like to change the overall totals by 5,000 and see what requirements that places on the individual product family sales. Mondrian also supports this; it's common for budget and planning workflows to look at year totals, then have those spread down to the month-by-month expenditures, and so on. Mondrian scenario support even allows various options on how the change is allocated to children (weighted allocation, weighted increment, equal allocation, and equal increment).

**SCENARIO SUPPORT IN SAIKU AND PENTAHO ANALYZER**  Currently Saiku is the only visual client to Mondrian that supports Scenarios. Scenarios aren't available via XMLA either; only OLAP4J has support for using scenarios.

Pentaho Analyzer currently has no support for Scenarios whatsoever; scenario support is not currently in a planned Pentaho Analyzer release.

Lastly, there exists a requirement to create a hanger dimension to allow the scenarios to be used in MDX. Refer to section 5.4.2 for more information on how to define a hanger dimension. Readers are advised to look at the Saiku sample Mondrian schema files for the Sales Scenario cube for a working example of creating this hanger dimension for use with scenarios.

Now that we've looked at how to do what-if analysis with Mondrian, we'll look at how to do some real high-powered data mining (DM) and machine learning (ML) using tools that specialize in this analysis.

## 11.3 Statistics and machine learning

Now that we've looked at some of the statistics you can do inside Mondrian (using MDX) and the ability to explore what-if scenarios, let's explore what companies like Adventure Works do when they need more advanced statistics or machine learning. For instance, though MDX helps understand growth, ratios, and simple linear regressions, it's nearly impossible to do a forecasting algorithm that includes commonly needed bounds and confidence intervals. For instance, what are the upper and lower bounds of my predicted sales figure with 95% confidence? These DM and ML packages help answer questions that Mondrian doesn't endeavor to; they're complementary.

Let's explore, at a high level, some common use cases that would best be addressed with DM or ML packages:

- Predicting future values with ranges and confidence figures using regression and other techniques
- Clustering of similar customers together to segment customers by similar behavior and attributes
- Market-basket analysis to determine which items are often purchased together, even if they seem unrelated
- Fraud detection and analysis to determine outliers or unusual behavior
- Classic statistical descriptions of confidence in values such as the + or - 3% qualifiers typically seen in polls based on sample sizing

Mondrian doesn't have any integrations directly with any data mining (DM) or machine learning (ML) packages. The approaches we cover here include how these systems are used in combination to create the end result functional requirements. This approach is not only the only practical method of integrations, but most users tend to find it perfectly reasonable and even preferable.

The most common method of combining Mondrian and DM tools is by simply using them on the same data. This is most often, and easily, achieved by using the different tools on the same source data. Mondrian uses a star schema (chapter 3) as the source for its multidimensional data, which also makes a perfectly good source for DM tools. This common approach makes sense: most of a company's investment in building an analytic solution involves data integration, restructuring, and loading (ETL and modeling) into the database. Using the ETL and modeling work along with data enriched with additional lookup attributes is a great source for DM tools.

> **DATA MINING PURISTS ON STAR SCHEMAS** Data mining purists may disagree that the star schema, cleaned and loaded from original source, represents the best data to perform machine learning and data mining on. Why? With one level of cleanup and enrichment (fitting into categories

and hierarchies), correcting data quality issues introduces some level of bias/effect on the data. Though this is true, in practice, DM practitioners often do some level of data preparation themselves for their modeling and do some similar things. Though not perfect, DM on star schemas (and their various aggregations/samples) is common, especially when the DM tool is to be used alongside Mondrian.

We'll cover, at a very high level, two data mining tools commonly used in conjunction with Mondrian solutions and when to use them. The tools, R and Weka, are also open source themselves, which is part of the reason they're so often used with Mondrian.

### 11.3.1  R

*R* is a language and environment for statistical computing and graphics (http://www.r-project.org/about.html). It's a widely and commonly used package for data preparation, modeling, and statistical analysis. That's worth noting: R is a language and set of tools that focus on statistics. It excels at classifying items, clustering like items together, and developing forecasts with confidence intervals. It's the "go to" tool for many data scientists to use classic statistical methods on their dataset.

Like previously mentioned, the most common method for using R with Mondrian is to use them side by side. You can download the R software, including the UI, connect it to your database, retrieve sets of data, and then continue the analysis in R. It's not necessary, or even that beneficial, to think of R connecting directly to Mondrian, since R tends to want to see the base level. In some cases, R (or the users of) would like to see some level of aggregation on raw events; in that case, it makes sense to point R at the aggregate tables inside the database already prepared for Mondrian performance (see section 7.3 for more on Mondrian aggregate tables).

An extensive community supports the R tool, including some commercial companies that offer support packages. R is primarily for statistics, but it also does have some capabilities for machine learning; there's some overlap between R and Weka. You should choose whichever package fits your DM or ML needs in general. If you're not sure, and you're looking for more statistical based algorithms and don't require any operational integration with Pentaho Data Integration, choose R. If you're looking for a greater focus on machine learning algorithms or need operational integration with PDI, you should consider Weka, which we'll discuss next.

### 11.3.2  Weka

*Weka* is a machine learning framework and tool (see figure 11.18). Similar to R, it provides UI tools for acquiring, managing, and filtering data for modeling. Models are built and evaluated using a dataset from a variety of data sources. Weka can use the star schema that any DM tool can access (like R), but it also has the advantage of being integrated into PDI as a series of useful plugins for doing common tasks. More on that later in this section.

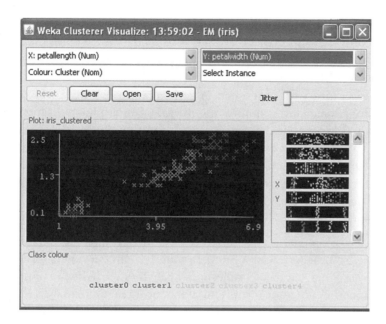

Figure 11.18 Weka clustering output

Weka excels and is best known for its capabilities on machine learning algorithms. It's well known for its large catalog of classification techniques, given its providence as a university project. Many researchers use Weka as their tool of choice for testing new algorithms, so there's no shortage of available supervised and unsupervised learning algorithms. In fact, this large volume of available techniques and algorithms is sometimes daunting to those new to data mining.

Given the specialized knowledge of data mining, it's difficult to get started. By far, the easiest way to get started with Weka is to use the prepackaged plugins available in Pentaho Data Integration to do common DM tasks. By using the PDI plugins to do some time-series forecasting and market-basket analysis, you'll learn the basics of DM without extensive training. For the common use cases that are deployed alongside Mondrian, that's a great way to start. With PDI's ability to query Mondrian (http://wiki.pentaho.com/display/EAI/Mondrian+Input) and stream results to further steps, this is the closest direct integration between Mondrian and a DM tool.

Hopefully you have a good sense of the tools available to use in conjunction with Mondrian for more advanced data mining and machine learning use cases. It should be clear how R and Weka fit in an overall solution with Mondrian; we'll now delve into a very Big (pun intended) topic and see where Mondrian fits in the Big Data space.

## 11.4 Big Data

Big Data, and the various technologies and skills involved, have garnered much attention in the past couple of years. These tools and technologies, the companies that produce them, and the practitioners that use them represent a huge segment of businesses that are looking to handle data that has

- *Volume*—Adventure Works needs to handle data volumes, where the total number of records they will manage two years from now will be more than 10x the data they manage now. The traditional databases they used to build their applications and analytic systems won't always do so effectively on billions of records.

- *Variety*—Adventure Works will need to get data from existing corporate documents, NoSQL data stores, online resources, and multiple applications within the firewall. Gone are the days of applications storing things solely in relational SQL databases, but there exists an increasing amount of unstructured (or hierarchically structured) data.

- *Velocity*—Adventure Works needs to handle a constant and increasing stream of data, and time to analyze and present that data is shrinking. Things are happening faster on both the processing of records and analysis side.

Mondrian is a nice complement and is used in conjunction with Big Data tools constantly. Mondrian is, in its own way, a Big Data tool. It helps customers analyze large amounts of data (caching, aggregate tables), do analysis on varied types of data (your dimensions and metrics are your own), and allows near-real-time analysis with some advanced cache management APIs (see section 7.4 for more on caching and APIs). Mondrian's focus on the OLAP space specifically, and leaving the heavy duty storage and aggregation to an RDBMS (see section 2.4.1 for more on ROLAP), provides significant benefit for nearly all companies; it's easy to find a relational database in use somewhere in a company. This reliance on a SQL RDBMS does tie Mondrian closely with SQL data storage systems and limits the data stores that Mondrian can use directly to those that speak SQL.

> **MONDRIAN NEEDS SQL**  Mondrian requires a database that speaks SQL to work properly. Even if your back-end database has the same capabilities through an API (filtering, aggregation by fields, and so forth), it can't be plugged in behind Mondrian. Users looking for connecting their NoSQL system with Mondrian should consider the work being undertaken at the Optiq project. Optiq is for creating a SQL layer on top of any data source (requiring a developer to write only the specific implementation) and is a practical method to connect Mondrian with a non-SQL source. Julian Hyde, coauthor of this book and lead developer of Mondrian, is also the project lead for Optiq (https://github.com/julianhyde/optiq).

### 11.4.1 Analytic databases

Mondrian fits with many Big Data systems that speak SQL. In particular, there's an entire breed of databases that use SQL as their interface but have specialized storage and processing methods for analytics. These systems are typically column-oriented (store like data together) and often include the ability to scale out to multiple servers. Mondrian is known to work with the following analytic databases:

- Vectorwise
- Greenplum
- Infobright

- InfiniDB
- LucidDB
- MonetDB

These databases are purpose-built for performing a workload very compatible with Mondrian. Mondrian generates many SQL statements to run in the RDBMS, from dimension lookups to aggregation plus group by SQL statements. These databases are purpose-built to execute the exact type of query that Mondrian generates. Though Mondrian will work with adequate performance on most traditional OLTP databases (Oracle, MySQL, PostGres, and so on), it'll perform much faster, and certainly much faster with more data, on an analytic database.

### 11.4.2 Hadoop and Hive

Hadoop is a *very* popular system for doing data processing; as a framework, it addresses all the V's (volume, variety, and velocity) as part of a large open source community. Hive is a SQL layer on top of Hadoop that allows users to run a SQL-like syntax on top of HDFS and Hadoop data. This provides significant benefit to Hadoop users performing an analytic workload on top of Hadoop. Mondrian has experimental support for Hive and will work functionally on top of Hive soon.

But unless a system like Cloudera's Impala or an additional query latency improvement system is also utilized, Adventure Works would likely be disappointed with the performance of Mondrian on top of Hive. Mondrian often issues many SQL queries to a database to look up dimension members, children, and get aggregations. Hive experiences high latency with often simple queries as well (5–10s); Mondrian makes an assumption that some queries run fast (lookup members in a dimension) while the aggregations hitting facts are slow.

> **HADOOP/HIVE SUPPORT** Hive support is being developed; even if Mondrian is functional on top of Hive, the latency for dimension member and similar lookups is a challenge for making an overall high-performance OLAP system with Mondrian and Hive.

Though Hive is a popular way to access data in Hadoop, there are other ways of using Hadoop and Mondrian together. When Hadoop is used, without Hive, it looks similar to the general NoSQL approaches we cover next.

### 11.4.3 NoSQL systems and Hadoop

Mondrian, being a system which requires SQL and a whole new class of systems that don't speak SQL (NoSQL = Not Only SQL), creates a natural question for Adventure Works: How do these things work together? Adventure Works has a mobile application that uses Cloudant (a hosted version of CouchDB) for storage; it's a popular document-based storage service for mobile developers. Adventure Works needs to do some reporting on a huge amount of documents stored in Cloudant, and Mondrian matches the reporting needs of the users.

Two methods are available to Adventure Works to use Mondrian on data in this NoSQL system. One is extremely common, not terribly sophisticated, and gets the job done today using a SQL database in between. The second is a sophisticated and cutting-edge technique to put a SQL driver in front of any system or API. We'll cover both approaches here.

**NOSQL AS A DISTRIBUTED CACHE**  It's worth mentioning that the two techniques covered in this section explore using NoSQL as the primary source for data in Mondrian. There's another technique that integrates NoSQL technology into Mondrian, but not as the primary storage and aggregation engine. NoSQL systems have been used by the pluggable cache API to allow Mondrian to share its cache among individual servers in a multiserver environment. Though this might not help users do reporting on top of NoSQL, it can certainly leverage some of the fantastic key value scalability and performance for managing Mondrian's cache (see section 7.4.2 for more on using an external segment cache).

**ETL DATA INTO SQL DATABASE**

This is the most common solution in practice today; for those who want to do ad hoc, high-performance analytics on top of data with NoSQL and Mondrian, the solution isn't really one at all. Adventure Works can take the data in CouchDB, run a periodic ETL process to capture the relevant data for the analytic solution, and push that data into a SQL database. Once in the database, Mondrian performs its analysis on top of the data, without modification or need to connect with the NoSQL system, as shown in figure 11.19. Most users will only export some sort of first-level sort and aggregation to reduce the dataset to the daily (or hourly) aggregations at the lowest level of aggregation.

There are some advantages to this approach. First is that the technologies involved are all mature, with years of deployment knowledge and experience. Second is that it has the same virtue as the traditional DW in that it offloads the analytic processing (which is different) to another system. It reduces the load on the source systems and separates out different kinds of use cases and workload.

There are also some disadvantages. The data is now stored separately, and there's an inherent staleness to data from the NoSQL system and the data presented to Adventure Works users. Another disadvantage is that some of these NoSQL systems are very scalable and handle the storage and aggregation as good as or better than their RDBMS peers. In other words, we could leverage some great, free, and open source

**Figure 11.19   NoSQL plus database architecture**

technology to act as the primary aggregation engine for our Mondrian solution, but we're simply putting it back into a less scalable SQL database.

**SQL ACCESS TO NOSQL SYSTEMS**

This is the less commonly used approach; similar in approach to accessing Hadoop data via Hive, this approach suggests that creating a way to "speak SQL" to NoSQL systems is interesting and is being used by many commercial tools. There's even an up-and-coming open source project being developed by an author of this book (Julian Hyde) providing a general JDBC driver for any system.

Speaking SQL to a NoSQL system has some advantages. SQL is a widely known language; its dominance in BI tools is unmistakable, and Mondrian is no exception. If a NoSQL system can offer the basic semantics that Mondrian SQL requires (filtering, grouping, and aggregation), then it can act as the primary storage and aggregation engine in Adventure Works' solution. Some of these NoSQL solutions do this (or are very close) and provide some remarkable scaling and performance compared to their RDBMS peers.

It's not without some drawbacks as well; you lose some of the richness of the native API for the NoSQL system. SQL, in particular the SQL Mondrian generates, represents a "least common denominator" for accessing data in a data store. The NoSQL systems often offer additional capabilities (intermediate group results in hierarchies) that aren't expressed in Mondrian SQL.

## 11.5 Summary

In this chapter we've looked at how we can do advanced ratios, percentages, and time-based calculations in Mondrian. This provides Adventure Works a basis for calculating many advanced analytics inside Mondrian with great speed and efficiency. We then looked at how Mondrian and Saiku can support basic "What If" analysis, making changes on the fly to see the effects of different scenarios.

We then continued to see what options Adventure Works has if they're looking to do more advanced data mining and machine learning. We introduced R and Weka, the most commonly used tools with Mondrian. Lastly we helped place Mondrian in the proliferation of new technologies wrapped in the Big Data moniker. We introduced how Mondrian is currently being used as, and in conjunction with, Big Data systems.

# appendix A
# Installing
# and running Mondrian

There are two ways you can get Mondrian to follow along with the examples in this book. The first and easiest is to download the virtual machine we've created. The virtual machine runs Ubuntu and has Pentaho CE configured with Mondrian, Saiku, and CTools. It also contains the Adventure Works data running in MySQL and a Mondrian 4.0 schema.

To use the virtual machine, you need to download a copy of VirtualBox, which is available as a free download from www.virtualbox.org/wiki/Downloads. Once you have VirtualBox installed, you can download the *Mondrian in Action* VM from www.manning-source.com/back/vm.html. Be sure to download the most up-to-date version of the VM. Use VirtualBox's import capabilities to start the machine. If you're prompted for a password to log in, it's *mondrian.*

> **UPDATES TO THE EXAMPLE PLATFORM** At the time of this book's authoring/ review, Mondrian 4.0 wasn't GA software, along with a variety of other components that were changing as Mondrian 4.0 completed its debut. You *must* check the forums (www.manning-sandbox.com/forum.jspa?forumID=823) for the latest information for the training platform, because we expect that by the time you read this, the VM and contents may have changed to enhance stability and cohesion.

The alternative is install Mondrian yourself. There are a lot of good reasons to do this, such as the following:

- You want to understand how Mondrian and Pentaho are installed.
- You want a different configuration than the one provided.
- You want to run Mondrian on a server other than Pentaho.
- You want to run locally and not in a VM.

Because there are a large variety options for installing Mondrian, we can't cover them all. But we can talk about a few that you may find useful when learning Mondrian. We don't give the instructions for installing each component because they change frequently and the sites have the instructions.

## A.1  Somewhere to store the data

The data warehouse can be stored in any database that's supported by Mondrian. The Pentaho InfoCenter contains a list of databases that are supported at http://mng.bz/2cJM. MySQL and PostgreSQL are popular free databases. The scripts for creating the database examples in this book are for MySQL.

## A.2  Just getting Mondrian

If you just want Mondrian, you can download the latest stable version from http://mondrian.pentaho.com. Instructions on how to install it are available at http://mondrian.pentaho.com/documentation/installation.php. If you want the very latest and greatest, you can visit https://github.com/pentaho/mondrian and download from there. Note that this approach requires building the code, but if you're a developer and don't mind such things, it's a great way to stay up-to-date with the most recent developments.

## A.3  Mondrian with Pentaho

Many of the examples in this book use Pentaho, and Pentaho will continue to be updated to work with Mondrian. An easy approach, then, is to download Pentaho. You can find downloads of the Pentaho BI Platform at http://community.pentaho.com/projects/bi_platform/. There are two versions: the manual version that you can install into your webapp server and the non manual version that comes bundled with Tomcat and MySQL. This is the quickest way to get up and running. Download the package, and unzip it into a convenient location.

> **PENTAHO 5.0 AND MONDRIAN 4.0**  At the time this book was written, Pentaho was on Version 4.8, which didn't support Mondrian 4.0. If you're using Pentaho CE and Saiku, this isn't a major issue, because you can have a different version of Mondrian for Saiku. But Enterprise users can't use Mondrian 4.0 with Analyzer. Pentaho 5.0 will add support for olap4j but probably won't incorporate Mondrian 4.0 until Pentaho 5.1.

## A.4  Adding C-Tools to Pentaho

You can also install C-Tools with Pentaho. Download C-Tools from WebDetails at www.webdetails.pt/index.html#ctools. The site contains a link to the `ctools-installer`. This installer is run from the command line and downloads, installs, and configures the various C-Tools. Read the installation instructions closely; it's not difficult, but you do have to be accurate.

## A.5   *Mondrian with Saiku*

You can get Saiku directly from http://analytical-labs.com. If you just want Mondrian with Saiku, you can download the standalone server. If you prefer to use Saiku with Pentaho, there is a plugin you can download and deploy. Instructions for both can be found on the Saiku site.

# *appendix B*
# *Online resources*

As an open source tool, Mondrian has an active online community and resources. This appendix contains links and descriptions for many resources you can use to continue to learn and use Mondrian.

**Table B.1  Mondrian and OLAP**

| Site | Link | Description |
|------|------|-------------|
| Mondrian | http://mondrian.pentaho.com | Documentation and links to the Mondrian source. |
| Mondrian schema reference | http://mondrian.pentaho.com/ documentation/xml_schema.php | Reference guide to each XML element in Mondrian's schema. |
| Mondrian source | http://github.com/pentaho/ mondrian | Mondrian source code repository with the latest versions. |
| Mondrian office hours | http://mng.bz/8tYc | Hours for Mondrian IRC chats with Julian Hyde and others. |
| *Mondrian in Action* | http://www.manning.com/ mondrianinaction | Information about the book and links to the forums. |
| *Mondrian in Action* Forum | http://www.manning-sandbox.com/ forum.jspa?forumID=823 | Discussion forum for Mondrian in Action. |
| olap4j | http://olap4j.org | Documentation for olap4j and links to download the source. |
| XMLA for Analysis (XMLA) via MSDN | http://mng.bz/3oEo | Microsoft's XMLA site. Probably the best reference site for XMLA. |
| xmla4js | https://github.com/rpbouman/ xmla4js | Documentation and code for xmla4js. |

**Table B.2  Pentaho resources**

| Site | Link | Description |
|------|------|-------------|
| Pentaho | www.pentaho.com | Pentaho's main site. |
| Pentaho community | http://community.pentaho.com | Pentaho's community site with links to related projects, documentation, and source. |
| Pentaho source | http://source.pentaho.org/ | Pentaho's open source page. Note that much of the code is being migrated to GitHub. |
| Pentaho forums | http://forums.pentaho.com/ | Pentaho forums that are a good source of past questions and online help. |
| Pentaho InfoCenter | http://infocenter.pentaho.com/ | Primary source of Pentaho Enterprise documentation. Most is relevant to the Community Edition as well. |
| WebDetails, a Pentaho Company | www.webdetails.pt | Maker of C-Tools. |
| Saiku | http://analytical-labs.com | Saiku software. |
| Pivot4J | http://mysticfall.github.com/pivot4j/ | JPivot replacement. |

**Table B.3  Blogs of interest**

| Author | Link | About the author |
|--------|------|------------------|
| Julian Hyde | http://julianhyde.blogspot.com | Lead architect for Mondrian and one of the authors of this book |
| Luc Boudreau | http://devdonkey.blogspot.com | Lead engineer for Mondrian at Pentaho |
| Nick Goodman | www.nicholasgoodman.com/bt/blog/ | One of the authors of this book |
| Bill Back | http://billonbi.wordpress.com | Director of OEM Services at Pentaho and one of the authors of this book |

**Table B.4  MDX resources**

| Site | Link | Description |
|------|------|-------------|
| Mondrian online MDX documentation | http://mondrian.pentaho.com/ documentation/mdx.php | The definitive resource to Mondrian MDX support. Provides the functions, their signatures, and a brief description of each function. Also covers the known divergences from the XMLA specification and Microsoft's MDX implementation. |

**Table B.4    MDX resources** *(continued)*

| Site | Link | Description |
|------|------|-------------|
| Microsoft MDX language reference | http://mng.bz/47m0 | The most comprehensive online resource for MDX. Covers language basics (operators and so on) and has an extensive function reference. Much of the documentation can be used as is, with no adjustment for MSFT versus Mondrian specifics. MSFT diverges from the specification frequently, so not all functions and documentation apply, but most do. |
| *Fast Track to MDX* by Mark Whitehorn, Robert Zare, and Mosha Pasumansky (Springer, 2005) | http://amzn.com/1846281741 | An introductory, and dated, book on MDX. If MDX looks like gibberish and you want to understand the basics, this is a good book to start with. |
| *MDX Solutions* by George Spofford et al. (Wiley, 2006) | http://amzn.com/0471748080 | Covers MDX extensively, providing huge numbers of practical exercises. Chapter 7 in particular is a gold mine of recipes for doing interesting things in MDX. Most of the MDX works as is or with minor adjustments, because this book was written for Microsoft instead of Mondrian. |
| Chris Webb's blog | http://cwebbbi.wordpress.com/category/mdx/ | MDX trainer and guru Chris Webb has lots of posts on MDX. He's into all Microsoft BI technologies, so you'll find many other topics in addition to MDX, but he has some solid info on MDX (check out his older entries). |

*appendix C*
*Schema shortcuts*

There is often more than one way to write something in Mondrian's XML schema format. Mondrian provides shortcuts to allow you to write concise XML. These are particularly useful if you're writing XML by hand.

| Name | Example |
|------|---------|
| `Attribute.nameColumn` default | An attribute's name defaults to its key (if the key has a single column) or the last column of its key (if the key is a composite). For example,<br><br>`<Attribute name='Year' keyColumn='year'/>`<br><br>is equivalent to<br><br>`<Attribute name='Year' keyColumn='year'`<br>`    nameColumn='year'/>` |
| `Attribute.keyColumn` for `Attribute.Key` | If an attribute's key is a single column, you can use the key-Column attribute. For example,<br><br>`<Attribute name='Year' keyColumn='year'/>`<br><br>is equivalent to<br><br>`<Attribute name='Year'>`<br>`    <Key>`<br>`        <Column name='year'/>`<br>`    </Key>`<br>`</Attribute>` |

| Name | Example |
|---|---|
| `Attribute.nameColumn` for `Attribute.Name` | If an attribute's name is a column (not an expression), you can use the `nameColumn` attribute. For example,<br><br>```<Attribute name='Day' ... nameColumn='day_of_month'/>```<br><br>is shorthand for<br><br>```<Attribute name='Day' ...>\n    <Name>\n        <Column name='day_of_month'/>\n    </Name>\n</Attribute>``` |
| Default table for hierarchy | The attribute `Hierarchy.table` lets you omit the `Column.table` attribute in all enclosed elements. |
| Default table for level | The attribute `Level.table` lets you omit the `Column.table` attribute for all enclosed elements. |
| `Attribute.ordinalColumn` default | If you don't specify an ordinal expression, it defaults to the name. For example,<br><br>```<Attribute name='Product Name'\n keyColumn='product_id'\n    nameColumn='product_name'/>```<br><br>is shorthand for<br><br>```<Attribute name='Product Name'\n keyColumn='product_id'\n  nameColumn='product_name' ordinalColumn='product_name'/>``` |

# *index*